TEEN LIFE IN THE MIDDLE EAST

TEEN LIFE IN THE MIDDLE EAST

Edited by Ali Akbar Mahdi

Foreword by Richard M. Lerner

Teen Life around the World
Jeffrey S. Kaplan, Series Editor

GREENWOOD PRESS
Westport, Connecticut • London

Library of Congress Cataloging-in-Publication Data

Teen life in the Middle East / edited by Ali Akbar Mahdi, foreword by Richard M. Lerner
      p. cm.— (Teen life around the world, ISSN 1540–4897)
  Includes bibliographical references and index.
  ISBN 0-313-31893-X (alk. paper)
   1. Teenagers—Middle East—Social conditions.   2. Adolescence—Middle East.   I. Mahdi,
Ali Akbar.   II. Series.

  HQ799.M628 T44   2003
  305.23'235'0956—dc21   2002075327

British Library Cataloguing in Publication Data is available.

Library of Congress Catalog Card Number: 2002075327

ISBN: 0-313-31893-X
ISSN: 1540–4897

First published in 2003

Greenwood Press, 88 Post Road West, Westport, CT 06881
An imprint of Greenwood Publishing Group, Inc.
www.greenwood.com

Printed in the United States of America

The paper used in this book complies with the
Permanent Paper Standard issued by the National
Information Standards Organization (Z39.48-1984).

10 9 8 7 6 5 4 3 2

*For working teens whose lives are reduced to seeking a livelihood
in crowded city streets and working farm women whose struggle
for sustaining their families is unending*

Ali Akbar Mahdi

CONTENTS

FOREWORD: TOWARD A WORLD OF POSITIVE YOUTH DEVELOPMENT

In these early years of the twenty-first century a new vision and vocabulary for discussing young people has emerged. Propelled by the increasingly more collaborative contributions of scholars, practitioners, advocates, and policy makers, youth are viewed as resources to be developed. The new vocabulary is legitimated by scholarly efforts at advancing what are termed "developmental systems theories." These models emphasize the plasticity of human development, that is, the potential for systematic change in behavior that exists as a consequence of mutually influential relationships between the developing person and his or her biology, psychological characteristics, family, community, culture, physical and designed ecology, and historical niche.

The plasticity of development legitimizes an optimistic view of potential for promoting positive changes in human life and directs emphasis to the strengths for positive development that are present within all young people. Accordingly, concepts such as developmental assets, positive youth development, moral development, civic engagement, well-being, and thriving have been used increasingly in research and applications associated with adolescents and their world. All concepts are predicated on the ideas that *every* young person has the potential for successful, healthy development and that *all* youth possess the capacity for positive development.

This vision for and vocabulary about youth has evolved over the course of a scientifically arduous path. Complicating this new, positive conceptualization of the character of youth as resources for the healthy development of self, families, and communities was an antithetical theoretical approach to the nature and development of young people. Dating within science to, at least, the publication in 1904 of G. Stanley Hall's two-volume work on adolescence, youth have been characterized by a deficit view, one that conceptualizes their behaviors as deviations from normative development. Understanding such deviations was not seen as being of direct relevance to scholarship aimed at discovering the principles of basic developmental processes. Accordingly, the characteristics of youth were regarded as issues of "only" applied concern—and thus of secondary scientific interest. Not only did this model separate basic science from application but, as well, it disembodied the adolescent from the study of normal or healthy development. It also often separated the young person from among those members of society that could be relied on to produce valued outcomes for family, community, and civic life. In short, the deficit view of youth as problems to be managed split the study of young people from the study of health and positive individual and social development.

The current scholarly and applied work that counters the historical, deficit view of adolescence, and in turn builds upon developmental systems theory to advance the new, positive vocabulary about young people and the growing research evidence for the potential of all youth to develop in positive ways, is both represented and advanced significantly by the *Teen Life around the World* series. More so than any other set of resources currently available to young people, parents, and teachers, the volumes in this series offer rich and engaging depictions about the diverse ways in which young people pursue positive lives in their families, communities, and nations. The volumes provide vivid reflections of the energy, passion, and skills that young people possess—even under challenging ecological or economic conditions—and the impressive ways in which adolescents capitalize on their strengths to pursue positive lives during their teenage years and to prepare themselves to be productive adult members of their families and communities.

Across the volumes in this series a compelling story of the common humanity of all people emerges, one that justifies a great deal of hope that, in today's adolescents, there exist the resources for a humane, peaceful, tolerant, and global civil society. To attain such a world, all people must begin by appreciating the diversity of young people and their cultures and that, through such diversity, the world possesses multiple, potentially productive paths to human well-being and accomplishment. Readers of the *Teen Life around the World* series will be rewarded with just this information.

Ultimately, we must all continue to educate ourselves about the best means available to promote enhanced life chances among all of the world's youth, but especially among those whose potential for positive contributions to civil society is most in danger of being wasted. The books in this series constitute vital assets in pursuit of this knowledge. Given the enormous, indeed historically unprecedented, challenges facing all nations, perhaps especially as they strive to raise healthy and successful young people capable of leading civil society productively, responsibly, and morally across the twenty-first century, there is no time to lose in the development of such assets. The *Teen Life around the World* series is, then, a most timely and markedly important resource.

Richard M. Lerner
Eliot-Pearson Department of
Child Development
Tufts University
Medford, Massachusetts
September 3, 2002

SERIES FOREWORD

Have you ever imagined what it would be like to live in a different country? What would it be like to speak a different language? Eat different foods? Wear different clothes? Attend a different school? Listen to different music, or maybe, the same music, in a different language? How about practicing new customs? Or, better yet, a different religion? Simply, how different would your life be if you were born and raised in another region of the world? Would you be different? And if so, how?

As we begin the twenty-first century, young people around the world face enormous challenges. Those born to wealth or relative comfort enjoy technological miracles and can click a button or move a mouse and discover a world of opportunity and pleasure. Those born without means struggle just to survive.

Education, though, remains a way out of poverty and for many privileged young people it is the ultimate goal. As more and more jobs, including those in the manufacturing and service sectors, require literacy, and computer skills, brains are increasingly valued over brawn: In the United States, entry-level wages for people with only a high-school education have fallen by more than 20% since the 1970s. Job prospects are bleaker than ever for youths who do not continue their education after high school. And, to be sure, while there are exceptions—like the teenager who starts a basement computer business and becomes a multimillionaire—working a string of low-paying service jobs with no medical insurance is a much more common scenario for those with limited education. And this seems to be true for adolescents in most post-industrialist countries around the world.

Adolescent girls, in particular, are at a disadvantage in many nations, facing sex discrimination as an obstacle to obtaining even basic education and social skills. In the Middle East and South Asia, girls are more likely to be pulled from school at an early age, and are thus less likely to develop critical literacy skills. Across most of the world, girls face more demands for work in the home and restrictions on movement that constrain their opportunities to gain direct experience with diverse social worlds. Similarly, as rates of divorce and abandonment rise worldwide, so do the chances in the workplace lessen for young women who fail to obtain skills to function independently. And as adults, they are increasingly vulnerable to poverty and exploitation.

ADOLESCENCE AROUND THE GLOBE

Adolescent life is truly plagued by difficulties and determined by context and circumstance. Anthropologist Margaret Mead (1901-1978) may have been the first social scientist to question the universality of the adolescent experience. When Mead contrasted the experience of North American and South Pacific young people in terms of sexuality, she found their experiences and attitudes toward sexuality dramatically different (South Pacific adolescents were more tolerant), and, she contended, adolescence should be seen in the contexts in which people live and dwell. In fact, for Mead and other social scientists, the only definition that can best describe adolescence is at best, restricted to a "period of transition," in which young people are no longer considered children, but not yet considered an adult.

Adolescence is generally understood as the period between the ages of 15 to 19, with some scholars referring to it as up to age 24. The term young adult is the most apt term for this age group, and without doubt, the many biological, psychological, and behavioral changes which mark this age, make this a concept that is continually dynamic and fluid in its change. Depending on which region of the world, the concept of adolescence or young adult is either emerging, or already well established. Most Western European societies use legal markers to underline the passage to adulthood, commonly set at age 16, 18, or 21. Thus, from country to country, there are minimum legal ages for marriage, for consensual intercourse, and also for access to sexual and reproductive health services without parental consent.

In many developing countries, though, the concept of adolescence has either been nonexistent or is relatively new in concept and understanding. Rather than define adulthood by age or biology, children become adults through well-established rites of passage—for example, religious ceremony, or marriage. In India, for example, especially in rural areas, many girls enter into arranged marriages before the onset of their first menstruation cycle, and then, have their first child at around 16 years of age. For these young Indian girls, there is no adolescence, as they shift so quickly from childhood to motherhood Similarly, in traditional Sri Lankan society, young people—once they enter puberty—are expected to get married, or in the case of a male, wear the yellow robe of a monk. To remain single is not held in high esteem because it is considered "neither here nor there."

Yet, the world is changing. Traditional patterns of behavior for young people, and what is expected of them by the adults, are in a state of flux, and in more open societies, adolescents are emerging as a powerful force for influence and growth in Africa, Asia, and Latin America. In these regions, massive economic, institutional and social changes have been brought about by Western colonial expansion and by the move toward a global society and economy. With more young people working in non-agricultural jobs, attending school longer, delaying marriage, adolescents are holding their own with adults.

In Indonesia, for example, young boys in urban areas are no longer tied to the farm and have started forming peer groups, as an alternative to life spent entirely inside the immediacy of their families. Similarly, in the urban areas of India, many girls attend single-sex schools, thus spending more time with peer groups, eroding the traditional practice of arranged marriages at an early age. In Nigeria, young people attend school for longer periods of time, thus preparing for jobs in their now modern economy. And in many Latin American countries, where young girls were once hurried into prearranged marriages, now, young girls are staying in school so they too can prepare for non-agricultural jobs.

And yet, those without means can only fantasize about what they see of mainstream material culture. As always, money is the societal divide that cruelly demarcates and is unrelenting in its effects on social, cultural, and psychological behavior. Young people living in poverty struggle daily with the pressures of survival in a seemingly indifferent, and often dangerous world. And access to wealth, or the simple conveniences of modern society, makes a considerable difference in the development of the young people. In rural areas in Zimbabwe and Papua New Guinea, for example, simple changes such as the building of a road or highway—enabling the bringing in of supplies and expertise—has had profound effects on young people's lifestyles.

When young people must leave their homes—either because of poverty, or increasingly, due to civil war—the result is often unprecedented numbers forced into bonded labor and commercial sex. For example, in the Indian cities of New Delhi, Mumbai, and Calcutta, thousands of young people take on menial jobs such as washing cars, pushing handcarts, collecting edibles from garbage dumps, or simply, begging. In Thailand, still more thousands of young girls earn their living as prostitutes. And in many countries of Eastern Europe, tens of thousands of young people are believed to be not attending school or formally employed, but instead, engaging in drug trafficking. Worldwide, the streets and temporary shelters are home to between 100 and 200 million children and adolescents, who are cut off from their parents and extended families (World Health Organization, 2000). What is it like to be them? What is it like to be young, scared, and poor?

Since the 1980s political and civil rights have improved substantially throughout the world, and 81 countries have taken significant steps in democratization, with 33 military regimes replaced by civilian governments. But of these fledgling democracies, only 47 are considered full democracies today. Only 82 countries, representing 57% of the world's population, are fully democratic.

Economically speaking, the proportion of the world's extremely poor fell from 29% in 1990 to 23% in 1999. Still, in 1999, 2.8 billion people lived on less than $2 a day, with 1.2 billion of them surviving on the margins of subsistence with less than $1 a day. In 2000, 1.1 billion people lacked access to safe water, and 2.4 billion did not have access to any form of improved sanitation services.

And armed conflict continues to blight the lives of millions: since 1990, 3.6 million people have died as a result of civil wars and ethnic violence, more than 16 times the number killed in wars between states. Civilians have accounted for more than 90% of the casualties—either injured or killed—in post-Cold War conflicts. Ninety countries are affected by landmines and live explosives, with rough estimates of 15,000 to 20,000 mine victims each year.

TEEN LIFE AROUND THE WORLD—THE SERIES

The Greenwood series *Teen Life around the World* examines what life is like for teens in different regions of the world. These volumes describe in detail the lives of young people in places both familiar and unfamiliar. How do teens spend their days? What makes their lives special? What difficulties and special burdens do they bear? And what will be their future as they make their way in their world?

Each volume is devoted to a region or regions of the world. For the purpose of this series, the volumes are divided as follows:

- Teen Life in Africa
- Teen Life in the Middle East
- Teen Life in Europe
- Teen Life in Central and South America and the Caribbean
- Teen Life in Asia

Readers can see similarities and differences in areas of the world that are relatively close in proximity, customs, and practices. Comparisons can be made between various countries in a region and across regions. American teens will perhaps be struck by the influence of American pop culture—music, fashion, food— around the world.

All volumes follow the same general format. The standardized format highlights information that all young people would most like to know. Each volume has up to fifteen chapters that describe teen life in a specific country in that region of the world. The countries chosen generally are representative of that region, and attempts were made to write about countries that young people would be most curious to learn more about.

Each chapter begins with a profile of the particular country. Basic political, economic, social, and cultural issues are discussed and a brief history of the country is provided. After this brief introduction to the specific country, an overview of teen life in that country is given, with a discussion of a teenager's typical day, family life, traditional and nontraditional foods, schooling, social life, recreation, entertainment, and religious practices and cultural practices. Finally, each chapter concludes with a list of resources that will help readers learn more about this country. These resources include nonfiction and fiction, Web sites, other sources to find information on the country, such as embassies, and pen pal addresses.

Although these chapters cannot tell the complete story of what it means to be a teenager in that region of the world and recognizing that perhaps there is no one typical lifestyle in any country, they provide a good starting point for insight into others' lives.

The contributors to this series present an informative and engaging look at the life of young people around the world and write in a straightforward manner. The volumes are edited by noted experts. They have an intimate understanding of their chosen region of the world—having either lived there, and/or they have devoted their professional lives to studying, teaching about, and researching the place. Also, an attempt was made to have each chapter written by an expert on teen life in that country. Above all, what these authors reveal is that young people everywhere—no matter where they live—have much in common. Although they might observe different social customs, rituals, and habits, they still long for the same basic things—security, respect, and love. They still live in that state of the half child/half adult, as they wait anxiously to become fully functioning members of their societies.

As series editor, it is my hope that these volumes, which are unique in publishing in both content and style, will increase your knowledge of teen life around the world.

Jeffrey S. Kaplan
Series Editor

REFERENCES

Dehne, K. L., & Reidner, G. (2001). Adolescence: A dynamic concept. *Reproductive Health Matters*. 9 (17), 11–16.

Baru, R. (1995). The social milieu of the adolescent girl. In S. Mehra (ed.) *Adolescent Girl in India: An Indian Perspective*. Saket, New Delhi. MAMTA, Health Institute for Mother and Child.

Caldwell, J. C.; Caldwell, P; & Caldwell, B. K. (1998). The construction of adolescence in a changing world: Implications for sexuality, reproduction, and marriage. *Studies in Family Planning*. 29(2), 137–53.

Deutsche Gesellschaft fur Technische Zusammenarbeit (1997).*Youth in development cooperation: approaches and prospects in the multisectoral planning group "Youth"*. Eschborn: GTZ.

Disanyake, J. B. (1998). *Understanding the sinhalese*. Columbo: Chatura Printers.

Larson, Reed. (2002). The Future of Adolescence: Lengthening the Ladders to Adulthood. *The Futurist*. 36(6), 16–21.

McCauley, A. P. & Salter, C. (1995). Meeting the needs of young adults. *Population Report*, Series J. 41:1–39.

UNAIDS (1999). *Sex and youth: contextual factors affecting risk for HIV/AIDS*. Geneva: UNAIDS.

UN Development Report (2002).

INTRODUCTION: TEENS, ISLAM, AND THE MIDDLE EAST

Ali Akbar Mahdi

TEEN AS A CATEGORY

Teen, as an age category, represents the ages from 13 to 19 and is also a socially constructed conceptual category. It is rooted in the Western world and English language. Historically, the use of the term in the English language dates to 1673.[1] It became a popular term in the United States in the late 1940s. A more scientific term referring loosely to the same age group is *adolescence*—a Latin word meaning "to grow to adulthood."[2]

Adolescence is a transitional stage between childhood and adulthood, covering roughly ages 11 to 21.[3] During these years adolescents experience drastic physical, psychological, and sexual changes generally defined as puberty. The experiences of this period for teens, as a social category, are often defined as the rites of passage—a time when new freedoms are offered to teens with lesser responsibilities and accountabilities than those expected from adults. Sociologically, this lack of correspondence between freedoms and responsibilities is defined as status ambiguity. Both adults and teens remain unsure of how to relate to one another as each tries to get the other to respond to its needs and expectations. On the one hand, whereas teens are socialized to adults' values, norms, roles, and statuses, they are neither treated as fully responsible adults nor given powers associated with those roles and statuses. On the other hand, teens' expectations in conforming to social norms and roles remain oriented toward their own needs and desires. As a result, both teens and adults remain unclear about the criteria by which teens' behaviors and performances are to be judged. As teen years begin, parents lose their influence to peers and the family loses its influence to society. As our societies become more risk oriented, multidirectional, and increasingly differentiated in roles and statuses, the identity of the young becomes subject to anxiety, uncertainty, and tension.[4]

Though relevant and meaningful, *teen* is not a uniform category. Young people's life conditions and cultural experiences are by no means identical. As such, *teen* has had neither a proper equivalent in the languages spoken in Middle Eastern countries nor a conceptual autonomy in the theological, philosophical, and cultural domains in those societies. Terms used for teens in these languages are vague in age equivalency and are often in reference to pre-puberty, pre-youth, and pre-adult, each with different age referents.[5] Whereas in the English-speaking world the idea of teen is associated with restlessness and rebelliousness,[6] in Middle Eastern cultures it connotes immaturity and imperfection. Childhood is often characterized by the absence of "reason" (*aql*). Just as the conceptual category of teenager in the Western world is a product of modernity and modernization of social life,[7] in the Middle East it is the product of the region's exposure to Western culture in the past 150 years. It was modernity that gave importance to the individual, gave birth to the ideology of adolescence, and established concrete boundaries between childhood, adolescence, and youth. A close look at the historiographies of countries in the region show that traditionally teens, like women, have been generally ignored in historical accounts. The written history of the region has been the story of male adults, especially notable ones.

Traditionally, most Middle Eastern societies had no transitional stage between childhood and adulthood. Puberty served as the dividing line between the two periods. Given the old structure of social life whereby children worked with parents, preparation for adulthood took place alongside them as well, either within the home or in parents' occupations. With the modernization of society and the emergence of secular schools, children spent a good number of years in the school system. This new period of transition expanded the time between biological maturity and recognition of adulthood, exposing children to modern education, technology, Western lifestyles, and new ideas. The combined effects of the latter factors gave rise to adolescents' social expectations and the development of a new identity as "teenager."

Traditionally, the life cycle of an individual in the Middle Eastern cultures, based on the Islamic traditions, is divided into two stages: childhood and adulthood. Puberty, with its various rites of passages in different cultures in the region, marks the transition from childhood to adulthood. In Islam, girls are said to reach maturity (*bolooq*) at the age of 9 and boys at the age of 15. Once reaching puberty (*baaleq*), boys and girls become *mokallaf*, that is, they are responsible for performing all their religious duties as an adult. Interestingly, this individual religious status may not conform to the person's civil or legal status in society. As these societies have become modernized and influenced by Western legal concepts, most define legal age as 18. For instance, in Iran a girl is eligible to marry at the age of 9 but cannot vote until she reaches 15. This same girl cannot obtain a driver's license until she reaches 18. If a boy commits a crime prior to the age of 15, he will be tried in a juvenile court. However, a female delinquent at the age of 11 will be tried as an adult, not a juvenile.

TEENS AND RELIGION IN THE MIDDLE EAST

Religion is one of the most influential forces shaping the lives of people in the Middle East. Except for Israel, whose official religion is Judaism, and Lebanon, whose Christian population makes up 30 percent of the population, all other countries of the Middle East are predominantly Muslim.[8] However, whether Muslim, Jew, Christian, Zoroastorian, or Bahai, teens in the Middle East are influenced and governed by religious rules and guidance, though in different forms and to different extents. To understand the effects of religion on teen life in the Middle East, it is important not to approach the issue from an "essentialist" perspective. An essentialist perspective views a community as a bounded whole characterized by uniform rules, values, practices, and traits. For example, if Islam dictates something, then one expects to see all Muslims abiding by it. This perspective ignores the multiplicity of life experiences and interpretations characterizing lives of religious believers around the world. It also ignores the fact that religious behavior, like other types of behavior, is subject to accommodations, changes, mistakes, shortcomings, and outright failure.

The normative effects of Islam on teen behavior should be observed at two levels: universal and particular. At the universal level, there are laws, rules, and principles enunciated by Islam as relevant to the life of all Muslim youths. At this level, Islam is an all-encompassing religion in which the entire individual's life is played out from cradle to grave. No part of individual behavior is outside of religious influences or can be conceived as outside the divine authority and framework. Allah is both creator and the master of the world (*Rabb al-Aalamin*). He is all-knowing and "encompasses everything in knowledge."[9] The cosmos within which a Muslim lives, moves, and leads his or her life is created and guided by Allah. Of course, a Muslim has a choice to (1) follow Allah's guidance and lead a faithful life, or (2) ignore religious rules and lead an unfaithful life.

At the particular level, there are two other sets of norms, rules, and attitudes: national and local. At the national level, Islam in each Muslim country is perceived and implemented differently. Saudi Arabia follows a version of Islam known as Wahhabism. In many respects Wahhabi Islam, a form of Sunni Islam (the majority sect in Islamic countries; see below), is quite different from Sunni Islam found in other Arab countries. Or, Shia Islam (the minority sect), as understood and practiced in Iran, is quite different from Shia Islam in Lebanon, Turkey, and Syria. For instance, as a universal rule, the consumption of alcohol is prohibited in Islam. However, the only Muslim country that comes close to the definition of a dry country, where alcohol is hard to find and harder to consume without impunity, is Saudi Arabia. Wealthy, Westernized, and secular Saudis who drink, do so outside the country. In most other Muslim countries, alcohol is available, either legally or illegally, and is consumed by teens in varying degrees.

These differences at the national level are augmented by differences at the local level, where the implementation of general principles is subject to local considerations. Although important, the universal principles do not always reflect what happens at the national or local levels, for general principles have to be interpreted and applied to particular circumstances in which many other factors play a role. Rural Muslims are often known to follow what social scientists have termed "folk religion." Folk religion derives its beliefs more from superstition than from the injunctions in Islam. For instance, most Turkish Alawaits (a subsect of Shi'ism) believe in the evil eye (the idea that some people's gaze is capable of inflicting harm. Numerous objects are designed and worn by people in order to ward off evil) as a part of their religious belief, a matter totally unrelated to Islam. Whereas Shias in Iran believe that women should cover all their body except their face and hands, Sunni women in India wear traditional Indian dress (*sari*) where some parts of their body may remain exposed.

Still, it is important to understand the general framework laid down by Islam for all Muslims, including teenagers, as a basis for moral growth. To be a Muslim, a person has to believe in the fundamentals of Islam, which include acknowledgment of the oneness of Allah, Mohammed as the last prophet, revelations from Allah, and the Day of Judgment. Commitment to these principles is manifested in following the five pillars of Islam: belief in God or Allah and acknowledging Mohammed as his prophet (*Shahaadah*), performing five daily prayers (*Salaat*), paying alms (*Zakaat*) for the poor and needy, making a pilgrimage to Mecca (*Hajj*) at least once in a lifetime, and fasting (*Sawm*) from sunrise to sunset in the month of Ramadan. All Muslims believe in these principles and are required to abide by them.

After the death of the Prophet Mohammed, the Muslim community managed its religious life by relying on Quranic injunctions, traditions set by the Prophet, and his statements (*hadiths*) regarding the course of action to be taken in specific situations. Muslims differed in their interpretations of these traditions and statements, resulting in different schools of religious laws. Over the course of years, four schools of thought developed, each named after founding jurists: Shafi'i, Hanafi, Maleki, and Hanbali. The major schism among Muslims came about due to the question of succession to the Prophet. After Mohammed's death on 8 June 632, Sunnis believed in the tradition of electing the eldest and wisest man close to the Prophet as the leader of the community (*Ummah*). They also believed that the community leadership should remain in the Qurayshi clan. The first leader (*khalif*) was Abu Bakr, the second Omar, the third Othmaan, and the fourth Ali ibn Abu Taleb, the Prophet's son-in-law. A group of Muslim followers known as Shias (i.e., party) believed that the leadership of the Islamic community should remain in the family of the Prophet, thus recognizing Ali as the rightful successor to the Prophet. From here on, Muslims divided into two major sects of Sunni and Shia. The majority of Iranians are Shia, although Shia minorities are found in almost all other Middle Eastern countries. The dominant sect in the Arab countries is Sunni. There are a few other divisions among these sects reflecting historical, theological, and doctrinal differences that emerged in later times.

Rules governing the lives of Muslims are drawn from the holy book, the Quran, the sayings of Prophet Mohammed, traditions established by the Prophet and his primary disciples, and the judgment of religious leaders (*ulama* or *imams*). Once regarded by religion as mature, teens must perform all their religious duties from prayers to codes of conduct. The five daily prayers are performed in the morning before the sunrise (*fajr*), at noon (*zuhr*), afternoon (*asr*), evening (*maghreb*), and night (*ashaa*). Many Muslims perform noon and afternoon, as well as evening and night, simultaneously. Teens are also to observe the codes of honor and modesty in the Islamic community. These codes demand segregation of sexes and social spheres. Muslim girls are to end their interactions with non-relative male teens at around the age of 9 and begin to cover themselves with a veil. The nature and type of the veil are subject to local adaptation, but its necessity is not in question for Muslim believers. Unmarried males and females are not allowed to have physical interaction with each other. Males and females are not allowed to enter into social spheres designed for the opposite sex.

In addition, Muslim males are expected, but not required, to participate in Friday prayer performed collectively in the mosque. Although daily prayers are required, not all Muslims are dutiful in this regard. Devoted Muslims observe their daily prayers and make sure their children do the same. The extent of teens' conformity to parental expectations depends on the family's degree of religiosity, education, lifestyle, and social class. Whereas Sunni women usually pray in the seclusion of home and do not participate at the mosque, Shia women have always prayed in the mosque—however, in a secluded area behind men, and never in front of them.

Islam obligates parents to attend to their children by choosing an appropriate name for them, feeding and caring for them, teaching them about Allah and His religion, and preparing them for their adult roles in society. To perform these duties, parents are allowed to use corporal punishment in moderation. Teens also have responsibilities toward their parents. Generally, their religious responsibilities are blended into the local cultures, reinforcing each other at all levels of social interaction within society. Here are some of those responsibilities.

Islam expects teens to obey their parents' instructions, respect and care for them in health and illness, and remain subservient to the interest of their family. The Quran states:

> And your Lord has decreed that you worship none but Him. And that you be dutiful to your parents. If one of them or both of them attain old age in your life, say not to them a word of disrespect, nor shout at them but address them in terms of honor. And lower unto them the wing of submission and humility through mercy, and say, "My Lord! Bestow on them Your Mercy as they did bring me up when I was young."[10]

The same respect and obedience should be offered to older siblings. As stated by a religious authority, "the right of the elder sibling over the younger sibling is like the right of the father over his child."[11] Prophet Mohammed is also quoted as saying, "Be dutiful toward your mother and your father, and your sister and your brother, then those closest to you, followed by those next to closest to you."[12]

Islam puts a great deal of emphasis on education and the correct ways of raising teens. This responsibility is assigned to parents—a responsibility that is becoming increasingly difficult in the face of challenges from modern educational systems. The exposure of Muslim youth to non-Islamic culture and education, often derived from Western sources, has become a major source of irritation for Muslim parents and educators. In response to this threat, Muslims have begun producing educational materials based on Islamic principles and specific books explaining the duties of Muslim children and youth.[13] The opposition to the Pahlavi regime in Iran by the religious leaders, which resulted in the overthrow of that regime and its replacement with an Islamic theocracy (a government ruled by religious leaders and guided by religious laws) in the late 1970s, was based on the fear that the modern education established by the Pahlavi dynasty (1925–1979) had contaminated Iranian youth with decadent Western values.

Across the Middle East, religiously conservative parents view the exposure to Western culture as detrimental to Muslim education. The rising wave of fundamentalism in the region has resulted in the establishment of educational schools based on Islamic principles. In Turkey, the development of these schools became a major threat to the secularization program followed by the government and resulted in efforts to eradicate these schools. The rise of the Taliban in Afghanistan in 1996 resulted in the expansion of the Wahhabi version of Islam in that country. Wahhabi Islam, as explained in the chapter on Saudi Arabia, is the official form of Islam adopted in Saudi Arabia. Wahhabism rejects Western culture, mingling of the sexes, interacting closely with non-Muslims, and tolerance of Muslims of other sects in Islam. It emphasizes outward behavior and is in favor of public punishment of sinners, minor or major, through flogging or execution. The Taliban established an Islamic regime in Afghanistan and also harbored Osama bin Laden, a Saudi dissident who has championed a crusade against foreigners and infidels in the region—a crusade that took his fight and soldiers all the way to the United States and inflicted the most horrific act of terrorism in history on September 11, 2001.

TEENS IN THE MIDDLE EAST

Sociologically, there are four areas of concern necessary for the healthy growth of teens: education, social services, family support, and health care. Looking at the statistics provided by the United Nations, one can easily see that no single country in the Middle East can hope for full satisfaction of these concerns. Even in Saudi Arabia, one of the richest countries in the world, the high birthrate has resulted in a huge population below the age of 15, and unemployment has reached 30 percent, putting pressure on an economy whose income from oil is now half of what it was in the early 1980s.[14] Many countries in the region lack adequate resources for ensuring a healthy future for their growing population of teens. There are alarming reports regarding the economic hardships experienced by teenagers in the region.[15] Teens from poor families are forced to work on the streets and interact with the adult world without much of a protective shield against economic exploitation, sexual abuse, and exposure to crime and violence.

There are numerous variables contributing to the increase in the ranks of teenagers in search of jobs in the cities: economic decline and increasing unemployment, higher rates of population growth, uncontrolled rural exodus, frequent earthquakes in countries in the region, and displacements due to war in Iran, Iraq, Lebanon, Palestine, and Afghanistan. Some of these teens are drug addicts, some are homeless living in abandoned vehicles and buildings, and some are victims of traffickers who rent them for economic exploitation or kidnap them from rural areas and transfer them to cities to work as beggars or maids. Most work as itinerant merchants, wash car windshields, beg in the streets, or offer to shine the shoes of passersby. Most are physically, psychologically, and sexually abused. For them, life itself is an abuse.

Globalization has had many positive aspects and has brought many countries, especially the Western ones, huge material and social comforts. Unfortunately, for many teens in the Middle East the fruits of globalization are not shared equally, and many young people in these countries do not find globalization helpful to their economic status. Many have left their dying communities in rural areas and come to the cities to find themselves in the traps of poverty and war. Although there is no going back for these teens, there is little with which they can move forward. In parts of the region, there are too many teens without access to schools, either due to economic conditions or to cultural and religious restrictions imposed on female children. In Afghanistan, the Taliban regime banned women from the public arena and closed schools for girls. In 1996, fully 90 percent of Afghani girls and nearly two-thirds of boys were left out of school.[16] The life of female teenagers left at home, and at the mercy of adults whose major concerns are chastity and a good future husband, leaves very little for these teens to look forward to. The increasing rate of suicide and runaways among young females in Iran is a testimony to the negative effects of the isolation imposed on women.[17]

A major issue related to the safety and stability of the environment within which Middle Eastern teens grow is the political instability caused by government repression, war, or occupation. The region has been and continues to be gripped by war: civil, national, and international. In the past two decades, thousands of teens have lost their lives, become permanently disabled, or been injured in armed conflicts between Iran and Iraq, Israel and the Palestinians, Israel and the Lebanese, Afghanis and Soviets, and various civil wars in the region. In Afghanistan, the proportion of teen soldiers has "risen in recent years from roughly 30 to at least 45 per cent."[18] The latest war in that country is being fought by many young Afghanis as young as 13 years old. The five-decades-old conflict between Israelis and Palestinians has now become a "teenage war." Teens make up a large segment of refugees from these conflicts, whether in Afghanistan, Iraq, Palestine, or Kurdistan. Economic sanctions imposed on Iraq by the United Nations for Iraq's invasion of Kuwait in 1990 have resulted in massive malnourishment among teens in that country and have wiped out the possibility of a meaningful future for them.[19]

While globalization increases pressure on older traditions and challenges traditional identities, new technologies and opportunities provide newer forms of identities based on individual choice and accountability. More and more young people view their own decisions as a choice rather than an unquestionable constraint imposed by culture, society, and traditions.[20] As demonstrated in various surveys of Iranian youth, more and more teenagers seek immediate gratification by fending for themselves and challenging pressures from traditional norms. As these societies move away from traditional structures toward modern institutions in polity, economy, and education, the life and experiences of their youth reflect the cultural anxieties associated with this transition.[21]

Whereas Western culture is obsessed with youth, marketing products to a growing population of teenagers, Middle Eastern societies are still obsessed with issues of an older generation whose desires for prosperous and democratic societies remain unfulfilled. Two generations of Middle Easterners, who have been struggling with modernity and its aftermath, are still in search of finding a balance among native cultures, modern technologies, economic development, and political democracy. Whereas Western corporations continue to look for new products to sell to this growing population, Middle Eastern leaders are trying hard to find ways to limit teens' access to Western products deemed incompatible with the local culture or religious values. Middle Eastern parents are wary of popular culture from the West—a culture selling violence and sex packaged in movies, music, and clothing. As these cultures clash, the gulf between Middle Eastern parents and their teenagers grows wide.

The population in all Middle Eastern countries is young. Those under the age of 25 make up between 40 and 63 percent of the population in different countries of the region. A cursory look at images of crowds of protesters, soldiers, and rebels involved in various forms of fighting in these countries shows a very angry young population. The anger of these young people is often loosely articulated and vaguely understood. Large pockets of frustrated teens remain a ticking time bomb in Middle Eastern political landscapes. They are young, inexperienced, impatient, and desirous. If their expectations and needs are not met, they will be a major source of political instability and unrest in decades to come. These frustrations are breeding grounds for militancy and attraction to extremist groups and ideologies.

STRUCTURE OF THE BOOK

This book follows the series format. As a reference, chapters deal with the same issues in the same sequence: Introduction, Typical Day, Family Life, Traditional and Nontraditional Food, Schooling, Social Life, Recreation, Entertainment, Religious Practices and Cultural Ceremonies, Conclusion, and Resource Guide, with Nonfiction, Fiction, Web sites, and Pen Pal/Chat information.[22] This uniformity is very useful in comparing various aspects of teen life in different countries in the region as well as with other regions in the world. Its disadvantage is the limitation placed on what could or could not be covered. For instance, the format is very effective in capturing the life experiences of teenagers in urban areas attending schools. However, in a region with a high rate of child labor, there are many teenagers whose typical day is more similar to that of working adults than to their city counterparts attending schools. Furthermore, the format did not leave much room for discussing child abuse—a phenomenon no less widespread in the Middle East than in other parts of the world. To compensate for these limitations, authors were asked to pay attention to these issues; most chapters allude to them in the context of proposed issues.

Culturally, the term *Middle East* has been used for areas from Afghanistan to North Africa. However, the more familiar political usage of the term refers to the following countries: Bahrain, Cyprus, Egypt, Iran, Iraq, Israel (and/or Palestine), Jordan, Kuwait, Lebanon, Oman, Qatar, Saudi Arabia, Syria, Turkey, the United Arab Emirates, and Yemen. Conventionally, social scientists have often studied Cyprus in the context of Mediterranean societies, Egypt of Africa, and Afghanistan of Central Asia. In this series, Egypt is included in the book *Teen Life in Africa*.

Starting this project in April 2000, authors who are either native to the country or currently live there were sought to write chapters for each of the countries. Unfortunately, my efforts, despite numerous attempts, did not result in full coverage of all countries. The war in Afghanistan made it difficult to find a scholar willing to write about teens in that country. My efforts to cover Kurdish teens, who do not receive adequate representation in the chapters on Turkey, Iran, Iraq, and Syria, were also fruitless.

Given the spread of Kurdish people in four countries of the region, and the complexities of Kurdish culture, it would have been difficult to develop a cohesive chapter for this volume.

NOTES

1. See the *Oxford English Dictionary*.

2. In 1904, Granville Stanley Hall termed *adolescence* a physical life-stage characterized by "storm and stress." See his book, *Adolescence: Its Psychology and Its Relations to Physiology, Anthropology, Sociology, Sex, Crime, Religion and Education* (New York: Appleton, 1904).

3. Social scientists divide adolescence into three stages: early adolescence (11–14), middle adolescence (15–18), and late adolescence or youth (18–21). See Laurence Steinberg, *Adolescence* (New York: Alfred A. Knopf, 1989).

4. For theoretical discussion of these issues see: Franco Moretti, *The Way of the World: The Bildungsroman in European Culture* (London: Verso, 1987); and Ulrich Beck, *Risk Society: Towards a New Modernity* (London: Sage, 1992).

5. In Persian, *javaan* means young and *nojavaan* means adolescent or early youth. The most authoritative dictionary in Persian, *Dehkhoda*, refers to youth as 15 to 34 years old. In Arabic, *Al-Shabaab* refers to youth and *Al-Moraaheq* refers to the period prior to puberty for boys. In Turkish, *yeni yetme* is a rarely used term referring to a person newly grown up. None of these terms have accurate reference to ages 13–19.

6. See E. Greenberger, and L. Steinberg. *When Teenagers Work: The Psychological and Social Costs of Adolescent Employment* (New York: Basic Books, 1986).

7. See J. F. Katt, *Rites of Passage* (New York: Basic Books, 1977); and John R. Gillis, *Youth and History: Tradition and Change in European Age Relations, 1770–Present* (New York: Academic Press, 1974).

8. Given that Islam is the official religion in all countries covered in this book except Israel, our discussion in this introduction is limited to Islam. For a detailed discussion of Judaism and its effects on teens, see the chapter on Israel.

9. Quran, Chapter 33 (Sura *Al-Ahzaab*), verse 63.

10. Quran, Chapter 17 (Sura *Osara*), verses 23–24.

11. This statement is from Al-Baihaqi and is quoted in Sh. Abu Bakr Al-Jazairi, *Islamic Etiquette* (Houston: Darussalam Publishers and Distributors, 1998), 57.

12. Quoted in ibid., p. 57.

13. For examples, see *The Children's Book of Islam* produced by the Islamic Foundation in London or *Islam for Children*, written by Adur Rauf and published by the Islamic Educational, Scientific, and Cultural Organization in 1991.

14. See Elaine Sciolino, "U.S. Pondering Saudis' Vulnerability," *New York Times*, 4 November 2001.

15. See reports regarding the children in Iran at www.geocities.com/icsofla/main.html.

16. Quoted in Gene Sperling, "Educating the World," *New York Times*, 22 November 2001.

17. See Jim Muir, "Iran's Girl Runaways," British Broadcasting Corporation, 14 December 2000.

18. The United Nations Department for Policy Coordination and Sustainable Development (DPCSD) at gopher://gopher.un.org/00/ga/docs/51/plenary/A51-306.EN.

19. See Christopher S. Wren, "U.N. Report Maps Hunger 'Hot Spots,'" *New York Times*, 9 January 2001.

20. Anthony Giddens, *Modernity and Self-Identity: Self and Identity in the Late Modern Age* (Oxford: Polity, 1991).

21. Moretti, *The Way of the World*.

22. A useful pen pal Web site for all the countries is World Pen Pals, P.O. Box 337, Saugerties, NY 12477. 845-246-7826. www.world-pen-pals.com.

Chapter 1

IRAN

Malihe Maghazei

INTRODUCTION

Iran is one of the oldest and largest countries in the Middle East. Located in an important geopolitical position on the crossroads of the East and the West, it is bounded on the north by Azerbaijan, Armenia, Turkmenistan, and the Caspian Sea; on the east by Pakistan and Afghanistan; on the south by the Persian Gulf and the Gulf of Oman; and on the west by Turkey and Iraq. It has an area of 636,300 square miles and vast natural resources. In some ways, Iran is unique in the Middle East because it is the only country in the region that uses the Islamic solar calendar, its official language is Persian with a modified version of the Arabic alphabet, and the majority of its population groups believe in Shi'a Islam. Iran is also a multilingual and culturally heterogeneous country in which almost half of the population speak non-Persian languages and dialects. Officially recognized religious minorities are Zoroastrians (0.05%), Jews (0.02%), and Christians (0.13%); Bahais are a small religious minority whose religion is not recognized by the government. Iran has a diverse climate allowing for different economic activities such as agriculture, fishing, hunting, forestry, business, industry, and services. During the last two decades the country experienced a surge in population growth and a significant migration from rural to urban areas. The population is 60,055,488, of which 61.30 percent live in urban areas.

Under the current political system, Iran is an Islamic republic, established after the popular Revolution of 1979. The Revolution overthrew the Pahlavi reign (1925–1979), ended the centuries-old monarchical system, and brought about a completely unprecedented form of government in the country. Pahlavi was a centralized, dictatorial, and pro-West regime. Its founder was Reza Khan, a former officer in the Iranian army, who came to power after a coup d'état in 1921. In 1925, Reza Khan declared himself a monarch, ended the Qajar dynasty and founded the Pahlavi dynasty. Reza Shah "embarked on vigorous programs of state-sponsored reforms and promoted an unprecedented degree of secularism in public life."[1] He enforced mandatory unveiling of women and adoption of Western clothing, and built a modern army and reduced the power of the clergy (*ulama*), who were popular and had spiritual as well as political influences on the common people.[2] To accomplish his goals he circumvented the legislative process, and the parliament functioned, in his era, only as a rubber stamp.[3] In order to sustain his reforms he fostered a sense of loyalty to the nation based on glorification of the pre-Islamic era. He suppressed all ethnic and political opposition movements, outlawed all political parties, and arrested or killed many outspoken intellectuals. Finally, because of his pro-Nazi tendency, he was forced to abdicate by the Allied forces that occupied Iran in 1941 and was succeeded by his young son, Muhammad Reza Shah (1941–1979), the last monarch before the Revolution.

In the initial years, Mohammad Reza's reign was weak; therefore a number of opposition groups, including the nationalist oil movement under the leadership of Mohammad Mosaddeq, emerged. Being a threat to the interests of Western oil companies, especially the British and Americans, Mosaddeq's elected government was overthrown by a U.S.-planned coup d'état in 1953. After the coup the Shah began to follow his father's policy of absolute rule. He restricted political activities, banned opposition parties, and established a secret police called SAVAK with the CIA's aid. The United States provided the Shah extensive military supplies, economic aid, and diplomatic support; in fact, the United States "became the dominant power in Iran."[4] The Shah initiated a policy of reform from above, including promulgation of the Family Protection Law (which reduced men's unilateral prerogatives in divorce and polygamy), enfranchisement of women, land reform, expansion of modern secular educational and governmental institutions, and so on.

The rapid secularization and modernization policy of the Pahlavis brought about a "two-cultures phenomenon" in Iran, separating elite and popular cultures in terms of dress, music, lifestyle, and so on.[5] The Shah's cultural policy, increasing political repression, an economic recession in 1976–1977, and growing discontent among different sections of the Iranian people eventually led to open opposition to his rule beginning in 1977.[6] Iranian writers, poets, journalists, lawyers, teachers, and clergy initiated public demonstrations and civil disobedience leading up to the

Revolution. Ayatollah Ruhollah Khomeini, a religious leader who had been previously sent to exile by the Shah, orchestrated mass opposition to the Pahlavi rule, forcing the Shah to depart Iran in January 1979, Khomeini emerged as the undisputed leader of the Revolution and returned to the country.

Shortly thereafter, a referendum was held to choose between a monarchy and an Islamic republic; the population overwhelmingly voted for the latter. Most of the Shah's reforms, including the Family Protection Law, were suspended. Women were barred from the judiciary and certain other jobs. Veiling became compulsory; segregation in transportation, sports, and many public places was imposed; and some discriminatory laws were introduced or reimposed.[7] The clergy quickly gained control of the state and gradually restricted the press and undermined other groups. The Islamic Constitution based on the concept of *Velayat-e Faqih* (Supreme Jurisprudent) was written in the first year after the Revolution. The new Islamic government combined theocracy and a parliamentary system with a centrally planned economy and a large public sector.[8] The government today consists of three branches: executive, legislative, and judicial. The president, who is popularly elected for a four-year term, heads the executive branch. The 290 members of the legislative body, the Islamic Consultative Assembly, which includes representatives of the recognized religious minorities, are also elected for four-year terms. The judiciary branch consists of a Supreme Court, a Supreme judicial, and several lower courts. According to the Constitution, all activities of the government are directly or indirectly under the supervision of religious custodians. The Islamic supreme jurist (*Vali-Faqih*), as the leader of the people, is granted wide-ranging constitutional powers.

TYPICAL DAY

Iran has a tremendously young population. Since the Revolution, the population has increased at an unprecedently high rate, rising from 33.7 million in 1976 to 60,055,488 by 1996. Now almost 70 percent of the population is under 30 years old, and there are 32 million people under 20 years of age.[9]

This young population is not homogenous. Despite the effort of the government toward Islamization of the society, they behave according to their own interests, social class, religion, ethnicity, and so on. Due to heterogeneity of the population, there is no typical Iranian teenager; therefore there is no typical teenager's day. In the urban areas most teenagers go to school. A typical day for children of upper- and middle-class families

Iranian girl. Courtesy of Ali Akbar Mahdi.

during the academic year is as follows: they go to school every day from Saturday to Thursday. Students go by bus, walk, or get rides to school from their parents. Some rich kids have their own cars. After school they rest, watch TV, and have dinner with their families. Most students have to spend a big part of their evening on homework. Many high school students take extra courses outside of school, such as foreign languages and computer skills. Some have private tutoring in the evenings as well. On weekends these teens go to the theater, parties, parks, or go hiking and so on. During the summer they take all kinds of classes, including art, sports, foreign languages, or school subject classes in order to review or prepare for the next academic year. Some studious teenagers in the last two years of high school also take courses in preparation for the university entrance exam.

In theory, all Muslim boys from age 15 and Muslim girls from age 9 should observe religious practices. These age specifications are actually the religious puberty ages, based on the assumption that boys and girls become physically and mentally mature at these ages and are ready to do the rituals. However, in practice not all Muslim teenagers strictly follow the rituals. An Iranian teenager's religious behavior is influenced by his or her family background, neighborhood, peer group, and so on. Some, under the influence of school, family, and the media become very religious, but only for a limited period. In general, whether the youth believe in Islam or not, in public arenas such as school they have to follow the rituals. The followers of other religions have freedom to do their own rituals in their houses or in their own public religious places.

Unlike American teenagers, who work to cover their own expenditures, Iranian teenagers never go to work unless their family's financial situation requires it. The kind of jobs the youth undertake also depend on their family's status and parents' occupations. In the urban areas, modern middle-class teenage girls rarely work: they often wait to finish high school or even get a university degree before they start working. Alternatively, lower-class teens, especially boys, whether they go to school or not, often support their families. Many impoverished teens from rural areas come to cities, with or without their families, in search of jobs. They do all kinds of work in order to support their families: they become vendors or work in shops, restaurants, houses, mechanic shops, and the like. Overall, participation of the youth in the Iranian economy is noticeable. According to the latest census, 18.5 percent of the workforce in agriculture, 28.5 percent in the industrial sector, and 19.7 percent in the service sector are young people (between ages 15 and 24); in other words, the breadwinners of almost 5 percent of Iranian households are youths between the ages of 15 and 24.[10]

In the rural areas, when the teens come home from school, they do their homework and help their parents on the farm, with handcrafting (weaving carpets or making other handicrafts), or with other economic activities. When there is no work to do, they do their homework and watch TV. In summer time, children cooperate with their parents in various village activities including farming, caring for animals, gathering fruit, and so on.

FAMILY LIFE

Because it is a heterogeneous country, there is no typical family life in Iran and there are various family styles. The mode of life in small and traditional cities is very different from that in major cities. Even within the major cities, lifestyles differ greatly among upper-class families, secularly educated families, highly religious families, and illiterate lower-class families. In the rural areas, especially in the north, where agricultural conditions are good, both men and women work on the land, and sometimes women work harder. There is not as much sex segregation in villages in terms of work. Girls, as well as boys, participate in most of the village activities.

In the urban areas, especially in big cities like Tehran, both parents usually go to work, particularly in lower- and middle-class families. Lower-class women take different kinds of jobs, whereas educated women from the middle class occupy various professional positions. In more religious and traditional families, many women participate in the family economy by sewing, handicraft making, carpet weaving, and so forth, and a small percentage of them work outside the home. In these families, usually women do traditional female chores. Children of families with both parents working outside the home are more independent. Many youngsters, when at home, prepare or heat their own food, and the older children help younger ones with homework. Eating schedules are more flexible in these families. In traditional families in which men work outside the home and women are housewives, the members of the family often wait for the men to come home and then they all eat together.

Many modernized wealthy women have their own businesses; others are active in cultural and artistic activities like writing, painting, playing music, sculpting, and so on. The mealtimes of these families are flexible too, because all members are busy with different activities. Some teenagers from these families have their own cars or drive their parents' cars (the legal driving age is 18). Although the current law forbids the consumption of alcoholic beverages, some teens drink and smoke. According to a male high-school principal, "smoking has become a common and widespread phenomenon among boy students."[11] In recent years drug addiction has also been growing among the youth of all classes. These addicts use hashish, opium, and heroin. Teens with addicted parents are more exposed to drugs. There are almost 1,200,000 drug-addicted youths in the country.[12] Even some university students use drugs. According to one report, some 1.8 percent of male students and 0.7 percent of female students are addicted to drugs.[13]

TRADITIONAL AND NONTRADITIONAL FOOD

Different parts of the country have different traditional cuisines. For example, seaside people eat more fish, and people living in desert areas consume more red meat. However, there are a number of traditional foods that all Iranians like and eat regularly. Most of these include plain rice with different kinds of stews. The ingredients of most stews are lamb or beef, mixed with different kinds of cooked or fried vegetables (fried eggplant, green vegetables, etc.). There is also rice cooked with green beans or lentils, barberries, or green vegetables; this is usually served with cooked chicken, beef, or lamb. However, some people in the north and other parts of the country have a number of meatless cuisines. Modern families sometimes cook foreign cuisine such as steak, Indian, Japanese, or Chinese foods. By and large, Iranian Muslims do not eat pork because Islam forbids it.

Fresh fruits and vegetables constitute an important part of the daily Iranian diet. Vegetables and herbs like radishes, green onions, basil, and fresh mint are often served with main dishes. Yogurt is also commonly served with food, either plain or mixed with cucumber, salt, pepper, raisins, walnuts, and/or dried mint. Feta cheese is very popular; it is one of the main constituents of breakfast.

In most families the women cook, even those who have an outside job. In urban areas groceries are bought from marketplaces. There are many modern supermarkets in major cities such as Tehran, the capital. In rural areas people usually grow vegetables in their own yards or farms, and they bake bread. They also have their own natural dairy products. Bakeries, meat shops, and groceries have opened in many big villages in recent years. Villagers eat meat less frequently than city people do.

There are different tastes among Iranian teenagers. In general, they are used to the kinds of foods they eat at home. However, many teenagers in urban areas love certain kinds of Western food like pizza and hamburgers. Spaghetti is a favorite dish among children of all ages. With the growing popularity of Western food, there arise differences in food preferences between teenagers and their more traditional parents. In Tehran and other major cities, there are all kinds of restaurants representing different national and ethnic foods. Teenagers who can afford to go out eat their favorite food at these restaurants, with or without their parents.

SCHOOLING

For children between the ages of 6 and 14, education is compulsory. The literacy rate has increased in Iran since the Revolution. According to the latest estimate, the rate of literacy (between 6 and 14 years) in urban areas is 94.55 percent; in the rural areas it is 91.37 percent. The total number of students in the country (including primary, junior high, and high school) has increased from almost 8 million in 1979 to 18.6 million in the academic year 1996–1997, which is almost one-third of the population. About 68.8 percent, or 12.8 million students, study in the urban areas and 31.2 percent, or 5.8 million, in the rural areas.[14]

The educational system includes five years of elementary school, three years of junior high, and three years of high school. Students' field of study in high school is determined in junior high school. Those who intend to go to a university take an additional year of pre-university courses. Those who do not intend to go to college receive their diploma at the end of the third year of high school. High school students can major in science, humanities, biology, or a vocational program.

All schools are sexually segregated. Before the Revolution there were a few mixed schools, but immediately after the Revolution they were closed. The majority of students go to public schools, which charge almost no tuition. Classes in public schools, especially in urban areas, are very crowded, sometimes with 45 to 50 students in one class. Teachers have a hard time covering their subjects and often do not have time to know all students adequately. Public schools start at 8 A.M. and end at 1 P.M.

There are a number of private schools in urban areas, in which children of well-off families are enrolled. The tuition fees of these schools vary. Some charge a very high tuition. Because of the low-quality education of many public schools, educated middle-class families who are concerned about their children's education endure economic hardship in order to send their children to private schools. Admission to these schools is generally based on entrance test scores and grade point averages. Private schools keep their students for longer hours, some until 2:45 P.M. and others even longer. These schools have better teachers and fewer students (between 20 and 25 in each class). The total number of students enrolled in private schools is 704,000, that is, 3.8 percent of all students.[15] Those who go to public schools often have to choose a school near their residence. Those who go to private schools have more liberty in choosing the school they want. Besides public and private schools, there are a number of special education schools for highly talented students, physically handicapped students, and students with learning disabilities.

In general, students have a heavy daily homework load, whether they attend public or private schools. Parents often help their children with homework. In the Iranian education system, a great emphasis is placed on memorization and there are not enough supplementary learning facilities. One of the most emphasized subjects in the curriculum is mathematics because it is viewed as essential for pursuing science and engineering.

Most teachers are strict and expect great respect and hard work from their students. When the teacher arrives in the classroom, everybody stands up as a sign of respect. They are expected to remain silent in the class until they are called on. In some private schools, teachers are more flexible and friendly. However, in both public and private schools, moral standards are rigidly enforced. If a student gets into any trouble—including being disrespectful to the teacher, fighting with other students, smoking, drinking, exchanging videotapes or CDs, not following the school dress code, and the like—a meeting will be arranged between the school principal, the student, and his or her parents. In the meeting the student is advised to behave; if not, she or he will be expelled from school.

In Iran, there are no coed schools and women are not allowed to teach in boys' high schools. Women teachers and girl students have to strictly observe the Islamic clothing code in schools. They have to cover their hair and wear long-sleeved robes of dark colors. Female students and teachers have to wear a uniform (often black, blue, dark green, or brown with pants to match).

The students take exams in all their subjects two times during an academic year, one at the end of each semester. The minimum passing score for each subject is 10 out of a maximum of 20, but the grade point average should not go below 12. Grades are very important in Iran, and students are under heavy pressure from both their teachers and parents to get the highest grades. The high-quality private schools require the highest possible grade point average for admission—a score of at least 19 out of 20 (equivalent to an A). In order to get the highest grades, many students have to hire a private tutor or attend private supplementary classes in the evenings.

One of the main worries of high school students is admission to a university, which is extremely competitive, especially in fields like engineering and medicine. If they do not pass the university entrance exam, they have to take it in the next academic year. Some take the exam several times and consequently get depressed, especially when their parents blame them. Many high school students practice the exam questions, starting in their junior, or even sophomore, year of high school. They take summer courses, and during the academic year they study textbooks from all four grades of high school and review previous exam questions and guidelines. All kinds of educational supplementary materials—including videotapes, CDs, cassette tapes, handbooks, and Web sites—have been produced for this purpose by private agencies. However, this is most common among middle- and upper-class students in the urban areas who have access to these facilities. Many lower-class students, especially in rural areas, do not pursue university education because of financial or academic reasons. In recent years the ratio of girls to boys participating in the entrance exam has increased: 57 percent of the participants in 2000 were girls and 43 percent were boys.[16]

SOCIAL LIFE

Since the Revolution of 1979, great changes have been made in Iran in terms of social relationships. The Islamic republic has attempted to replace secular and modern norms with Islamic norms and values through all means, including school textbooks, media, religious preaching, and lectures given by authorities. The young people are always reminded to follow "Islamic principles." In fact, "the Iranian Revolution is categorized as an 'ideological Revolution,' defined as one in which cultural issues are at the core of the revolutionary movement and cultural transformation is of primary importance."[17] All textbooks in the academic year 1981–1982 were rewritten according to the principles of the Islamic republic, and since then, no major changes have been made to these books. The new books reflect the state ideology and give guidelines for an "ideal Islamic citizen and Islamic society." An ideal individual or a good citizen, introduced in the textbooks, is one who has a simple life, is honest, has a sense of responsibility, believes in chastity and modesty, and avoids material desires, pleasure, or Western style of life.[18] "One of the most important values transmitted by social studies books is the belief in martyrdom. Schoolchildren are told that in Islam and especially in Shi'ism, a martyr ... gives his/her life for the betterment of the society and the welfare of the people."[19] In these books Iran is presented as a homogenous society with devoted Muslim people; there is almost no mention of political, cultural, and religious diversity.[20]

After the Revolution all nightclubs were shut down, intimate and public relationships between unmarried couples became illegal, and veiling for girls from 9 or 10 years old and up became compulsory. Girls have to cover their hair and wear modest, long-sleeved clothing, preferably of a dark color, in public places. All means are used to make the youths believe the Islamic moralities and rules. TV and radio programs, which are controlled by the government, advise the youth to be good Muslims.

In spite of all these measures, teenagers act according to their own wills and their immediate social and cultural environment. They wear different styles of dress outside of school. Modern teenagers from the middle and upper classes wear very fashionable clothes. Boys wear jeans with all kinds of T-shirts in public, and girls wear fancy European-style and designer dresses at family parties. But in smaller traditional cities, teen girls have to observe veiling more strictly and follow family rules. However, in recent years many teenagers with traditional family backgrounds have broken family rules and have been attracted to Western-style clothing and entertainment. Therefore, they often have arguments with their parents regarding this matter.

Furthermore, in Iranian culture youths are expected to respect their parents and follow their family traditions. However, teenagers pursue their own private interests in secret. They have developed all kinds of ways of doing this, including hiding their favorite music tapes, going to their friends' houses to listen to music and date, or even pretending to hate the opposite sex in order to gain more freedom to go out.[21] They also have developed a kind of slang, drawing from classical Persian poetry to butcher's lingo to western action hero like Arnold Schwarzenegger to communicate with each other, without anyone else able to understand. Through this slang they talk about their secrets, including arranging dates. But, in fact, in contemporary Iranian society the state rules are more important than family rules, and it is harder for kids to get away with the former than the latter. Moreover, because of the state pressures, many parents, including traditional ones, have become more flexible than in the past. They protect their kids from the government or school authorities if they get caught, even though they may not agree with their kids. However, some traditional families are still strict in their beliefs and rules; for example, they consider socializing between girls and boys a great sin and punish their kids for wrongdoing. Consequently, the teenagers who belong to these families have to either hide their feelings, interests, and relations or end up running away from home or even committing suicide.

Research on Iranian male and female students shows that girls, compared to boys in elementary and junior high school, are more conformist. However, in high school this trend becomes reversed. High school girls, compared to boys of the same age, are more affected with psychological, physical, moral, and educational problems—for example, depression, anxiety, suicide, violence, stealing, cheating, involvement with the opposite sex, verbal and visual problems. On the other hand, boys of all ages are more involved in using and distributing drugs, cigarettes, and alcoholic beverages.[22] Teenagers arrested for committing various crimes are sent to juvenile centers where they are rehabilitated for a period of time.

Except for universities, all schools, sports clubs, and even beaches are segregated by sex. Men and women are separated even at wedding ceremonies and other social events held in public places such as hotels and restaurants. Those wishing more freedom hold their parties at home. Despite all restrictions imposed by the state, girls and boys, in modern parts of urban areas, socialize with each other in parks, theaters, public libraries, friends' houses, shopping malls, and so on. Since relationships between girls and boys are prohibited in public, some modern families let their teenagers invite their friends from the opposite sex to their birthday or other occasions so that they can have healthy relationships with supervision. At the parties, teenagers exchange telephone numbers and e-mail addresses. Sometimes mixed-sex groups of teenagers go hiking together, even though this is also illegal in Iran and may result in occasional arrests

and punishment. In general, whether urban or rural, rich or poor, educated or uneducated, Iranians do not believe in premarital sex and
encourage their children to say no in all circumstances. Even modern and
secular families, who give more freedom to their kids, do not believe in
premarital sexual relationships.

Traditional and religious families, who deeply believe in segregation of
the sexes and forbid their children from socializing with the opposite sex,
follow the custom of arranged marriage. In this case, parents or adult family members select proper mates from among relatives or friends for the
youth. Because of the importance of marriage and family in Islam, the
government encourages young people to marry and has tried to remove
obstacles to the marriage of young people. Despite this encouragement,
the average age at marriage has gone up in recent years, mostly for economic reasons. The average age at marriage for women increased from
20.9 in 1991 to 22.4 in 1996, and for men from 24.6 to 25.[23]

RECREATION

Socializing with family and friends, going to restaurants, and strolling in
bazaars, streets, or parks are the most common recreational activities
among Iranians. The parks in Iran used to be the gathering place for old
people, but in recent years all parks are full of youths who walk and chat
with each other. The most common sports among teenagers are soccer,
basketball, tennis, table tennis, and swimming. Skiing is an expensive
sport, and only a minority of teenagers from rich families can afford it.
Wrestling used to be the most popular national sport in Iran. However, in
the last three to four decades soccer has become the most popular sport
with all ages, particularly teenagers. Some teenagers like hiking, especially university students. Many schools have sports teams that compete
with other school teams. Two hours a week of physical education is part of
school curriculums. However, in general, sports are not taken seriously in
schools, especially in public schools. In some schools, students even use
the time for physical education to do their homework. There are a number of sports clubs in each city, but not everyone can afford to pay the
monthly fees. Therefore, teen boys always play soccer in the streets
around their houses. In major cities there are a few playgrounds. In many
small cities and villages there are no playgrounds, stadiums, theaters, public libraries, or even parks; so, young people often walk in the streets or
watch TV.

The two most famous and oldest soccer teams in the country are based
in Tehran and have survived the changes of the Revolution. Players on

the teams Pirouzi (Victory) and Isteqlal (Independence) are national heroes, often participating in international soccer matches. Many young people are their fans and buy their posters and hang them in their rooms. In fact, throughout the country most teenagers are followers of one of these two teams. When these teams compete with each other, most people sit in front of the TV and watch, and more than 100,000 people, mostly teenagers (of course, all male) go to the stadium. Stadiums are all male unless female sports teams compete; then the audience is exclusively female.

In fact, there is a big difference between girls and boys in terms of sports. In general, there are fewer sports centers for girls. The government applies very strict sex segregation rules for sports in public. On the beach girls can swim in fenced places. Anyone who violates the rules will be arrested. The most popular sport among Iranian girls is volleyball. A few schools have teams that compete with each other. But these competitions are never shown on national TV. In recent years girls have been attracted to soccer, and a few soccer-training classes have been opened. There are not many national sports heroes among girls. They are also not allowed to play in public. They can only go to women's gyms.

ENTERTAINMENT

In general, Iranian families prefer their children to have family-centered entertainment, like visiting relatives, going on picnics, going to the theater, and taking trips to other cities, especially seaside areas. Some well-off families have houses by the beach. They go there in the summer, on weekends, or on most holidays. Some teens from rich families travel to Europe or other parts of the world with their families. One of the most common and affordable entertainments for Iranian teens is going to the movie theater. Some teens in the major cities, especially in Tehran, also go to plays, which are offered regularly.

The main evening entertainment for most Iranians is watching TV. However, TV programs are not appealing to teenagers. Some programs are boring, repetitive, and very didactic. In most TV programs, especially movie serials, traditional male and female roles are reinforced. Therefore, many teenagers in urban areas watch American or European movies, on video or CD player, and some have satellite TV (although it is not legal) at home. Middle- and upper-class urban teenagers also entertain themselves with computer games. They buy, copy, or exchange music CDs with each other. In some families teens have access to the Internet, so they chat, send messages to each other, and download the latest pop music.

Iranian teens, especially girls, are also interested in reading novels and poetry. Some novels are very popular, especially those dealing with women's lives. Some of the very popular poets and writers are those who have been condemned by the Islamic republic. However, their books have been reprinted many times. In fact, often books that are opposed by the government become more popular among the youth.

Iranian teenagers listen to all kinds of music. Their favorite music varies by the social groups they belong to. Family taste is an important element in the kind of music teenagers are attracted to; however, some teens may favor music disliked by their families. Some like traditional Iranian music, some prefer pop music, and some love folk music. Others are attracted to rap and heavy metal. Sometimes popular male singers sing in large concert halls. Tickets are not cheap, but these concerts still become very crowded, sometimes having audiences of up to thousands of young boys and girls. Women singers are not allowed to sing in public, but sometimes they hold all-female concerts in concert halls.

Some teens from the middle and upper classes in urban areas take music lessons, either privately or in music institutes. Most of them take traditional Iranian music lessons. However, a small percentage of modern affluent families favor Western classical music; their children take piano or violin classes, mostly privately at home. At present there are no dance clubs in Iran, and girls and boys dancing together is not allowed in public. Some teenagers with a modern family background dance with each other at birthday parties, weddings, or other private parties. The government condemns these behaviors, and the police sometimes disrupt these events and punish those who take part in them.

RELIGIOUS PRACTICES AND CULTURAL CEREMONIES

Shi'ism, being the dominant religion in Iran, has some popular religious ceremonies that the youth overwhelmingly participate in. The most typical ritual in the Shi'i tradition is the popular annual mourning in commemoration of the martyrdom of Imam Hussein, the third Shi'i *Imam* (religious leader) and the Prophet Mohammed's grandson. Imam Hussein was killed at Karbala, Iraq, in a battle against Yazid on the tenth day of the lunar month of Muharram (known as Ashura) in 61 A.H. (A.D. 680). Shi'is interpret Imam Hussein's death as a voluntary sacrifice for the struggle against injustice and oppression. Each year, during the month of Muharram, people mourn Hussein's death by wearing black clothes, gathering in mosques, and listening to the story of his martyrdom told by the clerics. In these meetings, listeners commonly break out in tears, and some, while crying, beat themselves. Since Shi'a Islam became the state religion in Iran in the sixteenth century, various kinds of commemoration ceremonies, including religious passion plays (called *ta'ziya*), have been developed. These plays are performed in the streets, and people gather to watch. On Ashura, all schools, shops, offices, and restaurants are closed. National radio and TV do not broadcast music on this occasion.

Many youths participate in these ceremonies. However, like all aspects of teen life in Iran, the degree of their participation varies by region, family environment, and religiosity. In small and more traditional cities, youths are more active in these commemorations. Local mosques undertake the duty of organizing these events. On these occasions the youth, often boys, organize mourning meetings, distribute food, march in the streets, perform religious dramas, and participate in other related activities. In the large cities the youth from modern and affluent families are less interested in these ceremonies. Apart from the religious dimension, these ceremonies are mostly regarded as occasions for socialization by Iranian youth.

In contrast to commemorative customs, there are several popular religious and national customs among Iranians that express joy and happiness. The Islamic government often attempts to reinforce the commemorative ceremonies and downplay national ceremonies. In the textbooks martyrdom is dramatized; schoolchildren are told that a martyr is a person who gives his or her life voluntarily to stop injustice and bring about prosperity for the people. However, since the Revolution, as a reaction to the Islamization of the society and the strict state control of their daily social lives, people celebrate joyful ceremonies with more enthusiasm.

The most popular national Iranian holiday that all people love, regardless of their age, sex, or religion, is the ancient Persian New Year, called Noruz—the first day of spring, which is March 21. Iranian people deeply believe that Noruz is a time for joy and celebration. The origin of Noruz goes back several thousand years and is based on the rebirth of the earth and its crops. All customs associated with Noruz reflect this idea of renewal. People begin to prepare well in advance. For example, before the New Year begins, people clean and some even paint their houses, and they buy new furniture and clothes. Noruz shopping in Iran is like Christmas shopping in Western countries. Because Noruz is a national holiday, schools are closed for thirteen days. On the thirteenth day of the new year, people go outside to picnic. During the Noruz holiday, people visit each other and give gifts or money to the kids.

The other important religious ceremony is the annual celebration of Mohammad's call to prophecy, called *Eid Mab'ath*. This is a very important day for all Muslims. Both Shi'i and Sunni Muslims celebrate this day and consider it more important than Mohammed's birthday, because they believe that on this day the Prophet went through a rebirth. Each year on this day people decorate trees with lights, are happy, go out, and listen to music. Some people believe that this is a good day to hold wedding ceremonies. In Iran, every region in the country celebrates the day of Mab'ath differently according to local customs. For example, in the central part of the country children chant and walk in the neighborhood, and then people come out and give them something to eat such as candy and fruit (like Halloween in the United States).

An official religious practice initiated by the Islamic government since the Revolution is the celebration of reaching the age of Islamic puberty for girls, called *jashn-e taklif* ("obligation ceremony"). This happens at the end of the third year of elementary school (when girls are 9 years old). All girls' religious obligations, including veiling, daily prayer, fasting, and so forth, begin at this age. A girl of 9 is expected to act like an adult woman even though her family and the society still consider her a child. This paradox brings about some problems for girls at this age. Girls react differently to this practice, and family environment is an influential element. Some become ultra-religious for a period of time, but others disregard it and continue their childhood. In fact, this is not a popular religious ceremony.

CONCLUSION

One of the important aspects of contemporary Iran is its young and diverse population. Since the Revolution the Islamic establishment has made unsuccessful attempts to bring about uniformity within the diverse young population. In general, the youth in contemporary Iran are under the influence of religious culture (through family and the official culture), family environment, neighborhood or peer groups, unofficial culture (including literature, art, films, etc.), and the world culture (through travel, satellite TV, videos, Internet, etc.) even though there are all kinds of contradictions among these sources. Therefore, Iranian youth constantly have to deal with a number of dualities: government rules versus family style, individual interests versus school rules, individual desires versus family expectations, and imposed official ideology versus the society's reality. There are even a number of conflicting ages of adulthood: official religious puberty is 9 years old for girls and 15 years for boys. The voting age for both sexes is 15, and the legal age (for getting a driver's license, opening a bank account, getting a passport, working, etc.) is 18. Confronting these contradictory sources and rules, Iranian teenagers have adopted various strategies. Compared to previous generations, they have become more pragmatic, more independent, less conformist, and more world conscious.

NOTES

1. William L. Cleveland, *A History of the Modern Middle East*. (Boulder, CO: Westview Press, 1994), 65.

2. Gholsm-Reza Vatandoust, "The Status of Iranian Women during the Pahlavi Regime," in *Women and Family in Iran*, ed. Aghar Fathi (Leiden: E. J. Brill, 1985), 185.

3. Joseph M. Upton, *The History of Modern Iran: An Interpretation of Iran* (Cambridge, MA: Harvard University Press, 1961), 58.

4. Nikki R. Keddie, *Roots of Revolution: An Interpretive History of Modern Iran* (New Haven and London: Yale University Press, 1981), 142.

5. Ibid, p. 183.

6. Ibid, p. 231.

7. Afsaneh Najmabadi, "Hazards of Modernity and Morality: Women, State and Ideology in Contemporary Iran," in *The Modern Middle East*, eds. A. Hourani, P. Khoury, and M. Wilson (Berkeley and Los Angeles: University of California Press, 1993).

8. Amir H. Mehryar, *Sustainable Human Development in Iran* (Tehran: Institute for Research on Planning and Development (IRPD), 1994).

9. Statistical Center of Iran (SCI). *Sar-Shomari-y Omoumi-I Nofoos, Maskan—1375: Natayedj Tafsili* [National Census of Population and Housing—1996: Detailed Results] (Tehran: SCI, 1996).

10. Ibid.

11. "Dar barabar-e Asibhaye Ejtemaa'i Chegouneh Nojavaanaan ra Masoun Negahbedarim" [How to Protect the Youth from Social Malign], *Iran* (daily newspaper in Persian), 23 February 1997.

12. "Javaani Jam'eiyat Keshvar: Ham yek forsat va Ham yek Tahdid ast" [Youthfulness of the Country's Population: An Opportunity and a Threat], *Hamshahri* (daily newspaper in Persian), 15 February 2001.

13. Ibid.

14. SCI [National Census].

15. Majlis va Pajouhesh, Amouzeh va Parvaresh-i Keshvar dar sal 1377 [a pamphlet, Education and Discipline in Iran in 1998], 30 January 1998.

16. *Peyk-i Sanjesh* (weekly journal in Persian), No. 187, 31 July 2000.

17. Golnar Mehran, "Ideology and Education in the Islamic Republic of Iran," *Compare* 20, no. 1 (1990): 53.

18. Golnar Mehran, "Socialization of Schoolchildren in the Islamic Republic of Iran," *Iranian Studies* 22 (1989): 35–50.

19. Ibid.

20. Ibid.

21. Sa'id Peivandi, "Tajroubeh Tahsili Doukhtaraan Javaan Dar Madaares Iran" [The Educational Experience of Young Girls in the Iranian Schools], a summary of a lecture at the Women Research Foundation of Iran at the University of California, Berkeley, January 2000.

22. Ministry of Education, Research Section. "Amar Ikhtelaalaat Guzaresh shodeh dar Madaares Shahr Tehran dar saal Tahsili 1378–79" [The Census on Deviation of Schoolchildren Reported in the City of Tehran in the Academic Year of 1999–2000], 2000.

23. SCI [National Census].

RESOURCE GUIDE

Books and Articles

Abrahamian, Ervand. *Iran between Two Revolutions.* Princeton, NJ: Princeton University Press, 1982.

Arjomand, Said. *The Turban for the Crown: The Islamic Revolution in Iran.* Oxford: Oxford University Press, 1988.

"Children of the Islamic Revolution." *The Economist,* January 18, 1997.

Ferdows, Adele K., "Gender Roles in Iranian Public School Textbooks." In *Children in the Moslem Middle East,* edited by Elizabeth W. Fernea, 325–336. Austin: University of Texas Press, 1995.

Friedl, Erika. *Children of Deh Koh: Young Life in an Iranian Village.* Syracuse, NY: Syracuse University Press, 1997.

Higgins, Patricia J., and Pirouz Shoar-Ghaffari. "Changing Perceptions of Iranian Identity in Elementary Textbooks." In *Children in the Moslem Middle East,* edited by Elizabeth W. Fernea, 337–364. Austin: University of Texas Press, 1995.

Keddie, Nikki R. *Roots of Revolution: An Interpretive History of Modern Iran.* New Haven and London: Yale University Press, 1981.

Khosrokhavar, Farhad. "Attitudes of Teenage Girls to the Iranian Revolution." In *Children in the Moslem Middle East,* edited by Elizabeth W. Fernea, 392–409. Austin: University of Texas Press, 1995.

Mahdi, Ali Akbar. "Children in the Iranian Culture and Society." *Iran Times.* March 21; March 28; April 4, 1997.

Mehran, Golnar. "Ideology and Education in the Islamic Republic of Iran." *Compare* 20, no. 1 (1990).

———. "Socialization of Schoolchildren in the Islamic Republic of Iran." *Iranian Studies* 22 (1989): 35–50.

———. "A Study of Girls' Lack of Access to Primary Education in the Islamic Republic of Iran." *Compare* 27, no. 3 (1997): 263–276.

Nafisi, Rasul. "Education and the Culture of Politics in the Islamic Republic of Iran." In *Iran: Political Culture in Islamic Republic of Iran,* edited by Samih K. Farsoun and Mehrdad Mashayekhi, 160–178. London and New York: Routledge, 1992.

Najmabadi, Afsaneh. "Hazards of Modernity and Morality: Women, State and Ideology in Contemporary Iran." In *The Modern Middle East*, edited by A. Hourani, P. Khoury, and M. Wilson. Berkeley: University of California Press, 1993.

Sayf, Sousan. "A Comparison between Problems of Iranian Adolescent Girls Residing in Iran and the United States." *Farzaneh* 1, no. 4 (Summer & Fall 1994): 169–174.

Fiction

Amirshahi, Mahshid. *Suri & Co.: Tales of a Persian Teenager*. Austin, TX: Center for Middle Eastern Studies, 1995.

Daneshvar, Simin. *Savushun: A Novel about Modern Iran*, trans. M. R. Ghanoonparvar. Washington, DC: Mage Publisher, 1991.

Parsipur, Shahrnush. *Women without Men: A Novella*, Trans. Kamran Talattof and Jocelyn Sharlet. Syracuse, NY: Syracuse University Press, 1998.

Rachlin, Nahid. *Foreigner*. New York: W. W. Norton, 1999.

———. *Married to a Stranger*. San Francisco: City Lights Books, 1993.

Web Sites

http://www.salamiran.org/Embassy/
Iranian Embassy. General information about the country, travel documents, tourism, and economy.

http://www.sci.or.ir
Statistical Center of Iran. Limited statistics about the country, population, cities, and commerce.

http://www.Iranian.com/
The Iranian is an Internet magazine based in California and updated daily. It is the first and most visited site by Iranians on the net. It contains news, photos, music, humor, and articles on all aspects of Iran. It provides a window to the thoughts and feelings of second-generation Iranians, especially in the United States.

http://www.un.int/iran/
The Permanent Mission of the Islamic Republic of Iran to the United Nations. Press releases, documents, and official statements by the government.

http://www.ankaboot.com/
Index of Iranian Web sites sorted in numerous categories including history, culture, arts, children and family issues, entertainment, society and culture.

http://www.badjens.com/
Bad Jens is a feminist magazine published in Iran. It deals with women's issues in contemporary Iran.

http://www.iranianchildren.org/
Iranian Children's Rights Society is a public nonprofit children's rights advocacy organization. Dedicated to improving the lives of children in Iran, the site

contains book reviews, articles, photos, and information on Iranian children.

http://www.payvand.com/

An indexed page providing news, photos, and cultural and historical information about Iranian society.

http://www4.ncsu.edu/~amsaleh2/iran/

The Iranian Web offers information and resource links about the Iranian culture. Categories include: business, education, news, radio/television, chat room, music, travel, culture, sports, publishers/publications, weather, and other related sites.

http://www.persia.org/

The Iranian Cultural Information Center was the first Iranian Web site on the Internet for learning about this new method of communication and teaching others about the rich culture of Iran. It now offers up-to-date tourist, cultural, and historical information about Iran.

http://www.zan.org/

Zan is an interactive Directory/Anthology of the arts and ideas of Iranian women. It also serves as a place where Iranian women network with one another.

http://www.ihrwg.org/

This is the official site of the Iranian Human Rights Working Groups. Numerous articles and statements of violation of rights of women and children can be found here.

Pen Pal/Chat

http://www.iranian.com/chat.html
http://www.payvand.com/board/
http://www.rahnema.com/chat/voice/

Chapter 2

IRAQ

Nadje Al-Ali and Yasmin Hussein

INTRODUCTION

Iraq is located in the area associated with one of the earliest civilizations of humankind: Mesopotamia—the land of two rivers (the Tigris and the Euphrates). With an area of approximately 170,000 square miles and a population of about 22 million, Iraq is the largest of the Fertile Crescent countries at the northern edge of the Arabian peninsula. Iraq is situated in the southwest region of the "near east" of the Arab world, bounded on the north by Turkey, on the east by Iran, on the west by Syria, Jordan, and Saudi Arabia, and on the south by Kuwait, Saudi Arabia, and the Persian Gulf.[1] The terrain included within the borders of Iraq is extremely diverse, ranging from swamps in the south to dry desert plains in central Iraq, fertile agricultural land along the two rivers, and inaccessible mountainous areas in the north.

Iraq was historically a multiethnic state with many ethnic and religious groups. Today's Iraq has a majority of Arabs (75–80%) and minorities of Kurds (15–20%) as well as Turkmans and Assyrians (about 5%). Arabic is the main language spoken in Iraq, followed by Kurdish and a small number of people speaking Assyrian and Armenian.

The nation-state of Iraq, formerly part of the Ottoman Empire, was created only in 1920, initially as a British mandate. Iraq became an independent kingdom in 1932, although it was subjected to another British occupation from 1941 to 1945. A revolution in 1958 ended with the proclamation of a republic. But it was the revolution of July 17, 1968 that brought the currently prevailing Ba'th Party into power. Its ideological origins were based on a strong belief in Arab unity (Arab nationalism) and a socialist-oriented transformation of society. The current president of Iraq, Saddam Hussein, is also the central party leader of the Ba'th Party. However, many Iraqi people would argue that the party and its leadership have diverged significantly from its original ideas and aims.

Saddam Hussein has been the president of the Republic of Iraq since 1979—the same year the Shah of Iran was overthrown in the course of the Islamic Revolution. In 1980, Hussein started a war with neighboring Iran that lasted eight years and cost many human lives on both sides. The Iraqi economy had been struggling due to increased oil prices in the late 1970s and early 1980s. However, the prolonged war with Iran resulted in a severe economic crisis as well as an enormous strain on social life for many Iraqi families. Only two years after the end of the Iran-Iraq war, Hussein ordered Iraqi troops to invade Kuwait in August 1990. Economic sanctions were imposed a few days after the invasion. The Gulf War of 1991 forced Iraq out of Kuwait. But it also resulted in the death of many Iraqis and the devastation of the Iraqi infrastructure. Continued economic sanctions and sporadic bombing of Iraq have had detrimental effects on both social and economic conditions in Iraq.

SPECIAL CONSIDERATION:
EFFECT OF ONGOING ECONOMIC SANCTIONS

This chapter reveals the universal concerns, aspirations, and anxieties of teenagers who live in Iraq, as well as the extreme conditions, difficulties, and suffering that are unique to Iraq and its adolescent population. At the heart of this contribution are the voices of several teenagers who were specifically interviewed for this chapter. They were asked questions related to their everyday lives, aspirations, and worries. There are several reasons to use a mainly qualitative approach to the exploration of teenage lives in Iraq: first, it is very difficult to obtain reliable statistical information in the Middle East in general and in Iraq, in particular. More significantly, the available statistics tend to conceal rather than reveal the actual experiences, attitudes, and life strategies of a group of people that has been silenced from within and without.

Through extensive in-depth conversations and interviews with a group of teenagers between the ages of 12 and 16, it is possible to get a sense of the present living conditions shaping their lives and restricting their choices, as well as a sense of the emotional landscapes of young Iraqis, their self-awareness, and attitudes toward "the outside world." The recorded interviews touch on a broad range of issues, varying from social change and transformations, problems with education, economic hardships, relationships with families and friends, gender relations, and identity questions. An underlying theme is the awareness that many of the difficulties facing young Iraqis today stem from an imposed sanctions regime that has not only devastated the economy but also affected the social and cultural fabric of Iraqi society.

References to "rapid social changes" and transformations of "normal lives" are common in the accounts of these teenagers. Despite indisputable political repression in the 1970s and 1980s, the majority of the Iraqi population at that time enjoyed high living standards in the context of an economic boom and rapid development, which were a result of the rise in oil prices and the government's developmental policies. Although signs of deterioration of living standards started to become evident during the years of the Iran-Iraq war (1980–1988), there seemed to be a prevailing belief that the situation would improve once the war stopped. And although many families lost sons, brothers, fathers, friends, and neighbors during this time, life in the cities appeared relatively "normal," with women notably playing a very significant role in public life.

Today's teenagers were born during these war years, when the Iraqi government encouraged everyone to fulfill "their duties" as citizens. While men were drafted in large numbers to the military, women were strongly encouraged to "produce" numerous children. Two relatively peaceful years were followed by the invasion of Kuwait (August 1990) and the Gulf War (January–March 1991). The latter was particularly traumatic for children, as night after night of heavy bombing not only disrupted their sleep and family lives but left many in deep shock and fear. Adolescent Iraqis have vivid memories of the Gulf War. Many spoke about ongoing nightmares, anxiety, and a great sensitivity to certain noises that could only remotely be mistaken for bombs. Unlike in other war-torn countries, like Bosnia-Herzegovina, post-traumatic stress syndrome is not a recognized medical condition in Iraq. Even if it were acknowledged, lack of resources and expertise make systematic treatment impossible.

While the memories related to the war in 1991, as well as political oppression by the Iraqi government, represent crucial elements in the pool of experiences that constitute the past of today's teenagers,[2] it is the comprehensive sanctions regime, in place since August 1990, that presents the most decisive factor in shaping the living conditions, options, and restrictions of Iraqi teenagers. Continuously high rates of child mortality (about 4000–5000 per month),[3] rampant malnutrition,[4] increased rates of leukemia, and various other forms of cancer, epidemic diseases, and birth deformities are among the most obvious side effects of the sanctions regime. The fear of disease and death is a real and a steady companion while growing up these days. The massive deterioration in basic infra-structure (water, sanitation, sewage, electricity) has severely reduced the quality of life of Iraqi families, who often have to get through the day without water and electricity. Not only have everyday lives changed with respect to the drastic deterioration of economic conditions and basic infrastructure, but the social and cultural fabric of Iraqi society has also been affected.

Alongside the drastic changes related to everyday lives, the intellectual and cultural isolation that accompanies ongoing economic sanctions affects teenagers in various ways. Some feel resentful and angry toward an international community that does not seem to care about the plight of ordinary Iraqis and seems to punish them for the actions of a government they did not choose. Others do distinguish between certain Western governments and the people and culture of these countries. In light of difficult, if not impossible, access to alternative media and education other than government propaganda, teenagers often do not have the analytical tools and background information that the previous generations had. This, par-adoxically, among other factors has strengthened the regime of Saddam Hussein. Yet a surprising number of teenagers blame not only the outside world but also their own government for the current situation. And many have just one wish: to leave their homeland as soon as possible and start a new life somewhere else. Hazim, a 14-year-old boy whose mother recently died, often dreams of leaving but finds strength in his faith:

> Sometimes I do think that our lives have become harder than before. But I have to remember that God is with us, and that we need to be strong to manage everyday life. But sometimes I really think that it would be better to escape to another place where life is easier and much happier.
>
> [Where do you think such life exists?]
>
> Everywhere in the world, apart from Iraq and maybe some places in Africa. I often give myself time to dream of living in another part of the world, and imagine myself living differently than this miser-able life. But I quickly remember that God has chosen this kind of life for me and I think it is some sort of test of my faith in God.[5]

Although empty houses have become a common sight, there are also those that seem to have been largely unaffected by the sanctions regime. Some people have even built huge houses during recent years. An emerg-ing class of nouveau riche war and sanctions profiteers, linked in various direct and indirect ways to the political regime, continue to lead the lav-ish lifestyle that characterized many Iraqi families during the 1980s. In stark contrast to most of the other teenagers that were interviewed, Farah (14 years old) and her brother Samir (13 years old) enjoy fully furnished bedrooms with the latest equipment ranging from computers, TV, and CD players to even a satellite dish. Both express very little sympathy for their peers who live in economic hardship and misery. But both also have hardly any contact with "ordinary Iraqis" as their schools, social worlds, and family are separate from the world of the majority of Iraqis.

TYPICAL DAY

Due to the unique circumstances in contemporary Iraq, it is very difficult to describe a typical day for an Iraqi teenager. In the past, young Iraqis would go to school in the mornings, return for lunch between 2 and 4 o'clock, have their main meal with their family, maybe nap for an hour or two (especially in the summer months), do their homework and study, and then enjoy themselves with friends and family. In the evenings, when life was still relatively ordinary and calm, teenagers would go out and walk the streets in groups, have ice-cream or *shwarma* sandwiches (sliced lamb or beef served in a thin bread), play games with their friends from the same neighborhood, visit their numerous cousins, watch TV, and listen to the latest hits.

These days, everyday lives are characterized by unpredictability and struggles for survival. Leila, a 16-year-old, expressed sentiments that many young Iraqis feel:

> I hope to finish my education and become a civil engineer, and would like to feel that I am a significant part of society. I would like to be economically independent but share the responsibility for raising a future family together with a man whom I will respect and love as much as he would respect and love me. I think this dream is a basic thing for many people, but it seems so hard to actually make true. Although I have strong faith in my heart and believe that I shall make it one day, I cannot deny that I fear the unexpected things that could change everything. Our lives in Iraq are so unpredictable, especially the economic situation, which has a decisive impact on all aspects of our lives. So my mood is swinging all the time. Sometimes I feel optimistic, but most of the time it is hard to ignore the reality of our lives. This is why I often get depressed. Now, for example, I am very disappointed by the results of my high school exams. I really believe that I have done all my best to pass this level with a satisfactory result, but that was obviously not good enough. And now I have to repeat the whole year in order to get better

grades. I truly believe that the examinations of the next year will be even harder than this year.

Leila's passionate account of her dreams and fears quite vividly illustrates the fact that teenagers in Iraq have a lot in common with teenagers in other countries all over the world: they worry about their grades in school, have ambitions for future careers, and think about love. Teenagers everywhere dream about having enough money, and many hope for a future spouse that will care for and respect them. And who has not met an adolescent who is experiencing and displaying mood swings—being very happy one moment and extremely down and depressed the next?

Yet despite the commonalities with teenagers in other parts of the world, most notably the Middle East, Leila and her peers in Iraq experience daily hardships and obstacles to their dreams that are unique to their surroundings. The devastation of two wars (the Iran-Iraq War of 1980–1988 and the Gulf War of 1991) and ongoing economic sanctions have left their country in a desperate situation. Leila's worries about the unpredictability of life in Iraq and "the unexpected things that could change everything" typify the fears and anxieties of a whole generation that grew up in times of extreme upheaval related to war, military threats, an oppressive regime, and economic sanctions that reduce everyday lives to a continuous struggle for survival.

FAMILY LIFE

Traditionally, Iraqi families—like most families within the region—played a significant part in young people's lives. Children and teenagers were brought up not only by their parents but also by their elder siblings and members of the extended family, like grandparents, aunts, and uncles. Families tended to be large and provided not only material but also emotional support for teenagers. Because of the size of most families, gatherings were generally not only an affair for adults, but children of all ages and teenagers were always present.

Although Iraqi families used to be very closely knit and supportive of each other, family relationships have been strained by envy and competition in the struggle for survival. More than a decade of economic sanctions has exhausted the Iraqi economy and most people living inside Iraq. In the past, teenagers grew up in the midst of their extended families, often spending time and sleeping over at houses of their grandparents, uncles, and aunts. These days, nuclear families have become much more significant in a context where everyone has to think first about himself or herself and those closest to them.

Some teenagers reported that they stopped visiting their relatives, as they did not want the relatives to feel embarrassed at being unable to provide their visitors with a meal. Hospitality, especially where food is concerned, is a very important aspect of Iraqi culture. These days, most Iraqi families cannot provide their guests with nice food because of unemployment, low salaries, and widespread poverty linked to the economic sanctions. This fact has had a damaging impact on family and social life in contemporary Iraq.

Class inversions related to economic sanctions have also affected family ties in ways unheard of during earlier times. Whereas the majority of the Iraqi population has been impoverished and has suffered greatly from the policies of its own government, the Gulf War, and the economic sanctions, a small percentage of people have actually managed to profit from the situation. These people are mainly working within the black market economy; they engage in smuggling of goods across the Jordanian, Syrian, Iranian, or Turkish border. These nouveau riche war profiteers tend to have close ties to the regime of Saddam Hussein. Living in luxury in the midst of widespread suffering and poverty asks for envy and contempt. So the few rich people that live in Iraq tend to stick to themselves.

Responding to the question of whether they had friends among their relatives, 14-year-old Farah answers the following:

> Almost all our relatives, from my father's side and my mother's side, are living outside of Baghdad. After we moved to Baghdad, we didn't really like to go there, and they don't come to visit us very often. My mother says that they are envious of my father because he is rich and because he is a businessman. My father used to visit my grandparents, but they passed away some years ago, so he does not go to our old city so often any more.

Her brother Samir (13 years old) agrees with her that they do not have friends among their relatives. He states:

> My mother told me that I should not mix with people who are different from us, and I agree with her. If anybody of our relatives comes to visit us it means that they need some help or money. We cannot give what my father is earning in hard work to people who want to get easy money. I think this is the reason why my mother is not so friendly with her two sisters who are always complaining about money.

It is important to stress that Farah's and Samir's experience is not representative of the majority of Iraqi teenagers. Despite the hardship and the everyday struggle for survival, families still try to be supportive of each

other. Yet there is definitely a change in that the nuclear family (parents
and children) has become the most significant unit within Iraqi society.
Extended families still have close relationships; but these days, people first
think of themselves and their own children.

TRADITIONAL AND NONTRADITIONAL FOOD

Food has traditionally played a major role in Iraqi social and cultural
life. Iraqi cuisine is varied and rich, ranging from saucy vegetable and
meat dishes, grilled *kebabs* (skewered chunks of grilled meat), and fish
from the Tigris (*masgouf*) to various kinds of *kubbeh* (minced meat, pine
nuts, raisins, and spices covered with rice or grains). The main staple food
in Iraq is long-grain rice (*timn*). It is prepared in different ways and with
different flavors. And all Iraqis, regardless of class and economic situation,
love rice. Another important staple is bread. No meal passes without lots
of bread on the table. Vegetables like green beans, fava beans, okra,
aubergine (eggplant), tomatoes, and zucchini are the basis of many tasty
vegetable dishes that are poured over the rice. Iraqis love meat as well,
especially lamb. Lamb *kebabs*, big chunks of lamb with green beans or
okra, and stuffed roasted lamb (*quzi*) are all-time favorites among Iraqis.

It is mainly women who prepare the food, but occasionally men help
out to prepare breakfast or lunch, especially if the wife has a paid job outside the home. The main cooked meal is lunch, which is usually between
2 and 4 P.M. Breakfasts tend to be light: bread, cheese or eggs, jam, and
date syrup. For dinner, people either just eat leftovers from lunch or have
some fruit or a sandwich. In the past, teenagers would often go out with
friends to have ice cream or *shawarma* sandwiches at night. These days,
many families are glad if they can manage to have one meal to feed everyone in the family. Very few families can afford to buy meat, chicken, or
fish because of the economic situation. Rice and bread are the main food
items that people can afford.

Prior to the economic sanctions, Iraq imported 75 to 80 percent of food
products, which were consumed at a cost of over $2 billon in 1989.
Through the 1980s, despite the war with Iran, Iraq maintained a very low
rate of malnutrition. Food was heavily subsidized by the state and in plentiful supply. As early as February 1991, a WHO (World Health Organization) UNICEF mission to Baghdad estimated that the daily per capita
calorie intake had fallen from the pre-sanctions level of 3,340 kilo-
calories to less than 1,000 kilo-calories (one-third of the WHO recommendation). But the daily per capita calorie increased in 1997 to 1,225

kilo-calories and has remained at this level until now (WHO/UNICEF Joint Team Report: A Visit to Iraq, February 1991).

Since September 1990, the main source of food has been the government food ration. The monthly amount of food ration per person after the oil-for-food agreement in June 1997 is: 7 kg flour, 1.25 kg rice, 0.05 kg sugar, 50 gr tea, 0.75 liter cooking oil.[6] Of course, in addition to that, there are open markets, supermarkets, and small corner shops (and the black market), where one can find almost all food products. Yet most people cannot afford to buy much extra food from the market or from shops, as they do not have much cash. Many Iraqis are unemployed as a result of the current economic crisis, but even those who have jobs receive extremely low salaries. Actually, the gap between food prices and monthly salaries is widening. A family of five would still need approximately 125,000 ID (Iraqi Dinar) monthly to purchase food, whereas the monthly salary of an average civil servant is between 3,000 and 5,000 ID.[7]

SCHOOLING

In the past education has generally been valued highly and sometimes is still perceived to be a "way out" of the difficult life conditions of Iraqi teenagers. Leila, for example, is very much aware of the grim prospects she is facing. Nevertheless, she stresses the importance of education:

> I know the salaries are so low and would probably not be enough to cover the basic food needs for a small family for a week; it is my ambition in life to become a civil engineer. In my family we have been taught to respect education. It is almost a holy thing for us. My father and my mother are educators and although they had to give up their jobs as teachers because of the low salaries, I still believe that their attitude toward education has not changed. My father was working so many extra hours in order to pay for my private lessons. And my brother, who is only two years older than me, is now studying economics and at the same time helping my father driving the taxi. He has the same support by my parents even though as an economist he would receive less salary than a civil engineer. I mean, the salary is not an issue here. But I also believe and hope that the situation in Iraq will change in the near future and that life will be back to normal.

Despite Leila's optimism where education and the future are concerned, many other teenagers who were interviewed clearly doubt that education will help in the present circumstances. Moreover, the educational system itself is subject to much anxiety.

One of the most long-term debilitating aspects of the current situation in Iraq is the disintegration of the educational system—a system that was formerly known within the Middle East for its resources and efficiency. State-induced policies in the 1970s and 1980s worked to eradicate illiteracy, educate men and women, and incorporate them into the labor force. These were the years of general economic boom and the emergence and expansion of a broad middle class.[8] In the context of a rapidly growing labor market, the Iraqi government actively encouraged education: many new schools were built, teachers were trained, and the necessary infrastructure (i.e., transportation and child care) were provided to make education accessible for all. Children generally started school when they were 6 years old and went to primary school for a compulsory six years. This was followed by three years of intermediate school and three years of high school. Many of those who finished high school would study hard for their final exams in order to be able to enter a university.

In 1974 a government decree stipulated that all university graduates—whether men or women—would be employed automatically. In certain professions, such as those related to health care and teaching, education itself entailed a contract with the government that obliged the students to take up a job in the respective profession.

These days, however, the Iraqi government acknowledges that about 23 percent of all school-age children (6 to 15 years of age) are no longer attending school and are working to supplement family incomes. According to a 1995 survey by the United Nations Children's Fund (UNICEF), only 87 percent of Iraqi children were enrolled in primary schools—down from 100 percent before the Gulf War, and the numbers have been going down year by year. Of those who enroll, only 58 percent finish primary school. Many are sent to work or to beg on the streets.

UNICEF estimates that more than 50 percent of schools in the south and center of Iraq are unfit for teaching and learning: "Schools are not being maintained and repaired and experience severe shortages of basic school supplies, classroom furniture, textbooks and teaching aids."[9] Many teenagers endure very difficult conditions in schools, where walls are crumbling and desks are falling apart. Not rarely, cardboard covers broken glass in the windows, library shelves are mostly bare, and children sit on cracked floors to read.[10] Paper and pencils are often unavailable, and textbooks are generally outdated.

The lack of adequate investment in teacher training, and in teaching and learning materials, has seriously affected the overall quality of edu-

Iraqi teenagers perform on stage next to a picture of President Saddam Hussein during a celebration in Baghdad, Iraq, marking International Women's Day, Sunday, March 8, 1998. (AP Photo/Peter Dejong)

cation. Teachers' salaries are grossly inadequate. This situation has prompted an increasing number of qualified teachers to leave the sector in search of better-paid jobs.[11] Especially in poor neighborhoods, where teachers cannot supplement their incomes with private lessons, many teachers have dropped out. Samira, 14 years old, says:

> This year, I had to take many private lessons because some teachers at our school have so suddenly left the school, and we were left behind without receiving many classes this year. So it was absolutely necessary to have private teachers in order to complete the curriculum of many subjects such as physics, mathematics, and chemistry. We could study other subjects, such as geography or English, alone.

Private lessons are an essential part of a pupil's education, and those who cannot afford it tend to fail their exams. Some teenagers reported that their parents have taken over the role of teaching them, as many educated Iraqis do not trust the current schooling system to provide an adequate education for their children. Yet despite the poor secondary education available to Iraqi teenagers, end-of-year exams are extremely demanding and nerve-racking affairs. Leila (age 16), who failed her final exams in high school, complains:

I think every year the state exams are becoming harder and harder, because the university has a limited capacity for new admissions. On the other hand, there are an increasing number of new students who would like to continue their education in university. This is why I think that the examinations are made intentionally hard. Admission to university is so difficult that a big number of young people, especially boys, are pressured to go for the military service. You know, when the boys are not at university, they have to do their military service, and many of these men stay in the military for the rest of their lives.

Ever since the Iraq-Iran war (1980–1988), being drafted into the army has become a very possible, and often frightening, reality for male teenagers. A place at a university, successful studies, and financial means help them to avoid being drafted into the army for a long period of time. For the majority of young Iraqi men, however, the encounter with the military starts very early in life and constitutes an ongoing threat and reality. Yet it is not only boys who suffer severe consequences if they fail the final exams of high school. For girls, this could also be detrimental:

If I am not able to complete my university degree, it means that I am going to sit at home all the time doing housework, and I will be isolated from the rest of the world. But, the worst of all is that the only option left is to get married. I would have no other things to do with my life except being a housewife. Imagine, what a future would I have then? I know some cases where the girls could not finish their education because of the same problem and they have been pressured to marry anybody, even without their consent. I also knew a girl who committed suicide after a long time of depression, sitting at home without any hope for a better future other than a marriage without love.

The fear of failure in their education increases the stress levels of a generation of Iraqis for whom trauma, worry, and anxiety are part of their immediate experiences. Despite the ongoing deterioration of the education system, Iraqis, in general, still value education greatly, and the sense of confidence and self of a young person is often bound up with his or her achievements in school and university. Especially middle-class parents, who particularly value education, might sell all their belongings to be able to help their children through school. Many parents work more than one job to make ends meet. Saad (a 15-year-old boy) rarely sees his father, as he is always out trying to make some money:

My father used to work at the biggest dairy factory in Baghdad, but the factory has been changed into a small family business. All the staff is laid off, as there was not enough work anymore. My father is doing freelance work now. He is doing different jobs: for example, he is sometimes selling vegetables, working on a construction site, or selling and buying various things. But in the evening, he is always polishing shoes in different parts of the city.

More and more frequently, it is the teenagers themselves who have to contribute to the daily costs of living, and particularly the costs of schooling. Ali, a 13-year-old shoeshine boy, explains why he is working:

These days, my family needs more money because of the opening of schools. We need to buy clothes, shoes, books, notebooks, and pencils for the whole family. My father cannot manage to make all this money, so my brother and myself are helping him. The re-opening of the Baghdad Fair[12] is a good opportunity to earn some money. There are many people, as you have seen yourself, visiting and celebrating the event. My brother is also working here with my father and me, but he only works in his free time. He is attending the second year at the medical school. I am really proud of him because he is going to be a doctor within four years. He is very busy with his studies, but he has to help also. [whispering] He is not working as much as I do.

SOCIAL LIFE

The social life of teenagers has also been negatively affected by the current conditions inside Iraq. Spending time with friends has become a privilege in and of itself. Many young Iraqis have taken on responsibilities that used to be only carried by adults in the past. Hazim (14 years old) started to work and look after his younger siblings when his mother died, which was three months before the interview:

My mother fell so suddenly ill and within only one week, we lost her. We still don't know what was the reason for her death. She felt tired, and one day she just did not wake up in the morning. This summer was the worst time ever for us because of my mother's death. We realized that everything changed. I felt that I grew older and that I had to share responsibilities with my father and my oldest brother. My mother did not like to see me working apart from doing homework. She believed that I should only study and care for my school, but this has changed now as she passed away. She used to share the responsibility of the household together with my father. Imagine, she was sometimes earning more in one week than my father's monthly income. She was a very strong woman.

The loss of loved ones has become a common aspect of the pool of experiences of today's teenagers. Two wars, ongoing political repression, widespread diseases, malnutrition, and a collapsed health system account for the great number of deaths that occur in present-day Iraq. Aside from sadness, depression, and sometimes anger, young people in Iraq are also remarkably fatalistic and have built up an incredible resistance to deal with pain and suffering.

As difficult as it has become to spend time with their friends, a number of teenagers did stress that they would talk over their problems and worries with their closest friends. As their parents are too busy dealing with "bigger problems," friends often become the only moral support, the main counselors, and the persons to confide in. Friendships are therefore valued greatly and frequently become the main point of reference in turbulent lives.

Over and over again, teenagers speak about changes related to socializing, family ties, and relations between neighbors and friends. Often, a parent or older relative was quoted as stating how things were different from the past when socializing was a much bigger part of people's lives. Zeinab, a 15-year-old from Baghdad, spoke about the lack of trust between people. She suggested the following as an explanation for the change in dress code for women and the social restrictions she and her peers experience constantly:

> People have changed now because of the increasing economic and various other difficulties of life in Iraq. They have become very afraid of each other. I think because so many people have lost their jobs and businesses, they are having loads of time to speak about other people's lives, and they often interfere in each other's affairs. I also think that because so many families are so poor now that they cannot afford buying more than the daily basic food, it becomes so difficult for them to buy nice clothes and nice things and therefore, it is better to wear *hijab* [headscarf]. Most people are somewhat pressured to change their lives in order to protect themselves from the gossip of other people—especially talk about family honor.

In addition to increased responsibilities and time restrictions related to economic circumstances, teenage girls complain about the increasing social restrictions and difficulties of movement. The most obvious change that has taken place over the past decade or so is the dress code of young women. Aliya is clearly unhappy about the changes:

I do think that our life was much more easy and happy in the past than it is now. My father used to be so open and believe in women's free- dom. He would let my mother go out without covering her hair when they visited our relatives in Baghdad. We only had to wear the abbayah[13] in Najaf[14] because it is a holy city. Some years ago, he started to change his attitude to many things. And lately he has become so conservative that he thinks covering the hair is not enough, and he demanded that my mother wear abbayah everywhere outside the home. He said that I also should keep the cover on my hair when I go to Baghdad. I am now not even allowed to go out with trousers outside our home. My mother and I have to wear long skirts with a long wide shirt covering the hips when we go outside our home.

As much as Aliya detests the imposed dress codes and her father's new conservatism, she understands the underlying reasons. She explains:

I know why my father is doing this and I am not angry with him. I discussed this issue with him many times, and I really do not blame him for this change in attitude. I think it is not only my father who is doing this, but that it may be all fathers in Iraq. They are doing the same in order to protect their daughters from the risks of becoming victims of bad rumors.

Increased social conservatism and the threat of gossip that would tar- nish one's reputation are a common complaint among Iraqi teenagers. Especially girls suffer in a climate where patriarchal values have been strengthened and where the state has abandoned its previous policies of social inclusion where women are concerned. Economic hardships have pushed a number of women into prostitution—a trend that is widely known and subject to much anguish in a society where a woman's honor is perceived to reflect the family's honor. Prostitution has recently been condemned by the government, thereby making it extremely dangerous.[15] Men often feel compelled to protect their female relatives from being the subject of gossip and from losing the family's honor. The increasing social restrictions imposed on young women have to be analyzed in the context of wider social changes, particularly with respect to gender relations.

Whereas the parents of the predominantly middle-class teenagers that were interviewed used to mingle relatively freely when they were the age of their children, today's young Iraqis find it increasingly difficult to meet each other. Schools are often segregated between sexes; but even in co- educational schools, interaction between boys and girls has become more limited. Girls are extremely worried about their reputation and often avoid situations in which they find themselves alone with a boy. According to 16-year-old Samira:

> Yes, of course, I would like to be able to speak with boys and get to know how they think about girls, but this is getting more and more difficult. I have heard some cases where a boy tried to drag a girl to speak with him by claiming that he was in love with her. But the truth is that he just wanted to show his friends that he had "a sexual affair" with her. This is a very dangerous thing to say about a girl in Iraq. Such incidents would mean that the girl has desecrated her family's honor—something for which she might be severely punished by her father or her brother. It would also mean that her chances of getting a husband become very slim.

Samira's fears might have been aggravated by nowadays not uncommon occurrences of so-called honor killings. Fathers and brothers of women who are known and often only suspected of having violated the morally accepted codes of behavior, especially with respect to keeping one's virginity before marriage, might kill their female kin in order to restore the honor of the family. Although this phenomenon is mainly restricted to rural areas and uneducated Iraqis, knowledge about its existence works as a deterrent for many female teenagers.

Others might be less worried about the most dramatic consequences of "losing one's reputation." For educated middle-class women from urban areas, it is less death they fear than diminished marriage prospects. Samira, who is avoiding boys as much as she can, states that she and her girlfriends fear them. But she regrets not knowing more about them and the way they think about girls:

> I cannot say that all boys are the same, but I would not take the risk to speak with any of them. I really think that boys do hate girls who are friendly with them, especially as I often hear about incidences where boys take revenge of girls who fall in love with them. I also know for sure that boys do not like to get married to girls who fall in love with them. They prefer girls who never had any history with a man.

The fact that in contemporary Iraq marriage presents a difficult undertaking is a consequence of both the current demographic imbalance between men and women and the ongoing economic crisis. The demographic costs of two wars, and the forced economic migration of men triggered by the imposition of economic sanctions, account for the high number of female-headed households and the difficulties for young women to get married. Polygamy, which had become largely restricted to rural areas or uneducated people, has been on the rise in recent years. There is also a growing trend among young women to get married to Iraqi expatriates, usually much older than they are.[16] There are numerous cases of women who could not cope with living abroad and who are feeling totally alienated from their husbands and the new environment they find themselves in. Others are being married to older men within Iraq, often to settle a debt within the family:

"Zahra used to be a happy girl and loved to be with her friends all the time, but in the last two months, she became a bit sad and preferred to be on her own," says Hannah, Zahra's best friend. On the day of her wedding, 16-year-old Zahra looks sad and withdrawn. She is about to leave her childhood friends and teenage life behind to get married to a man more than 20 years her senior. Rumor has it that her father was pressured to give his daughter into this marriage in order to save his business.

At the same time as marriage has become a relatively difficult under-taking, young women feel pressured by a new cultural environment that is marked simultaneously by a decline in moral values pertaining to honesty, generosity, and sociability and an increased public religiosity and conser-vatism. Many young women spoke sadly about the total inversion of cul-tural codes and moral values. Changes in the social and cultural fabric of Iraqi society have affected gender relations in various ways. Without doubt, Iraqi women lost some of the achievements gained in the previous decades. They can no longer assert themselves through previous channels, such as education and waged employment, as the education sector is dis-integrating and unemployment is rampant.

In the 1970s and 1980s—regardless of the government's motivations—Iraqi women became among the most educated and professional in the whole region.[17] The question in terms of how far access to education and the labor market had resulted in an improved status for women is more complex. As in many other places, conservative and patriarchal values did not automatically change because women started working. And there existed great differences between rural and urban women as well as women from different social class backgrounds.[18] In the 1990s and early twenty-first century, prospects for young women look much more bleak and less promising in comparison to the ones that were open to their mothers.

RECREATION

Like teenagers all over the world, Farah and Samir, the brother and sis-ter from a rich family mentioned earlier, enjoy the company of their friends and spend most of their leisure time hanging out, listening to music, watching videos, and playing computer games. They enjoy parties in each other's homes, go to picnics with their parents, and visit the sports club to go swimming. All their friends come from the same social background (rich business people or government officials) and attend the same school—a private school in one of the richest neighborhoods of Baghdad.

Obviously, Farah and Samir are not examples of the hardships and struggles for survival endured by most families, as they represent the living conditions of a privileged few. For the majority, the lack of economic means prevents them from engaging in activities considered normal for teenagers. Ahmed (age 15) spends all his free time trying to earn some money to support his family:

> I would like to play soccer in my free time, but I don't have enough time to play or to go outside with my friends. They are almost as busy as I am. We do go outside and play soccer during the school holidays sometimes, but it has been a long time now, we do not have time for such things anymore.

Before the Gulf War (1991) and the imposition of economic sanctions, Iraqi teenagers used to spend lots of their free time playing with friends and relatives on the streets, in back gardens, and inside their houses. The toys and gadgets that were used for playing depended on the economic and social standing of their parents. Sports was very popular among boys; soccer in particular was a favorite recreational activity (both to watch and to play).

ENTERTAINMENT

Due to all the reasons mentioned previously, the majority of Iraqi teenagers have few choices and little time for entertainment. Yet music is definitely a favorite among *shabab* (youth), who listen to it as much as they can. There are some contemporary Iraqi singers who combine traditional Arabic music with Western tunes and modern rhythms. Kazem Al-Saher is probably one of the most popular singers of this trend, and he is famous all over the Arab world. Some teenagers listen to Western pop music as well, but it is quite difficult to have access to the latest "top of the pops," as Iraq has been very much isolated. Internet and satellite dishes are not available for the general public, which limits most people to the government-controlled national TV.

A relatively new channel, Al-Shabab, controlled by Saddam Hussein's son Uday, is the only channel of entertainment for many Iraqi teenagers.

It is also one of the few means through which many Iraqi teenagers get exposed to the outside world. The channel regularly shows pirated copies of fairly recent Hollywood movies, which are subtitled in Arabic. A popular program on Al-Shabab shows home-grown music videos featuring young Iraqis trying to become famous singers.

Although isolated from the outside world, many young middle-class Iraqis are actually aware of the current trends and fashions emanating from Western countries. Despite the heavily censored media, recent Western movies and video clips are accessible, mainly via Al-Shabab. Pirated copies of the most recent Hollywood blockbusters reveal a world largely beyond reach. Yet they are a means of keeping in touch with the outside world.

Another means of information are Iraqi expatriates from all over the world, who not only support their families financially but also often send medicine, clothes, books, magazines, and music to their families back home. Occasionally expatriate Iraqis visit their families and bring not only goods of consumption but also stories and ideas related to life outside the very narrow confines of the Iraqi borders. Almost everyone today is aware of the Internet and e-mail, for example; but except for a very small group of elite Iraqis or those belonging to the regime, it remains an abstract idea to imagine and dream about. Even computers are an extremely rare sight in a country where schools and universities lack the resources to provide computer access to their students.

Dancing is popular among teenagers, but there are very few occasions when they can actually dance. Birthday parties and family get-togethers sometimes end up in teenagers dancing to popular tunes.

RELIGIOUS PRACTICES AND CULTURAL CEREMONIES

Although a precise statistical breakdown is impossible because of likely inaccuracies in the latest census (1997), according to conservative estimates over 95 percent of the population are Muslim. The (predominantly Arab) Shi'a Muslims constitute a 60 to 65 percent majority, while Sunni Muslims make up 30 to 35 percent (approximately 18 to 20% are Sunni Kurds, 12 to 15% are Sunni Arabs, and the rest are Sunni Turkomans). The remaining approximately 5 percent consist of Christians (Assyrians, Chaldeans, Roman Catholics, and Armenians), Yazidis, and a small number of Jews. The Shi'a, predominant in the south, are present in large numbers in Baghdad and have communities in most parts of the country. Sunnis form the majority in the center of the country and in the north. Christians are concentrated in the north and in Baghdad. Yazidis are located in the north.

Although Shi'a Arabs are the largest religious group, Sunni Arabs traditionally have dominated economic and political life. Arabs holding Sunni religious beliefs are at a distinct advantage in all areas of secular endeavor: civil, political, military, economic, and so on. However, it is important to stress that Shi'a and Sunni Arabs are not ethnically distinct and that many Shi'a have fought alongside Sunnis in various political struggles for or against the government.

Islam has grown to play a more significant role in Iraqi teenagers' lives nowadays than in the past. They visit the mosque on Friday for the weekly reading of the Quran and prayers, and they observe religious holidays. These religious holidays include Eid al-Fitr (end of Ramadan), Eid al-Adha (Feast of the Sacrifice), Ashura (Shi'a day of mourning), and Mawlid al-Nabi (the Prophet's birthday). Attention to religion and religious holidays has increased since the early 1980s. Until the early 1980s, Iraq was a relatively secular society where many people grew up without observing religious prescriptions like prayers and fasting. Very few young women would wear the headscarf (*hijab*), although the traditional black loose garment (*habay*) was common among older women and women of the poorer classes. These days, Iraqis have become much more religious and teenagers are much more interested in religion than many of their parents ever were. One of the most obvious aspects of these changes in Iraq since the 1980s and particularly during the 1990s, is the fact that even girls have started to cover their hair when going to school.

As in most other countries mentioned in this book, many Iraqi teenagers have learned how to do their daily prayers, although not everyone observes them. As in any other country, there are those who are pious and practicing and others who are not. But even those young Iraqis who are not particularly religious celebrate Muslim holidays and festivals, and most teenagers fast during the month of Ramadan. In addition to these Muslim holidays, there are official holidays that schoolchildren might have to celebrate on the order of the government. These include Army Day (January 6), Revolution Anniversary (February 8), National Day (July 14), and Ba'th Revolution Day (July 17).

CONCLUSION

As the various accounts in this chapter have shown, Iraqi teenagers are exposed to a number of difficulties and hardships that shape not only their daily lives but also their dreams and expectations for the future. Noticeable in the accounts of teenagers that were interviewed was a high degree of self-awareness but also a high level of sadness and widespread depression. Happiness is a fickle thing, especially for teenagers, wherever they live. Yet for Iraqi teenagers happiness has become a particularly rare and precious gift. Leila, who was quoted several times in this chapter, became defiant when asked about happiness:

> I am not a happy person! I am sorry, I cannot tell you otherwise. As I often see or hear that some people are dying of hunger, diseases, and war in this country [Iraq] or somewhere else, I start to blame myself for being so pessimistic and for not being a good believer in God. So, I am aware that some people are lucky while others, like me, are not, and that everything has a meaning. Knowing all this, I guess, does not make anybody happy.

Leila might be more self-reflective and articulate than many of her peers, but her words appear to echo the sentiments of many of them. However, it would be a fallacy to conclude that Iraqi teenagers are mere victims of circumstances, passively accepting their fate. Young people in Iraq are active agents, trying to shape their own worlds and trying to optimize their options and possibilities. They strategize to earn some extra money and to benefit from the little resources that are available with respect to education and access to information.

Many Iraqi teenagers are incredibly frustrated by their isolation from the outside world. Notwithstanding their inability to consume popular culture and access the virtual realities of the Internet, some are surprisingly aware of social and cultural trends on a global scale. Although probably not within their reach, many young people are aware of the significance of computers and the Internet, for example. Others do know about the latest fashion, even if only from magazines brought in by their expatriate relatives.

No doubt, the difficulties and hardships experienced by today's teenagers in Iraq cannot simply be reduced to economic sanctions. The economic crisis triggered by two wars, lack of democracy, and political repression by the regime as well as personal tragedies or mishaps are all factors contributing to the life experiences of young people in contemporary Iraq. Yet economic sanctions have augmented the hardships and have spiraled suffering into new dimensions. It is therefore not surprising that the issue of sanctions features highly in the anecdotes, complaints, and accounts of today's teenagers.

Despite frustration, depression, and feelings of devastation, one could not detect a prevailing sense of bitterness among the teenagers that volunteered in this research. Quite the contrary, one can easily be moved and humbled by an underlying current of hope and optimism that things will change—for the better. One hopes today's Iraqi teenagers will be adults in a more positive future.

NOTES

1. Phebe Marr, *The Modern History of Iraq* (Boulder and London: Westview Press, 1985), 1.

2. Ongoing bomb attacks by British and U.S. forces, especially in the south of Iraq, present a continuous source of fear and trauma for those who live in affected areas.

3. See United Nations Children's Fund (UNICEF), *Children and Women in Iraq: A Situation Analysis* (New York: 1997); Richard Garfield, *Mortality Changes in Iraq, 1990–1996: A Review of Evidence*, (London: Overseas Development Institute, 1999); "Changes in Health and Well-Being in Iraq during the 1990s: What Do We Know and How Do We Know It?" in *Sanctions on Iraq: Background, Consequences, Strategies*, Proceedings of the Conference hosted by the Campaign Against Sanctions on Iraq, 13–14 November 1999 (Cambridge, U.K.: 2000).

4. Nutrition surveys carried out by UNICEF and the World Food Program (WFP) last year show no improvement in the nutritional status of children since the introduction of the Oil for Food Program in 1996. One in five children in the south and center of Iraq remain so malnourished that they need special therapeutic feeding. Child sickness rates continue to be alarmingly high (New York: UNICEF, Iraq Donor Update, 11 July 2001).

5. All interviews were carried out by the authors in Baghdad, Iraq, in 2001.

6. The UN Oil-for-Food arrangement stipulates that Iraq can sell oil and use 72 percent of revenues to purchase humanitarian goods such as food and medicine.

7. UNICEF, *Children and Women in Iraq: A Situation Analysis*, 1997; April 1998.

8. The initial period after the nationalization of the Iraqi oil industry in 1972 was characterized by economic hardship and difficulties. However, the oil embargo by OPEC countries of 1973, known as the "oil crisis," was followed by a period of boom and expansion. Oil prices shot up considerably, and oil-producing countries started to become aware of their bargaining power related to Western countries' dependence on oil.

9. UNICEF, Iraq Donor Update, 11 July 2001.

10. See United Nations Children's Fund, Children and Women in Iraq: A Situation Analysis (New York: 1997).

11. UNICEF, Iraq Donor Update, 11 July 2001.

12. An annual international trade fair that was closed for ten years due to economic sanctions; it reopened in November 2000.

13. Traditional black loose garment worn by Iraqi women.

14. City in southern Iraq known for its Shi'a shrines and cemetery.

15. In an incident in November 2000, an unknown number of women were beheaded by government militia on suspicion of being involved in prostitution.

16. Nadje Al-Ali, "Sanctions and Women in Iraq," *Sanctions on Iraq: Background, Consequences, Strategies*, Proceedings of the Conference hosted by the Campaign Against Sanctions on Iraq, 13–14 November 1999 (Cambridge: CASI, 2000), 79–80.

17. Rather than abiding by some egalitarian or feminist principles, the policies of social inclusion of women by the Ba'th regime in the 1970s and 1980s were mainly driven by economic considerations. While most of the Arab Gulf countries relied on foreign labor after the "oil boom," the Iraqi government tried to mobilize its labor mainly among its own human resources.

18. Nadje Al-Ali, "Sanctions and Women in Iraq," p. 77.

RESOURCE GUIDE

Books, Articles, Reports

Ali, Mohamed M., and Iqbal H. Shah. "Sanctions and Childhood Mortality in Iraq.," *The Lancet* (27 May 2000): 1851–1857.

Al-Khayr, Misbah, and Hashim Al-Samira'I. "Iftah Ya Simsim [Open Sesame] and Children in Baghdad." In *Children in the Moslem Middle East*, edited by Elizabeth W. Fernea, 464–468. Austin: University of Texas Press, 1995.

Al-Radi, Nuha. *Baghdad Diaries*. London: Al-Saqi Books, 1998.

Arnove, Anthony, Ali Abunimah, eds. *Iraq under Siege: The Deadly Impact of Sanctions and War*. London: Pluto Press, 2000.

Burns, John F. "Baghdad Journal: Iraqi Youth, the Time Has Come to Rock." *New York Times*, 9 April 2001.

Byman, Daniel. "After the Storm: U.S. Policy toward Iraq since 1991." *Political Science Quarterly* 115, no.4 (Winter 2000–2001): 493–516.

CASI—Campaign Against Sanctions on Iraq. *Sanctions on Iraq: Background, consequences, strategies*. Proceedings of the Conference hosted by the Campaign Against Sanctions on Iraq, 13–14 November 1999, Cambridge. Cambridge: CASI, 2000.

Graham-Brown, Sarah. *Sanctioning Saddam: The Politics of Intervention*. New York: I. B. Tauris, 1999.

Kandela, Peter. "Baghdad 2000—Rubbish Heaps and Cesspits." *The Lancet* (27 May 2000): 1893. A brief eyewitness account.

Save The Children. "The Impact of Sanctions on Children and Young People in Iraq." Press release. 2001. http://www.scfuk.org.uk/pressrels/280201.html

Sluglett, Marion Farouk, and Peter Sluglett, eds. *Iraq since 1958: From Revolution to Dictatorship*. London and New York: I. B. Tauris, 2001.

Tripp, Charles. *A History of Iraq*. Cambridge: Cambridge University Press, 2000.

UNICEF. *The Impact of Sanctions: A Study of UNICEF's Perspective*. New York: UNICEF, Office of Emergency Programs, February 1999.

Fiction

Heide, Florence Parry, and Judith Heide Gilliland. *The House of Wisdom*. New
  York: D K Publishing, 1999.

Khedairi, Betool. *A Sky So Close*. New York: Pantheon Books, 2001.

Kishtainy, Khalid. *Tales from Old Baghdad*. London & New York: Kegan Paul,
  International 1997.

Web Sites

http://www.iraqi-mission.org

Permanent Mission of Iraq to the United Nations. Information about Iraq, press
  releases, and resouces about Iraq.

http://www.arab.net/iraq/iraq_contents.html

Information about the geography, history, culture, business, and transportation of
  Iraq.

http://www.odci.gov/cia/publications/factbook/geos/iz.html

CIA—The World Factbook. Information about Iraq's geography, people, government, economy, transportation, and traditional issues.

http://www.geocities.com/iraqinfo/index.html?page=/iraqinfo/sum/hist/history.
  html

Iraq resource information site. Information about news, latest reports, featured
  editorials, government, religion and people.

http://www.iraq4us.com/

Iraq4US: mission is to bring Iraqi/Arab people closer together. Information about
  chat rooms, the nation, food, discussions, films, sports, and games.

http://www.megastories.com/iraq/children/hospital.htm

Information about the poor and insufficient health system in Iraq, as well as the
  consequences.

http://www.igc.apc.org/globalpolicy/security/sanction/iraq1/irakids.htm

Iraq Sanctions Leave Mark on Children: Malnutrition, Unawareness Define
  Youth is an article written by Charles M. Sennott about Iraq's "lost generation."

http://www.unicef.org/newsline/Iraqi

Information about UNICEF activities in Iraq, voices of youth, as well as the highlights of Programs for Children and Women in Iraq.

http://www.msnbc.com/news/499015.asp

News, business, sports, health, technology, opinions, and weather.

Pen Pal/Chat

http://www.iraq4u.com/

http://www.iraqchat.com/

Chapter 3

ISRAEL

Rebecca Torstrick

INTRODUCTION

Located on the eastern shore of the Mediterranean Sea and bordered by
Lebanon, Syria, Jordan, and Egypt, Israel is about the size of the state of
New Jersey. It stretches about 290 miles from north to south and is 85
miles wide at its widest point to only 6 miles at its narrowest point.[1] Israel
has a population of over 6.2 million people, 78.5 percent of whom are
Jewish (most of whom came to Israel from other countries) and 21.5 percent of whom are Palestinian Arabs (the original native population).[2]
Since its founding in 1948, Jews have immigrated to Israel from over 120
countries in Europe, Asia, the Middle East, and North and Latin America. Israel's Jewish residents are often categorized according to their place
of birth. *Ashkenazim* are those Israelis whose parents immigrated from
countries in Europe, Russia, or the Americas; they make up 41 percent of
Israeli Jews. *Mizrahim* make up 31 percent of the Jewish population; they
are people whose parents immigrated from countries in the Middle East,
Africa, and Asia. *Sabras* are those whose parents were born in Israel; they
make up 28 percent of Israeli Jews. The country is thus ethnically quite
heterogeneous. The official languages are Hebrew and Arabic, although
English is widely taught and understood. One can hear a wide variety of
other languages spoken on the streets because the immigrants often preserve their native languages while also learning Hebrew. About 91 percent of the Jewish population lives in 200 urban centers, with another 5
percent living in *kibbutzim* or *moshavim*.[3] The Palestinian population is
largely rural (75%), with 60 percent living in villages in the Galilee, 30
percent in the Jenin-Nablus-Tulkarm area (called the Little Triangle),

and 10 percent in the Negev. Those who live in urban areas tend to be concentrated in the major Arab cities of Nazareth and Shfar 'Amr and in the so-called "mixed" cities of Acre, Haifa, Lod, Ramleh, Tel Aviv–Jaffa and Jerusalem (cities with both Jewish and Palestinian residents).

Most Jewish Israelis would say they are secular and not particularly religious, although the state religion of Israel is Orthodox Judaism.[4] Among Orthodox Jews, there are a number of different factions, each of which follows a different rabbi as its spiritual leader. Best known are the various Hasidic groups, which trace their roots to former Jewish communities in Eastern Europe, many of which were annihilated during the Nazi Holocaust. The Palestinian Arab population is Sunni Muslim (82%); over 30 different denominations of Christians, including Roman Catholics, Greek Catholics, Greek Orthodox, Russian Orthodox, Maronites, Copts, Armenian Catholics, and Protestants (9%); and Druze (9%).[5]

Israel has its origins in the nationalist movements that developed in Europe in the late 1800s. European Jews believed that the only way they would ever live free of persecution would be to have a state of their own. This movement, which came to be called Zionism, resulted in the emigration of Jews from different parts of Europe to Palestine, which was then a province of the Muslim Ottoman Empire. Ruled by the British government under a mandate from the League of Nations from 1922 onward, Palestine increasingly absorbed more Jewish immigrants. Under the British, who had indicated support for the creation of a "Jewish homeland" in Palestine in 1917, the Jewish immigrants were able to set up their own independent economic and political infrastructure. Friction with the Palestinian population was inevitable, as the arrival of new immigrants began to have negative effects on the lives of the native Palestinian people. Britain turned Palestine over to the fledgling United Nations in 1947, and the U.N. decided to partition the territory into two states—one Jewish and one Palestinian. At this time there were about 650,000 Jews in Palestine and 1.3 million Palestinians; Jews owned 7 percent of the land. The Israelis went on the offensive in 1947, and war broke out. When an armistice was finally declared in 1949, the new state of Israel controlled its territory and an additional 25 percent of what would have been the Palestinian state's territory. Israel existed; the Palestinian state was never created, and over 750,000 Palestinians found themselves refugees in nearby countries. Over a hundred thousand Palestinians remained within the borders of the new Israeli state and became Israeli citizens. This conflict and its outcome are the roots of the present-day conflict between Jewish Israelis and Palestinians.

Since the 1947–1949 war, Israel has been involved in outright war with its Arab neighbors in almost every decade: the 1956 invasion of Egypt; the 1967 Six-Day War with preemptive strikes on Syria, Jordan, and Egypt; the 1973 Yom Kippur War against invading Syrian and Egyptian forces; and the 1982 invasion of Lebanon and occupation of portions of the south from which Israel only withdrew in 2000. Although Israel has since signed peace accords with Egypt and Jordan, its relations with Syria and Lebanon remain tense. Since 1967, Israel has ruled over Palestinian populations in the West Bank and Gaza Strip as well as Druze populations in the Golan Heights (areas often referred to as the Occupied Territories). Palestinians in the West Bank and Gaza Strip rose in massive civil disobedience in 1988–1993 (the first Intifada; *intifada* is an Arabic word meaning "a shaking off") and are again engaged in protesting the continuing occupation (the ongoing Al-Aqsa *Intifada*, which began in 2000 and continues to the present.)[6]

In 1950 the state of Israel passed the Law of Return, which gives any Jew anywhere in the world the right to come to Israel and become a citizen. Under this law, Israel's Jewish population rapidly increased as immigrants came there from all over the world. The early state had to deal with providing housing, employment, health care, and education to these new immigrants. From 1948 to 1963, Israel's Palestinian citizens lived under military administration and were subject to restrictions on their freedom of movement. Although Israeli Palestinians no longer live under military occupation, their lives remain greatly affected by Israel's occupation of the Territories and the treatment accorded Palestinians there.

Israel is a parliamentary democracy along the model used in many Western European countries. Its political structure consists of a 120-member elected parliament (the Knesset), the office of the president, and the offices of the prime minister with a cabinet. Whereas the president is elected by the Knesset and serves as a ceremonial head of state, the prime minister is directly elected by popular ballot and serves as chief executive of the state. Unlike elections in the United States, which focus more on the candidates themselves, elections in Israel focus on the political parties and their platforms.

One of the major contradictions for the Israeli political system is its claim to be both a democratic state and a Jewish state; these principles often contradict each other when they are put into practice. Israelis have never adopted a constitution. Instead, the country operates under a system of Basic Laws. As of 2002, there were 11 Basic Laws that dealt with the Knesset, Israeli lands, the president, the state economy, the army,

Jerusalem, the Judiciary, the state comptroller, human dignity and liberty, the government, and freedom of occupation. In addition, there are a number of ordinary laws that govern areas of life such as nationality, the Law of Return, the education system, women's rights, and the courts. Although the Declaration of Independence asserts that all Israeli citizens will be treated equally, in practice Palestinians have a second-class status and are often harmed by ordinary laws that promote or accord to Jewish citizens rights or benefits not available to Palestinian citizens.

To further complicate matters, the state has turned over a number of governmental functions to entities called the "national institutions"—public-sector organizations such as the World Zionist Organization, the Jewish Agency, and the Jewish National Fund. These entities raise funds from Jewish communities outside Israel that are then invested within Israel in housing, social programs, educational enrichment, immigrant resettlement, and community development. Very little of this money is intended to support the needs of Israel's Palestinian citizens; in some cases, these organizations have rules that prevent them from assisting non-Jewish populations. Finally, Israel has no civil code regulating marriage, divorce, alimony, child custody, and inheritance. These matters fall under the jurisdiction of religious courts established for Jews, Muslims, Druze, and Christians. Unlike the Jewish religious courts (whose rulings may not be challenged in civil court), the final source of legal authority for Muslims, Druze, and Christians are the secular laws of the state.

SPECIAL CONSIDERATION: CONTRASTING TEEN LIFE

For teens living in this country, it matters a great deal who they are in terms of what their lives will be like. Jewish teens are more advantaged than Palestinian teens, who live as second-class citizens. However, *Ashkenazi* Jewish teens are more advantaged than *Mizrahi* Jewish teens. The majority of the country's economic, political, and social elite are *Ashkenazim*. More *Mizrahi* teens are likely to come from families that are large in size, struggling to make ends meet, and socially marginalized. *Ashkenazi* teens can look forward to careers running Israel's major corporate and governmental structures; *Mizrahi* teens will be the workers they pay and the voters whose votes they rely on. If a teen is a recent Russian or Ethiopian immigrant, he or she may also face a great deal of racism or hostility, as veteran Israelis are often angry at the generous assistance packages that the government or the Jewish Agency makes available to more recent immigrants. Israel saw its own wave of school-related violence during 1999, when numerous reports surfaced about beatings given to Russian immigrant children at the hands of their schoolmates.

One additional major difference that separates Jewish and Palestinian teens is military service. Jewish teens, male and female, go into the army right after they finish high school. Boys serve for three years and girls serve for two years.[7] Thus, by the time they are 18, Jewish Israeli teens are in the military. Muslim and Christian Palestinian teens are not drafted; even if they try to volunteer, they are unlikely to be admitted to military service because they are viewed by the state as security risks. Druze and Bedouin teens, like Jewish teens, are drafted. In the army, teens mix with people from all over the country and from a variety of social backgrounds. The ties forged there remain important to them for the rest of their lives, especially because Israeli males continue to serve reserve duty every year until they reach the age of 55. They will continue to be brought together on an annual basis with the friends they make during their initial period of service. Palestinian teens start at the universities or begin to work. By the time their Jewish counterparts leave the army, the Palestinian teens may already have married and begun to take on adult responsibilities. Because they do not serve in the army, a number of occupations are closed to them (employers want to see discharge papers; they cannot get security clearances) and they are excluded from state welfare programs that are given to those who do army service.

TYPICAL DAY

As with any country, what teens do depends on whether they are male or female, their family's social class, where they live, and what religion they are. Teens who live in the major urban areas of Israel have shops, cafés, movie theaters, and other opportunities available to them that teens who live in border settlements such as the *moshavim* or *kibbutzim* lack. Teens in the north of the country pursue different recreational opportunities than those who live in the more arid southern regions. Jewish teens have more freedom of movement than do Palestinian teens. And boys can do more and go to more places than girls in both communities.

For most Jewish teens, their day begins by getting ready for school. Their school week is 6 days (Sunday through Friday), and school starts at 8 A.M. Teens who live in outlying areas of the city, or who live in small communities and attend regional high schools, take the bus to school. Those who live nearer to the school walk or bike. In cities like Tel Aviv, where some teens attend specialized high schools, they take the bus. Students eat breakfast at home (usually bread, cheese, yogurt) and take a snack with them to school (*aruhat eser*, literally ten o'clock meal) that their mothers have prepared.

Once at school, what teens do depends on their grade level and school type. At lunch time, students go home to eat. The normal school day is until 1 or 2 P.M. until grade 7, a little longer in the later grades. What mainly changes after grade 7 is not the amount of time spent at school, but the amount of homework that students take home. After school, teens make their way home on their own. Once there, they may study, have private lessons, hang out with their friends, or go out to cafés, shops, or community centers in downtown. As a teen nears the end of high school, more of his or her free time is taken up with private classes and studying for the matriculation and psychometric exams. Passing these exams with high scores is necessary for university admission.

The weekend for Jewish teens runs from Friday evening through Saturday evening (the Jewish Sabbath begins Friday evening at sundown and ends Saturday evening at sundown). For secular teens, Friday and Saturday are popular nights to go out. It is not uncommon for them to stay out with friends until 4 or 5 in the morning. Saturday night, especially, is lively as many clubs, cafés, and shops reopen at the end of the Sabbath and people of all ages take to the streets to celebrate the weekend.

For Palestinian teens, a different weekly routine prevails. Mothers wake teens, prepare their breakfasts, and make sure they get safely to school. The Arab school system runs five days a week (Monday through Friday). Between 1 and 1:30, teens come home from school for the midday meal. After school, teens may attend activities at the municipal cultural center or neighborhood youth clubs, or join in a pick-up game of basketball or soccer at the YMCA. Girls go out less than boys; when they do go out, it is usually with relatives. At home, they help clean house, study, watch television, listen to music, or get into doing hair, nails, or clothing. Studying is one way to avoid some household chores. Mothers usually supervise homework and make sure that teens get it done. By early evening, everyone is gathering around the television. Teenage girls may help their mother prepare food. People eat while watching foreign programs like *The Simpsons* and Israeli Hebrew programs aimed at youth. Front doors are left open from 6 P.M. until 11 P.M., and a steady stream of visitors moves in and out of homes. Teens may listen in as conversations range from local news to discussions of developments in Israel, the Territories, Arab states, and the world at large.

Religion also determines part of a teen's routine. For the more religious Jewish teens, any homework brought home has to be finished before the

Sabbath begins as work of any sort is forbidden during the Sabbath. Friday night is spent at home with family. The family shares Friday night dinner together and welcomes in the Sabbath. They may attend synagogue on Saturday and then spend the rest of the day in quiet activities, such as reading or visiting with friends and family, so as not to violate the sanctity of the day. Muslim teens who are religious often rise before dawn in order to perform the morning prayer. On Fridays, they may go to the local mosque for participation in collective prayer and hearing the sermon. For Christian teens Saturday is a free day, but Sunday may be spent attending church services and then visiting with various family members.

FAMILY LIFE

Family is the major component of people's lives in both Palestinian and Jewish communities in Israel. It is not uncommon to see university students going home to visit their families every chance they get rather than taking advantage of free time to party with their friends. Children live at home with their parents until they get married and establish their own homes. In some cases, even once they are married, children continue to live in their parents' house. That said, it is important to realize that there are as many different family forms in Israel as there are different groups of people. Some teens live in nuclear families with both parents working and sharing equally in the household responsibilities. Other teens live in an extended family household, with their grandparents and other aunts, uncles, and cousins under the same roof and all contributing to the family's welfare. Still other teens belong to *kibbutzim* where raising children is seen as a collective responsibility; *kibbutz* families pool their resources and share the responsibility for childcare.

One major trend that can be seen in many families in Israel is that of male privilege and male control over the family, regardless of whether the family is Jewish or Palestinian. The head of the family is the man, and his word must not be challenged. Mothers are usually responsible for the care of the home and the children, but any major decisions about the children's lives are ultimately made by the father, although he does consult with his wife. In Jewish families, male privilege is tied in with the fact that men continue to do army service for years. Since men go off to war, women must do their part by supporting their fathers, brothers, sons, or husbands in these endeavors. When sons come home from the army on leave, their mothers, sisters, or girlfriends are often expected to cater to their every need. *Mizrahi* and Palestinian families tend to follow patterns present in Arab families overall. Israeli women, Jewish and Palestinian, often hold paid employment, but they still remain responsible for all the household duties as well. Israeli women are more likely to take positions that allow them to attend to their families first. Israeli working mothers do not report the same levels of stress about balancing work and household responsibilities as do American working mothers. Employers are expected to understand that the woman's family duties come first.

Family resonates deeply in Israeli lives for other reasons as well. For those Israelis who survived the Nazi Holocaust in Europe, establishing and raising a family was one way for them to cope with the trauma they had suffered. Such parents worked hard to make sure their children had everything they wanted. Their children often felt the need to excel in order to make their parents feel better or felt guilt at the fact that their parents had suffered in ways they never would. As this generation raises their own children, many of them are trying to come to terms with the legacy of the Holocaust in their lives so that their children can grow up without the burdens of guilt and parental expectations that they felt.

Palestinian parents too have their own burdens. Many Palestinians who lived through the events of 1948–1949 made a practice of not speaking of these times to their children in order to spare them. Life under military administration was demanding, and parents wanted to protect their children as best they could. It was better, many thought, not to talk of those times, to retreat into family and village life and remain detached from the outside world. The second generation of Palestinian Israelis therefore grew up knowing few actual details of what their parents had suffered. It is only with the third generation and recent changes in Israeli society that grandparents have begun to talk to their grandchildren about their history. This means that Palestinian teens today have a far different sense of their identity than their parents did.

Finally, children of immigrant parents face the same challenges as immigrant children in many parts of the world. Parents who were raised in more traditional ways may find it hard to adapt to the new country, its values, and its behaviors. It is often the children who lead the way. Family remains important as an anchor in the strange new land, but family structure also begins to change as the children are socialized into new ways of acting and thinking.

TRADITIONAL AND NONTRADITIONAL FOOD

Given that its citizens hail from over 120 different countries, each with their own established cuisines, eating in Israel can be quite an experience in diversity. While the traditional foods of native Palestinians, *falafel* (fried spiced chickpea balls) and *hummus*, (chickpea and sesame paste) have become famous as Israel's national dishes, one would be hard put to define uniquely Israeli dishes. Instead, it is the sheer diversity of possible foods one could be served that distinguishes Israeli food.

Food is an incredibly important part of life here. It plays a major role in every religious and national holiday. All Israelis enjoy eating, and eating is often a very social occasion. For some Israelis, to refuse food when it is offered would be considered a grave insult. When a guest comes to visit, he or she is usually served something to eat and drink almost as soon as he or she arrives—fruit, cake, or cookies; coffee or sodas. Over the course of the visit, the food and drink are replenished. If the visitor stays long enough, he or she may be invited for dinner.

Visitors to a family who hails from Morocco may find that dinner con- sists of a savory couscous (steamed grain) served with vegetables and chicken with harissa, a crushed hot pepper sauce, to spice it up. Guests in a Yemenite household may be served *malawach*, a bread eaten like we eat pancakes, with two hot pepper-based sauces, *zhug* or *hilbeh*. In an Ethio- pian household, dinner will certainly include a spongy pancake-like bread (*injera*) that is used to dip into a variety of lamb, chicken, or beef stews (*wats*) or into vegetable dishes such as buttery greens cooked with onions and peppers (*gonen*) or yellow split peas with herbs and peppers (*kik alecha*). In a Palestinian home, dinner might consist of a selection of sev- eral different appetizers (*mezze*) of traditional salads such as chopped pars- ley, tomato, and cracked wheat spiced with lemon (*tabouleh*), ground chickpeas with sesame paste, lemon, and garlic (*hummus*), or grilled egg- plant, tahini, olive oil, and lemon juice (*baba ghanoush*) served with pita bread and followed by a main dish of chicken and rice or meat. In the home of a family who immigrated from Australia, one might be served grilled steak and fries—food not so different from that served in a typical American household.

Different religious traditions affect the types of foods eaten. Under Jew- ish dietary laws (*kashrut*), as spelled out in the Bible, one is not allowed to mix meat and milk in the same meal, let alone the same dish. Certain types of meat or seafood (pork and shellfish, for example) are prohibited; those meats that are allowed must still be killed and prepared in a certain prescribed fashion. So, going to a kosher dining establishment for dinner means one would not find cheeseburgers or meats cooked with cream sauces on the menu. And one certainly would not be able to get a pep- peroni pizza. These prohibitions filter into the eating styles of even secu- lar Israelis. For example, it is not uncommon to find that a family eats one main meal a day with meat, either at lunch or dinner. The other meal usually consists of milk-based products—cheeses, yogurts, creamy salads, or eggs. Israeli Muslims also do not eat pork, while Christian Israelis face no prohibitions in terms of the foods they may eat.

The traditional Israeli fast food is a deep-fried patty of ground chickpeas and spices (*falafel*) that is served in pita bread with a variety of salad items to spice it up such as sweet or sour pickles, hot peppers, pickled turnips, hot sauces, lettuce, chopped tomato, and tahini sauce (sesame seed paste, lemon, olive oil) to drizzle over the top. *Falafel* stands can be found everywhere and are a popular stop for local teens looking for quick, inexpensive food. Some bakeries also serve a special pita bread (flat, pocket bread) coated with *zaatar* (an herb mixture of sumac, thyme, and sesame seeds) and olive oil (*manquusheh*). In the major cities, American fast-food establishments such as McDonald's, Burger King, Kentucky Fried Chicken, Domino's Pizza, and Pizza Hut have sprung up. While some of the establishments originally tried to observe Jewish dietary laws, most now serve cheeseburgers, which has created an uproar among religious Jews and become a political issue for the religious political parties like Shas. Teens are not as likely to frequent these fast-food restaurants on a regular basis because they are more expensive to eat at by local standards. Local pizza restaurants, like Sbarro's, draw a large crowd among Israeli teens. In Tel Aviv one can find a branch of the Hard Rock Café. Ethnic restaurants featuring Chinese, Italian, Indian, French, Thai, and Continental cuisine can be found throughout the country in the larger cities. Haifa even features an American-style pancake restaurant!

Even though Israelis love to eat, Israeli teenage girls face some of the same body image pressures that confront teen girls in the United States. According to the most recent cross-national survey on the health behavior of school-age children conducted by the World Health Organization, Israeli girls (together with girls in the United States and Austria) were the most likely to be currently dieting. In fact, levels of dieting are highest for Israeli girls in all age categories. In addition, the highest level of dieting boys at age 15 is found in Israel.[8] In July 2001, the Knesset Committee for the Status of Women asked the Health Ministry to approve a "No to Anorexia" campaign. Current statistics show that more than one-third of girls age 13 to 16 say they are on a diet. Eating disorders are on the rise, with 8- and 9-year-olds coming in for treatment.[9]

SCHOOLING

School attendance in Israel is free and required for students age 5 to 13. The earliest schools were closely linked to the major political parties, so they were often used as vehicles for gaining the votes of the students' parents. That practice was stopped in 1953, when the state passed a new law that established the Ministry of Education and made it responsible for all the schools and their curricula. This law also gave parents the right to supplement up to 25 percent of the school's curriculum according to their own philosophy. In practice, parents usually did not exercise that right. The 1953 law established three different school systems: a Hebrew secular state-funded track (*mamlakhtī*), a Hebrew religious state-funded track (*mamlakhtī-dātī*), and an Arab state-funded track (*mamlakhtīaravi*). The law also provided for "nonofficial recognized" schools and "exempt, unofficial, and unrecognized" schools (such as different types of orthodox Jewish religious schools as well as foreign and missionary schools).[10]

In 1968 the Educational Reform Act sought to integrate the Hebrew schools so that Jewish children of different social and ethnic backgrounds would be mixed in schools at as early an age as possible.[11] These reforms occurred mainly at the middle school level, through the establishment of regional or districtwide schools that drew a more diverse student population. Since 1968 the Israeli schooling system has consisted of a primary level of 6 years, a middle school level of 3 years, and a secondary level of 3 years.[12] Amendments to the Compulsory Education Law in 1978 and 1979 raised the age for mandatory schooling to grade 10, and a further revision in 1978 extended free education (but not compulsory education) through grade 12.[13]

Students attend elementary and junior high schools based on their place of residence. For high school, however, parents can, and often do, send their children to schools in other locations. The major limiting factor is the cost of transportation. State schools comprise 95 percent of formal education (*mamlakhtī*, 75%; *mamlakhtī-dātī*, 20%), with private religious schools accounting for most of the remaining 5 percent. State schools are divided into separate Hebrew and Arab systems, each with its own curricular requirements.[14] High schools offer an academic, a vocational/technical, or a low-level vocational focus, although some schools (the *māqīf*, or comprehensive) provide more than one track from which their students may choose. For each track, the Ministry of Education and Culture determines the minimum units required for a matriculation certificate. Within the academic track (similar to the American college-preparatory), secondary students select their program of study, choosing those subjects and areas for which they have both ability and interest. At the completion of their secondary studies, students sit for either final exams or matriculation exams. Successful students receive their diplomas. Students who wish to continue to university studies or to get a job in various occupations must sit for and pass matriculation exams (*bagrūt*). In recent years, about half a million jobs in Israel have required successful completion of the *bagrūt* examination as one of the minimum qualifications to enter that job; this is approximately one-third of the Israeli job market.

Responsibilities for the educational system in Israel are divided between the Ministry of Education, which provides all professional aspects (teacher licensing requirements, development and implementation of curriculum, hiring and firing of teachers), and the local authorities, which are responsible for providing and maintaining buildings, equipment, and furniture. In practice, though, since the municipalities also receive most of their budgets from the central state, schools are financed by the national government. Funding levels for the schools vary widely from place to place depending on the strength of the local government and its ability to get more money for its schools.[15] The Arab schools do not receive the same level of funding as comparable Jewish schools. For example, over the years the Arab school system in Acre, a mixed city, has struggled with lack of space, equipment, playground facilities, and books, whereas Jewish schools in the same community have been comparatively well provided for. Part of the funding difference arises from the role of external Jewish institutions such as the Jewish Agency. The Jewish Agency has, for example, partnered Jewish schools in particular communities with Jewish congregations in the United States that provide additional financial support for the school.

Except for some religious schools, most Israeli schools are co-educational. In the classroom, relations between teachers and pupils are relaxed; an outside observer might find the students' lack of manners toward the teacher rude. Classroom style is correspondingly raucous, and one might be tempted to think there are discipline problems in Israeli schools. The Arab school system maintains more formal relations between students and teachers, and classroom atmosphere is accordingly more disciplined. In the Jewish system a great deal of attention is paid to "social education," or education for citizenship. School newspapers, student government, class trips lasting several days, celebrations, parties, field trips, sports days, concerts, and performances are all organized to encourage students to be involved in their school and in their country. Students in the Jewish system are encouraged to develop critical thinking skills; teachers tend to lecture less and to devise more hands-on learning activities. In recent years teachers in the Arab system have also come to rely less on lecturing and more on promoting critical thinking. In addition, only within the last ten years have teachers within the Arab system been able to discuss current events and politics in their classrooms with their students. Prior to this, such discussions might have caused a teacher to lose his or her job.

Teens are tracked in junior and senior high school in Israel. The tracking is based on elementary grades, recommendation from the counselor, and family variables. Once on a track, students tend to remain there. Although in principle they are free to choose their high school and track, in practice students and their parents are counseled about what is available given the student's achievements.[16] Teachers and counselors have a powerful position in determining a student's life chances. In 1993, 47 percent of Jewish high school students were on the vocational track. In the last ten years, only about one-third of Jewish teens have been entitled to the *bagrūt* at the end of high school. In the Palestinian sector, matters are even worse. For example, in 2000, only 18.4 percent of Palestinian Arab 17-year-olds, compared with 40.4 percent of Jewish 17-year-olds, were eligible to attend a university.[17]

Students may begin to drop out of school starting in high school because school attendance is required only through grade 10 (age 15). In 1998–1999, for example, 0.3 percent of 14-year-olds, 5.8 percent of 15-year-olds, and 10.4 percent of 17-year-old Jewish students had dropped out of school.[18] Dropout rates are higher for students whose families recently immigrated and for *Mizrahi* students and students from working-class families. Dropout rates among Palestinian students are even higher: 7.4 percent, 20.6 percent, and 31.7 percent respectively for the same year and age groups. More Palestinian boys are likely to drop out once in high school than girls. Girls, however, are less likely to actually make the transition to attending high school. Part of this is a function of the distance they may need to travel to reach a high school.[19] Parents may be unwilling to let a girl travel on her own over long distances.

SOCIAL LIFE

A great deal of a teen's social life in Israel involves the family and family gatherings. Unlike teens in the West who may want little to do with their parents, teens in Israel stay quite close to their families and do not mind spending time with them. Children are valued by all Israelis and are often given a great deal of latitude, are spoiled, and are made the center of attention at family and other social gatherings. Well-to-do teens may travel outside the country with their family.

There are major distinctions in Israel by community when it comes to relationships between boys and girls. In the *Ashkenazi* and *Sabra* communities, it is not uncommon for teens to be pairing off with a member of the opposite sex as girlfriends or boyfriends by age 11. By age 14, they may be engaging in sexual intercourse. Teens choose their dates themselves; although if the relationship becomes serious, families may get involved to make sure that the potential spouse is suitable. In *Mizrahi* communities, boys may be encouraged to get girlfriends and engage in sex, but girls may be more tightly controlled and are expected to remain virgins until they get married. In some *Mizrahi* groups, arranged marriages are still common. In the Palestinian community, boys and girls are watched closely. Premarital sex is not sanctioned, and parents are very vigilant about their daughters. The daughter's behavior is a reflection on her family, and any inappropriate sexual conduct on her part will damage the family's standing in the community. Although more Palestinian teens are having a say about whom they will marry, parents' opinions still carry a great deal of weight in the final decision. It is not uncommon for marriages in different sectors of the Palestinian community to still be arranged. Girls who complete high school and who go on to college are more likely to be able to make their own decisions about whom they will marry.

The striking differences among the three communities send very different messages to teens about what is expected of them when it comes to sexuality. Palestinian boys who cannot go out with Palestinian girls may turn to the Jewish community and try to get a Jewish girlfriend. Jewish parents worry that their daughters will fall in love with Palestinian boys and want to marry them (although cross-group marriage is very rare and quite problematic in Israel). Muslim and Christian parents often note the loose morals they see in Israeli Jewish society and worry that their children will be tempted to experiment and will bring dishonor on the family. Jewish teens often note how rigidly Palestinian girls are raised and how little freedom they have to make their own decisions. Druze teens, who have been raised to avoid contact with girls, enter the army where they interact on a regular basis with Jewish female soldiers. Remarkably, teens are able to navigate these stormy waters. While they may experiment in their teen years by dating people of different backgrounds, by the time teens marry, they generally do so within their own religious community and social class.

One must be 18 years old to purchase alcohol in pubs, clubs, and restaurants in Israel. However, this does not prevent Israeli youth from drinking. Studies carried out in 1997 among Jewish teens (16–18) living in the north of the country and in 1998 among a national sample of Jewish 12- to 18-year-olds showed that 56–57 percent reported drinking in the previous year (not for religious purposes).[20] Among Arab youth in the north of the country the figures are also quite high, especially when one takes into account that Islam prohibits drinking. A 1996 study found that the rates of drinking in the last year among Muslim, Druze, and Christian males were about 32 percent, 50 percent, and 82 percent, respectively, with female rates of about 13 percent, 11 percent, and 37 percent, respectively. Whereas most Jewish adolescents drink in pubs, Arabs drink mainly at home and in restaurants.

For years, Israel served as a transit point for the illegal drug traffic in the Middle East with heroin and other drugs moving from Lebanon to Israel and then south to Egypt. Today, most of the drugs that enter Israel are intended for the local market and are coming from Lebanon or Jordan. In recent years, officials have reported increases in the availability of hashish (coming from the Egyptian Sinai) and heroin.[21] Among Israeli teens of all social classes and groups, drugs are "in"; at the same time, overall rates of drug use by Israeli teens are low (9.8% of Israeli teens reported using some drug in 1998, according to the Israeli Anti-Drugs Authority).[22] Many teens begin by smoking marijuana, which is perceived as a "soft drug" that will not harm one if used only occasionally.[23] Some teens then move on to heroin, various forms of cocaine, LSD, or Ecstasy and amphetamines. Teens who reported using drugs noted that they were fashionable and that the drugs made them "feel good." Officials report that drugs are available on the premises of most Israeli schools, including the religious schools. In Jerusalem, Kikar Zion (Zion Square, a popular teen gathering spot) is known as an area where one can find drugs; 70 percent of the young people who hang out there are taking drugs, according to one person who works with drug users in Jerusalem.[24] Overall, drug use is not tolerated by Israeli parents, and there is a fairly negative image of teens who take drugs as people who have problems and need help. Within the Palestinian community, drug use has been a major ongoing concern for years now. The drug culture flourishes in Palestinian areas in the mixed cities (Jaffa, Acre) that experience high poverty rates and high unemployment rates, where adults and children alike hold little hope for a different future. Teens growing up in such areas are often swept into the illegal drug trade, much like teens growing up in inner-city ghettos in the United States.

The percentage of teens smoking cigarettes daily in Israel more than doubled in four years, going from 5.5 percent in 1994 to 12 percent in 1998.[25] While only 7 percent of 15-year-old girls reported smoking daily, 17 percent of the boys were smoking daily (compare this to U.S. figures of 12% for girls and 13% for boys). There is no law in Israel that prohibits cigarette sales to minors. In August 2001, a ban on smoking in public places took effect. This ban is unique in the Middle East, where smokers light up almost anywhere. Given the prevalence of smoking in Israel, it remains to be seen how rigorously the ban will be enforced. Teens who can no longer smoke in school corridors now resort to smoking in the bathrooms. Smoking is more common for Palestinian boys than it is for girls.

For teens in Israel, there is no instruction in driver's education through the schools. To learn to drive, one must enroll for private lessons and these are expensive. The legal driving age is 17 and a half. Cars remain a status symbol for both teens and adults. Teens do not get cars until after their army service. They get around by using the public bus system, the train, and the fleets of service taxis (*sheruts*) running along fixed routes.

Israel has a thriving fashion industry of its own, and Israeli teens are also exposed to new fashion trends from nearby European countries. Shopping for clothing can take one from the noisy chaos of the shopping malls (*canyonim*) to open-air stalls in central city markets to small trendy and exclusive boutiques in more fashionable areas. Jeans are all the rage, although a pair of Levis may cost $85. Dyed hair and cool, gel haircuts are also in fashion. Body piercing has only become widespread recently. Most teens get ear or nose piercing, although some want their belly buttons or genitals pierced. Although Jewish religious law prohibits piercing, parlor owners are doing about 5,000 piercings each year. As single piercing has caught on, some teens want multiple piercings or to pierce unusual parts of their bodies such as the area underneath their bottom lip or between their nostrils. Many who pierce consider themselves "Modern Primitives" a social and cultural movement among young Jewish Israeli teens that embraces tattooing, branding, and other forms of marking the body.[26]

RECREATION

Israeli teens have a wide variety of recreational opportunities available to them. Even teens who live in more isolated communities can easily travel to larger nearby towns or cities in order to take advantage of the options for recreation there. Basketball and soccer are two tremendously popular sports for both Jewish and Palestinian male teens. They may play at the local community centers (*Matnasim*) or neighborhood youth clubs, through Maccabi sports clinics or clubs (an Israeli sports organization), or impromptu pick-up games in neighborhoods. Both boys and girls may play intramural sports at school. Outside of school, girls do not play soccer or basketball. The popular sports for girls include jazz dancing, dance, gymnastics, and competitive swimming. Israel has a number of attractive beaches and water parks. During the warm months, swimming and other water sports are very popular with teens. Among wealthier Jewish teens, swimming at the country club has become more popular than going to the beach; country club pools are perceived as "cleaner."

Jewish male teens may go to the local gym and work out in preparation for their army service. *Capoeira*, a Brazilian form of martial arts that incorporates dance movements, has become very popular recently. Teens can take classes and learn the movements employed in the dance; usually two people face each other, striking and parrying in time with the music.

Paramilitary training (*Gadna*) is still popular, although not as popular as it once was. Youth movements, especially those attached to political parties, are weaker than they used to be. Scouting remains the largest youth movement in both populations. Girls are more likely to stay involved in scouting during their teen years as leaders than are boys.

ENTERTAINMENT

Israel thrives on tourism, so there are numerous entertainment possibilities for teens. Dance clubs, pubs, theaters, cinemas, and cafés abound. The club scene is very popular among Israeli teens, although occasional bombings at clubs have caused some teens to stay away from these outlets. The clubs open at midnight, and teens may stay out dancing until 4 or 5 in the morning. Salsa dancing is the current craze, while Israeli folk dancing is now mainly restricted to the age 30 and up group. Another popular place for teens to congregate are the squares (*merkaz*) in the centers of many towns. Boomboxes provide the musical entertainment as teens dance, talk, and order pizza to be delivered.

Israeli teens also show interest in a wide variety of music, both Western and Eastern. Israel has become the world center of trance music, a type of electronic music, usually without lyrics, that blends the sound textures of ambient music with the fast drumbeats of rave and techno. The rave party scene is thriving, with foreign DJs coming to Israel to hold parties.[27] The Israeli version of trance music combines Eastern musical influences with 1970s disco and 1960s psychedelia. The Israeli trance act Mystica hit the British charts twice in one year, and another popular local performer is Ofaria. House music (electronic music) at the dance clubs is beginning to surpass the popularity of rock music for teens. Choopie, one of Israel's best-known DJs, plays to over 5,000 people every weekend at clubs in Tel Aviv's port area.

Teens can attend rock concerts in venues like Tel Aviv's Yarkon Park, where groups such as Irish boy band Westlife and British pop group 5ive come to play open-air performances to audiences of thousands. Among

Ethiopian teens, American rap music (Tupac Shakur, Biggie Smalls) and reggae (Bob Marley) are extremely popular. And Israel has produced its own local reggae/rap style musicians—artists such as Mook E, Fishi Hagadol, indie musician Mosh Ben Ari, and Yuval Banai.

Another strong musical current in Israel is Mediterranean music (also called *mizrahit* music), with roots in Morocco, Algeria, and Iraq. This music accounts for 60 to 70 percent of local Israeli music sales and features musicians such as Haim Moshe and the late Zohar Argov or groups such as Teapacks. Western-influenced rock is also strong with musicians such as Aviv Geffen or bands like Eifoh Ha-Yeled (Where's the Child) and Shabak Samech, influencing the whole field of Israeli popular music with their adaptations of Anglo-American "alternative" rock and hip-hop.

Israeli television for years was a government monopoly with only one channel broadcasting. The government eventually added a second channel that provided movies and some serials and opened up cable opportunities. By the end of 1998, over 70 percent of Israeli households had subscribed to cable.[28] Israeli teens watch a mean of 3.39 hours of TV on school days and almost 6 hours daily during vacations. American television shows such as *The Simpsons*, and *Beverly Hills 90210*, as well as The American MTV network are teen favorites as well as Israeli television serials such as *Ramat-Aviv Gimel* (a cross between *Beverly Hills 90210/Melrose Place* and *Dynasty/Dallas*) and *Florentene*.

Last but not least, Israeli teens also make good use of computers and the Internet. In fact, Israeli teens are well known in the community of computer hackers. In 1998, three Israeli teens were put under house arrest after they hacked into the Pentagon's computer system. In October 2000, Israeli teens launched a cyber attack on the Web site for Hizbollah (a Lebanese Muslim political movement that fought the Israeli army in Lebanon). In response, hackers in Arab countries attacked Israeli sites. In 2001, four teens from Nahariya admitted to writing and distributing the Goner computer virus, which tore through computer systems worldwide. Teens normally use their computers to connect to information for school projects; to access news, video, and music from around the world; and to make contact with teens in other countries.

RELIGIOUS PRACTICES AND CULTURAL CEREMONIES

Among many Jewish teens in Israel, their religion is taken for granted because they live in a Jewish state. Two-thirds to three-quarters of Israelis are not religious in observance or practice. Israeli teens who have visited the United States, for example, often note that they were more conscious of being Jewish here than they ever are in Israel. Jewish religious practices have been integrated into state frameworks such that teens do not have to think about being Jewish. Shops and businesses close on Friday/Saturday for the Sabbath, public buses and trains stop running (except in the north, where there is a significant non-Jewish population), and Jewish religious holy days are national holidays.

Jewish teens all go through a coming-of-age ceremony known as the *bar* (boys) or *bat* (girls) *mitzvah*. According to Jewish law, a boy reaches the age of moral adulthood at 13 and is then expected to follow all the commandments; girls reach this stage at age 12. While this ceremony has become a major celebration, this has occurred only within the last century. In Israel, teens invite their classmates, family, and friends for a party in a rented hall with a DJ, in addition to any ceremony at the synagogue, where the boy will be called to read Torah (the first five books of the Old Testament) for the first time. Another important rite of passage occurs with the graduation ceremony at the end of twelfth grade. Teens put together skits, songs, and even movies and sometimes organize parties. The final rite of passage celebration occurs right before teens are inducted into the army. Those last days of freedom are also occasions for parties before the teens begin rigorous basic army training.

National holidays celebrated in Israel include specifically Jewish religious holidays, such as the Day of Atonement (Yom Kippur), two days of New Year's (Rosh Hashana), Shavuot, Shmenei Atzeret, Sukkot, first and last day of Passover (Pesach), as well as Independence Day (Yom Ha'Atzmaut), Holocaust Remembrance Day (Yom Hashoah), and Remembrance Day for the Fallen Soldiers (Yom HaZicharon). The Jewish calendar is lunar, so the dates for these holidays vary from year to year. Teens get these days off from school and are free to celebrate with their families or friends. Some religious holidays are occasions to go on picnics and to the beaches or clubs; others are taken more seriously and are celebrated in more traditional fashion. Even secular Jews observe Yom Kippur and may fast or attend synagogue. Most Israelis welcome Pesach with a special Pesach dinner. Many families build small harvest huts (*sukkahs*) for Sukkot and take meals in them during the holiday. In some communities additional holidays may be given, such as Mimouna, a traditional Moroccan day of celebration after Passover.

The national holidays are celebrated differently among the Jewish and Palestinian communities. Teens may be expected to take part in ceremonies at their schools in honor of Israeli independence or remembering fallen soldiers. Failure to observe moments of silence when the sirens sound may bring censure on teens. Teens take part in processions and in municipal ceremonies that mark these events. Clearly, however, these holidays have different meanings for Jewish and Palestinian teens. Palestinians have developed their own "national" holidays. The first was Land Day, first celebrated on March 30, 1976, when Palestinians went on strike that day to protest seizures of Arab land. It continues to be observed in Palestinian communities throughout the country with gatherings, parades, speeches, and strikes. In the last few years, Palestinians have begun to celebrate a new day in response to Israeli Independence Day—Yom al-Nakba (Catastrophe Day, May 15).[29]

For Palestinians, the holidays they celebrate are also connected to their religious traditions. For Christians, Easter and Christmas are important celebrations. For Muslims, the Eid al-Fitr and Eid al-Adha are observed. Those who can may travel with their families to the Old City in Jerusalem to attend the Al-Aqsa Mosque for services.

CONCLUSION

Israeli teens, like teens everywhere, care deeply about their families, their communities, and their country. Throughout Israel, Jewish and Palestinian teens have been meeting through their schools and other programs in order to get to know one another better and seek a resolution to the ongoing conflict that structures all their lives. Every summer since 1993, Seeds of Peace, an American nonprofit, nonpolitical organization, has been bringing together Israeli, Palestinian, and other Arab youths in a camp setting in Maine in the United States in order to foster the teens' ability to see each other as human beings and to train them in conflict resolution and leadership skills. These teens return to their own countries and carry on with meeting and working together to further the cause of peace in the region. Since the outbreak of the civil disturbances in the Territories in September 2000, some Jewish teens have gone even further. In September 2001, 62 teens signed and published a letter saying they would refuse to do military service because they object to the military's policies with regard to Palestinians. The letter sparked a storm of controversy within Israel. Some Israelis spoke out against these students, but others supported them for their courage. There is a growing movement of conscientious objection among Israeli teens who are choosing jail over possible service in the Occupied Territories. The current generation of teens are taking an active and vocal role in determining their own future and the future of their country. Whatever else one can say about them, they are not apathetic—they are involved!

ACKNOWLEDGMENT

The author would like to thank Tania Forte and Laurie King-Irani who provided valuable information on teen life in Israel.

NOTES

1. These descriptions and this chapter refer to the pre-1967 boundaries of the country, an area often referred to as "inside the Green Line." For a discussion of what life is like for teens in the areas occupied by Israel since 1967—the Gaza Strip, West Bank, Golan Heights, and East Jerusalem—see the chapter on the Palestinian Territories.

2. *Statistical Abstract of Israel 2001*, Population. http://www.cbs.gov.il/shnatonenew.htm.

3. *Kibbutzim* are collective settlements whose members own property collectively. They pool their earnings and divide them up so that all members' needs are met. Jobs on the kibbutz usually circulate among all members. *Moshavim* are cooperative farming settlements where property is individually owned, but members may cooperate in certain activities such as harvesting or selling their products.

4. Several small Conservative and Reform congregations now exist and hold services, but they are not recognized or supported by the state.

5. All Israeli citizens carry identity cards, which include a listing of their nationality. For Jews and the Druze, their nationality is the same as their religion, respectively, "Jew" and "Druze." For Christian and Muslim Israelis, their nationality is listed as "Arab." The fact that the Israeli state does not recognize one single nationality—Israeli—for all Israeli citizens has been a major point of contention in Israel's political affairs.

6. The first uprising led to the Oslo Accords, the outcome of secret negotiations between the Israeli government and the Palestinian Liberation Organization (PLO) in 1993. Oslo established a set of principles to be used to guide Israeli withdrawal from the Occupied Territories and the creation of Palestinian control over these areas over five years. At the end of this five-year period, final status talks were to be held to resolve all the remaining issues (such as water rights, status of Israeli settlements, Palestinian refugee status, final borders between the two states, and the type of Palestinian political entity to be created). Israel began to withdraw form some areas and turned them over to limited Palestinian control but at the same time, they expanded their settlement activities and road building in other parts of the West Bank and Gaza. Final status negotiations, scheduled to begin in mid-1996, did not begin until mid-2000. By this point, it was clear to most observers that the Olso Accords were dead. When Ariel Sharon visited the Haram al-Sharif (Temple Mount) in Jerusalem's Old City in September 2000, Palestinians protested his presence at their holy place.

Six unarmed Palestinian protesters were killed by Israeli soldiers, which sparked the current uprising against Israel's occupation. One of the major differences between the two periods of protest is the level of force being used by both sides. During the first protest, Palestinians were limited in their access to weaponry— they fought with stones and Molotov cocktails. During the current uprising, they have access to more sophisticated weaponry. On the Israeli side, lessons learned in combating the earlier uprising have led to greater use of missiles, tank shells and other artillery, and helicopters. The consequence is that the death toll on both sides is much higher. For more information on the uprising, check out the Primer on the Uprising in Palestine published on the web by MERIP (Middle East Research and Information Project) at *http://merip.org/new_uprising_primer/ primer_intro.html.*

7. Youths who are religiously observant may be released from military service. Girls who do not want to serve may decide to get married (or pregnant) so they will be released. Not every girl is drafted. Any teen who scores low enough on the exams or who has a criminal record may also not be drafted.

8. Candace Currie, Klaus Hurrelmann, Wolfgang Settertobulte, Rebecca Smith, and Joanna Todd, eds., *Health and Health Behaviour among Young People* (World Health Organization, 1999). http://www.who.dk/document/e67880.pdf

9. "Israeli Parliamentary Committee Proposes Campaign against Anorexia," *Deutsche Presse-Agentur,* 12 July 2001.

10. Lynne R. Franks, *Israel and the Occupied Territories: A Study of the Educational Systems of Israel and the Occupied Territories and a Guide to the Academic Placement of Students in Educational Institutions of the United States* (Washington, DC: American Association of Collegiate Registrars and Admissions Officers, 1987), 10.

11. Nachum Blass and Benyamin Amir, "Integration in Education: The Development of a Policy," in *School Desegregation: Cross-Cultural Perspectives*, eds. Yehuda Amir and Shlomo Sharan (Hillsdale, NJ: Lawrence Erlbaum Associates, 1984), 70.

12. This "reform" has been slow to occur in the educational system. When Arnold Lewis studied the schools of Sharonia in 1975–1976, they were still operating under the old structure (8-4). A number of elite schools continue to follow the model of eight years of elementary and four years of high school (for example, the Reali School in Haifa and the Herzlia Gymnasia).

13. Franks, *Israel and the Occupied Territories*, p. 9.

14. The language of instruction in the Arab system is Arabic, although students also learn both Hebrew and English. Students who plan to attend a university must master Hebrew (and English), since there are no Israeli Arabic-language universities. Arab students at all levels have units on Arabic language and literature, Arab history, and Jewish/Israeli studies.

15. For ten years now, the Israeli government has acknowledged it spends more on educating Jewish students than it does on Palestinian students. Palestinian students are allocated only 60 percent of what Jewish students receive. United Nations Human Rights Committee (on 9 April 1998), paragraph 843, for discus-

sion of the disparities in funding, as well as the report from Human Rights Watch, *Second Class*: Discrimination Against Palestinian Arab Children in Israel's Schools, September 2001, p. 47. http://www.hrw.org/reports/2001/israel2/.

16. Nura Resh, "Track Placement: How the 'Sorting Machine' Works in Israel," *American Journal of Education* 106, no. 3 (1998): 416–438.

17. Human Rights Watch, *Second Class: Discrimination against Palestinian Arab Children in Israel's Schools*, September 2001, p. 32. http://www.hrw.org/reports/2001/israel2/.

18. Ibid, p. 30.

19. Ibid, p. 40.

20. These figures and those that follow are from the Web site of the Israeli Society for the Prevention of Alcoholism, http://www.ias.org.uk/ispa/.

21. United Nations Office for Drug Control and Crime Prevention, Egypt Regional Office, http://www.undcp.org/egypt/country_profile_israel.html.

22. Statistics from the table Developments in Drug Use among 12–18 Year Olds, 1989–1998, Israel Anti-Drugs Authority Web site, http://www.antidrugs.org.il/.

23. Marion Marrache, "Drugs and Teens—A Harsh Cocktail," *Internet Jerusalem Post*, 19 August 2001.

24. Ibid.

25. UNICEF, *The Progress of Nations 2000*, http://www.unicef.org/pon00/smoking.htm.

26. Lyn Duff, "Piercing in Israel," *Wiretap*, 15 May 2000.

27. For more about the Israeli trance scene, see http://www.isratrance.com.

28. The cable services offer approximately 40 channels, including Sky News (from Britain); CNN International; MTV; the German SAT1, 3SAT, and RTL; BBC Asia; Turkish channels; Russian channels; Spanish channel (TVE); Arab channels from neighboring countries; Eurosport; National Geographic; the French TV5; and Israeli stations. Israelis also receive the Christian Broadcasting Network (CBN) through the Middle East Network, which is located in southern Lebanon. The cable services also provide five special channels: the movies channel, the sports channel, the children channel, the family channel, and the nature/documentary channel.

29. For more information about the Nakba, see the following Web site: http://www.alnakba.org/.

RESOURCE GUIDE

Books

Elon, Amos. *The Israelis: Founders and Sons*. New York: Penguin, 1983.

Finkelstein, Israel, and Neil Asher Silberman. *The Bible Unearthed: Archaeology's New Vision of Ancient Israel and the Origin of Its Sacred Texts*. New York: Free Press, 2001.

Oz, Amos. *In the Land of Israel*. New York: Harvest Books, 1993.
Segev, Tom. *1949: The First Israelis*. New York: Free Press, 1986.

Fiction

Almagor, Gila. *Under the Domin Tree*. New York: Simon & Schuster, 1995.
Darwish, Mahmoud. *The Adam of Two Edens: Selected Poems*. Syracuse, NY: Syracuse University Press, 2001.
Dor, Moshe, ed. *After the First Rain: Israeli Poems on War and Peace*. Syracuse, NY: Syracuse University Press, 1998.
Habiby, Emile. *The Secret Life of Saeed: the Pessoptimist*. Northhampton, MA: Interlink Publishers, 2001.
Liebrecht, Savyon. *Apples from the Desert: Selected Stories*. New York: Feminist Press, 2000.
Matalon, Ronit. *The One Facing Us*. New York: Owl Books, 1999.
————. *Panther in the Basement*. New York: Harvest Books, 1998.

Web Sites

http://www.knesset.gov.il/index.html
Israel's government, the Knesset. A good source for information about the government, basic laws, and documents, as well as government links.
http://www.haaretzdaily.com/
Ha'Aretz, is Israel's premier newspaper. This is one of the most important sources of current news about Israel.
http://www.mof.gov.il/gpo/
National photo collection of Israel with educational activities for students and teachers.
http://www.kibbutz.org.il/eng/welcome.htm
A Kibbutz Industries Association site containing information about investment, plants, and so on. Also contains numerous links.
http://www.israel.org/mfa/go.asp?MFAH00190
Facts About Israel. Broad information about Israel, its culture, religion, history, economy, and society.
http://www.israelemb.org/chicago/links.html
Chicago Consulate links to sites on Israel. An important guide to government offices, academic sites, art and culture, economics and trade, Jerusalem, news and media, youth programs, tourism.
http://www.partner.org.il/malachi/otzmabook/
Israel in the Eyes of Its Youth. Numerous articles about Israel from its youths' perspective.
http://www.mfa.gov.il/mfa/go.asp?MFAH0h9w0
Israel at 53: a statistical glimpse at Israeli society. Data on geography, people, economy, education.

http://www.mideastweb.org/
Mid-East Web Gateway. Information about Palestine and its people, with links to
    articles on Palestinian society and culture.
http://www.ariga.com/index.htm
Ariga: links to peace groups in Israel. Information about peace activist connec-
    tions, links, and documents inside and outside Ariga.
http://www.israelpages.co.il/reut/
Re'ut/Sadaka: Jewish-Arab Youth Movement for Peace. An excellent site about
    the friendship between Jewish and Arab youths and the organization
    established for this purpose.
http://www.ipcri.org/index1.html
Israeli-Palestinian Center for Research & Information.
http://www.seedsofpeace.org/newclubhouse/
Seeds of Peace Clubhouse. Information about the world's news from different per-
    spectives; also links to different newspapers.

Pen Pal/Chat

http://web66.coled.umn.edu/schools/IL/Israel.html
Web66: International School Web Registry. Information about elementary and
    secondary schools in Israel, educational organizations, resources.

Chapter 4

JORDAN

Musa Shteiwi and Nahed Emaish

INTRODUCTION

Jordan, officially the Hashemite Kingdom of Jordan, is bordered by Palestine and Israel on the west, Syria on the north, Iraq in the northeast, and Saudi Arabia to the east and south. Amman is the capital and largest city. The total population of Jordan is estimated at 5 million in a 37,737 square meter area (97,740 sq. km). As a political entity, modern Jordan was established in 1921 under the British mandate and was called the Transjordan or the Emirate of Jordan. Prior to that, what is known today as Jordan was under the rule of the Ottoman Empire. The establishment of Jordan was affected by two important processes at the time. First was the Arab Revolt against the Ottoman Empire, which was led by Sharif Hussein Ben Ali. He was a Hashemite and a descendant of the Prophet Mohammed. He aspired to liberate the Arab land from the Ottoman occupation and establish an Arab government in parts of what is known today as Iraq, Syria, Jordan, and Palestine. His endeavor led him to cooperate with the "Allies" (Britain and France) against the Ottomans. After the defeat of the Ottomans, the Allies reneged on their promises and divided the Arab countries between them, and Jordan came under the British mandate.

After the evaporation of Sharif Hussein's dream, his son Abdullah directed his efforts at establishing a political entity in what is known today as Jordan. With the support of the local tribes and the British government, Transjordan was established and Emir Abdullah (later King) became the ruler of Jordan. Immediately after the establishment of Transjordan, the process of building up the central government institutions was started, but at a very slow pace. The new government had no resources (it was financially dependent on meager British financial aid) and was under the British direct rule. The British interest in Jordan was political and not economic because of Jordan's crucial geopolitical location in the region. The country gained its independence in 1946, and its name was changed to the Hashemite Kingdom of Jordan in 1949. This change reflects the country's acquisition of land west of the Jordan River during the Arab-Israeli war of 1948, which led to the establishment of the state of Israel in parts of historical Palestine. The rest of Palestine (the West Bank of the Jordan River) was officially united with Jordan in 1950. The Arabs in general and the Palestinians in particular (who lost their land and were displaced from it) deemed the establishment of the state of Israel in parts of Palestine illegitimate and unjust. This resulted in animosity between the Arabs and the Israelis. In 1967, the second Arab-Israeli war erupted and Israel further occupied parts of Egypt, Syria, and Jordan. Jordanian forces were routed in the 1967 war, and Jordan lost the West Bank. Since then Jordan has been composed of the East Bank of the Jordan River.

Jordan is a constitutional monarchy, where the king wields extensive power as the head of the state. The state has three branches: the executive, the legislative, and the judicial, which are supposed to be autonomous from each other. The government is appointed by the King but has to obtain the vote of confidence from the parliament. The constitution guarantees the political participation of individuals through political parties and civil society organizations. However, parliamentary politics came to a halt in the mid-1950s and remained so until 1989. Since then, regular parliamentary elections have been held three times and political parties have been allowed to function. Today there are more than 10 licensed political parties. In spite of the return to democracy, political parties and the political participation of citizens remain very weak. However, compared with other Arab and Third World countries, Jordan is considered to be one of the most dynamic states with democratic institutions in the region. Recently, November 1994, Jordan signed a peace treaty with Israel—the second Arab country to do so.

Jordan has suffered a great deal because of the Arab-Israeli conflict and the Gulf War in 1991. For one thing, the country has received two waves of mass migration from Palestine and one from Kuwait. Over 300,000 refugees fled to Jordan in 1948 and another 300,000 in 1967, settling in refugee camps. Most of them were granted Jordanian citizenship. Many have moved out of the camps since then, but a significant number are still living in 10 refugee camps around the country. In 1991, because of the Iraqi invasion of Kuwait and the subsequent Gulf War, more than 250,000

Jordanian expatriates (many of them of Palestinian origin) who were working in Kuwait were displaced and settled in Jordan. These waves of migration have exerted great pressure on the country's meager resources and changed the composition of the population to the extent that Jordanians of Palestinian origin make up almost half the population of the country.

With very little natural resources, Jordan has invested greatly in its human resources. Since its independence, the government has directed its attention to human resources by investing in the development of the educational system. It has one of the highest literacy rates in the region and the highest educational enrollment rates at all levels as well. Basic education is mandatory and free, and secondary education is very affordable. The country has 18 universities (8 governmental and 10 private). In this regard, the country has been an exporter of educated and skilled labor to the Arab Gulf countries. More recently, the country has embarked on an economic drive to make the country an information technology–based society.

The majority of Jordanians are of Arab ethnic background (98%), with the rest from Caucasian and Armenian origins. Muslims make up the majority of the population, with a significant Arab Christian minority. The country has a rich historical heritage with over 12,000 historical sites from different civilizations. Most of these sites date back to the Nabateans (pre-Muslim Arab civilization), Romans, Muslims, and crusaders. In fact, not one single month passes without discovering new archeological sites in the country. The most important of these sites is Petra (Nabatean city), Jerash (Roman city), Muslim desert palaces, and the site where Jesus Christ was baptized in the Jordan River (this site was declared by the Pope to be the official baptism site for Christians). In 2001, the oldest church in the world was discovered; it is being excavated north of Jordan.

TYPICAL DAY

The typical day for teenagers in Jordan varies according to region of the country, urban-rural, and social class. What all teens have in common is that most of them go to school and finish approximately at the same time. Schools start at 8 A.M. and end at 2 in the afternoon. Most students go to school by bus. Many schools are community based, so it is a short ride to school. However, some schools are far from the community where students live, and the ride to and from school can take a long time both in the morning and in the afternoon. Some students are driven to school by their parents (students of upper and middle classes). A third group walks to school, especially in the rural and pastoral areas; this can be difficult in the winter season. The weather in winter is rainy with cold temperatures dropping to zero Celsius. These conditions, coupled with the rather poor conditions of children in these areas, can make walking to school a hardship.

Most students are home between 2 and 3 o'clock in the afternoon, when lunch is served. In Jordan, like many Arab countries, lunch is considered to be the main meal of the day. After lunch, boys rest and girls help their mothers in the kitchen (some families have servants and maids, which frees girls from performing household duties). After getting some rest, students begin preparing their homework for the next day. Most schools give students a lot of homework that takes a lot of time to finish. Once the homework is finished, students either play with their friends, watch TV, or both. Light dinner is served early (between 7 and 8). During school time, students go to bed early and no later than 10 o'clock. In rural and pastoral areas teenagers help their fathers and mothers in either farming or herding activities. In big cities, it has become normal to see teenagers working in restaurants and shops. Many of those who work outside the home do so at their parents' establishments, but some work for outsiders. Most of those who work outside the home do it for financial reasons in order to get some additional money. However, most if not all teenagers are dependent on their parents for financial support, which makes them more dependent on them in general. Many teenagers now spend a lot of time in Internet cafés, where they go for chatting and communicating with their friends or listening to music or visiting other sites.

This typical day changes when schools are out. Then teenagers spend a lot of free time hanging out with friends, playing sports, and relaxing. The same does not apply to female teens. They normally do not engage in many activities outside the house. Instead, they stay at home to help their mothers in doing household activities. This does not apply to all female teens, because in the wealthy areas they have a chance to go out more freely.

FAMILY LIFE

Although the structure and the role of the family in Jordan are changing, the family remains the most important institution in the country and maybe in the entire Middle East. Until recently, the common form of the family in Jordan was the extended type. In this type of families, married and unmarried children live in the same house. Life in this type of setting is close to a communal way of life. People normally act as a unit whereby they support each other and share their resources. There is no privacy in such an arrangement, with very little room for individual freedom. The affairs of any individual are those of the family. For instance, marriage—which is taken for granted in the West as an individual choice—is a family affair in traditional families where every member of the family has a say. The same goes for other issues and concerns. Of course, in traditional families, males are the dominant members of the family. The father is the head of the family, but also the older brothers exert power over younger brothers and sisters. Women are disadvantaged in this type of family because men tend to interfere in most aspects of their life. Family honor is very important in Jordan, and it is linked to the sexual conduct of women. Women are not supposed to engage in emotional and/or sexual activities with men before marriage. In traditional areas women can be subject to violent actions if they are suspected of having such relations. However, this does not apply to the majority of Jordanians. More than two-thirds live as a nuclear family, and women go to school with and work alongside men. But the family still is the main unit for organizing the social life of its members. That is reflected in the fact that most social activities and entertainment take place within and between families. However, this varies according to the area of residence and social class. Youth in urban centers and in middle and upper classes have more opportunities to engage in activities without their families, much more than do youth of the working and poor classes or youth in the rural areas. Youth of the middle and upper classes are able to engage in many sports and entertainment activities similar to what youth have in most Western countries.

Like in most societies, Jordanian youths are experiencing the benefits and the pains of the changes of the value system in the country. In the last 50 years, the country has experienced tremendous and rapid transformations in all spheres of life. In the 1950s, most people worked and lived in rural areas, were mostly illiterate, lived without electricity, had primitive communication technology, and followed a very conservative value system. In contrast, today most people live and work in urban areas in a modern economy, with access to modern communication technologies including computers and the Internet. These transformations have contributed to a great gap in the value system between the older and younger generations. Unlike the older generation, the younger generation is more individualistic, less politically inclined, and more open to Western culture.

In spite of these changes, the youth are still largely controlled by their parents. The main reason for this is the continuing financial and social dependence of children on their parents. Parents are still responsible for providing support for their children's education throughout school and college. Youths live with their parents until they get married, and parents retain the responsibilities for most of the activities of their children.

TRADITIONAL AND NONTRADITIONAL FOOD

The traditional food in Jordan includes rice, lamb, chicken, beef, fresh vegetables and fruits, and Arabic bread on the side. The traditional food in Jordan is derived mainly from the agricultural and pastoral roots of the economy. Most of the fresh foods are produced all year round in the country with the exception of rice, which is imported. More recently, the country started importing more food from abroad. Fresh fish is not easily available in the country and is imported from neighboring countries, but frozen fish is available and readily consumed. Normally, people purchase their foods at specialized outlets (meat and poultry) and from supermarkets where they can talk and bargain. In the summertime, it is very common to find fresh fruits and vegetables displayed along the main streets. Fresh breads and pastries are bought directly from bakeries almost on a daily basis.

Aside from the class differences, there is little variation in the menu. Breakfast normally consists of Arabic bread, yogurt (*labaneh*), eggs, cheese, thyme seeds, olive oil, and tea. However, on the weekend a huge breakfast might be served that might include, in addition to the normal menu, chickpeas with sesame paste (*hummus*) and mashed broad beans with spices (*foul*). For most Jordanians, lunch is the main meal; it is usually served between 1 and 3. It consists of cooked lamb or chicken with rice and some vegetables: green beans, okra, zucchini, potatoes, or a spinach-like vegetable called *millokhiah*. Salad or yogurt is also served. Then fresh fruits (depending on the season) or desserts are served. The meal usually ends with tea. Most people (especially men) take a nap after lunch. A light dinner is served between 7 and 8 P.M.

Dinner can be a combination of foods served at breakfast and at dinner. There is one dish that is known to be the Jordanians' favorite and national dish, the *mansaf*. It is usually served on special occasions, for important and special guests, and in festivities. The *mansaf* is made of lamb cooked with fresh or dried yogurt. Rice is cooked separately. The *mansaf* is served by spreading the rice in special rounded trays, then putting the meat on top of the rice, and the yogurt sauce on top of the meat. Traditionally, people gather around the table and eat this dish by using their right hand to make a small ball of rice, but people can also eat it with spoons.

Fast-food places are spreading everywhere in the cities. Most popular fast-food Arab dishes are *shawarma* and *falafel*. *Shawarma* is sliced lamb or chicken served in thin bread as a sandwich. *Falafel* is a vegetarian mix of chickpeas and other spices served on pita bread. More recently, American fast-food restaurants have been introduced in the capital of the country. McDonald's, Burger King, Kentucky Fried Chicken, and Pizza Hut are some of the fast-food places in Jordan. Like in the United States, these fast-food places are favored by Jordanian youth over other types of restaurants and dishes.

SCHOOLING

In spite of the fact that Jordan is a poor country, education has been given a great deal of attention by the state since its independence. Public schools were established gradually in all parts of the country. Today, there is no part of the country that does not have access to primary education. Mobile schools cover even the remote, nomadic areas. Primary education is compulsory and free up to tenth grade. Secondary education is not free, but the cost is minimal. The state's emphasis on education helped transform the country from largely illiterate to mostly literate in about four decades. This is reflected in the 89 percent literacy rate that the country enjoys today.[1] At the primary and secondary levels of education, there is gender parity in school enrollments. Parallel to the state commitment to education, there is an equally important emphasis by the Jordanian people on education.

As for higher education, there are 18 public and private universities in the country. Education in public universities is not free but is partially subsidized and is affordable. There are also many scholarships that target children of various segments of the population such as teachers, members of the army, the poor, refugees, and so on. The majority of Jordanians go to public schools and universities. But in the last 10 years there has been a growing number of private schools and universities attracting teens of higher-income families. Although there were always private schools in Jordan, their number now is rather large. Consequently, there is a growing divide between those who go to public versus private schools. The middle and upper classes send their children to private schools, whereas the children of the poor, lower-middle, and working classes go to public schools. The surge of private schools has contributed to a decline in the quality of education in the public schools because these schools attract more qualified teachers, have better facilities, teach more foreign languages than public schools, and provide students with a wide range of additional activities that are important for the growth of children. Some of these schools are international such as modern American schools, Victoria College and others.

Jordanian schoolgirl. Courtesy of Ali Akbar Mahdi.

Most private schools are coed, whereas all public schools are sex segregated. However, the Ministry of Education prescribes the curriculum and all schools have to teach it. Private schools are allowed to add additional educational materials, if they choose. The curriculum includes the Arabic and English languages (French has also been approved to be taught in schools), science, math, biology, physics, history, computers, and civic education. Islamic religion is taught to Muslims, and Christian religion is taught to Christians.

After students finish the tenth grade, they have to choose one of the following tracks: scientific, literary, or vocational. Once students choose a track, they go to different classes or schools. The achievement level of the students determines the choice of the track. The choice of the track determines the students' field of study in college. For instance, if a student chooses the literary track, he or she cannot enter an engineering college; but the reverse is not true for those who choose the scientific track—they can choose any field of study they want. It is assumed that students of the scientific track are more intelligent than students from other tracks. Also, students from other tracks are not exposed to enough courses in physics, mathematics, and chemistry, which are necessary for future study at the university level. In the final year of high school, all students have to take a standardized national examination (called Tawjihi) that determines their chances of entering the university. The Tawjihi score is the sole criterion for acceptance at a university. As the only exam determining a student's future, it is very competitive and stressful for both students and their parents. Schools are generally responsive to the educational demands placed on them. They offer students a variety of subjects and experiences that prepare them for dealing with the modern and global way of life. Most students are bilingual and computer literate. Since schools are not community based, most students go to school by bus. However, wealthier parents drive their children to school in private cars.

SOCIAL LIFE

Although Jordanian society is almost culturally and ethnically homogeneous, it is beginning to exhibit sharp distinctions in the social life of its people—distinctions that are eventually reflected in teens' social life. The main differences can be noticed between different classes and the level of urbanization. Normally, teens socialize with their peers in school. Students of well-to-do parents usually drive their own cars and go out, sometimes with their dates, to coffee shops, restaurants, and dancing places. They also might have private parties in their homes. The legal age for driving is 18. In some instances, the parents know that their daughters are dating boys, but most often dating takes place without either the knowledge or the consent of the parents. Modern communication technology has made it easier for rich teens to evade parental control.

The spread of private cars, Internet service, and mobile phones is having a great impact on the social relations and social values of teens and the society at large. Internet cafés are widespread and very popular with young people. In a 1-kilometer stretch of one of the streets in Irbid, a city in the north of Jordan, there are more than 120 Internet cafés. In fact, this street was listed in the *Guinness Book of World Records* as having the highest number of Internet cafés in the world. Internet cafés are accessible to poor and rich people alike. Although boys and girls do not mix in these cafés, they meet in the premises. Like teens everywhere, they are mostly interested in chatting, sex, music, and sports.

As for teens from working-class and poor backgrounds, their social life is in contrast to that of their peers from rich backgrounds. They tend to socialize with the same gender, have little access to modern technologies,

Group of Jordanian girls after school. Courtesy of Ali Akbar Mahdi.

and have much less access to public facilities. However, males still have more advantages than their female counterparts from this background. Males still go outside with other males to public places like restaurants and cinemas and attend public events. They hardly are able to meet with females in public. The females are hardly able to go out to public places on their own. When they do, it tends to be with other females in the family or relatives. They mostly go shopping and occasionally to restaurants. These activities do not happen often. Otherwise, the females stay at home, if they are not at school or at the university. Social life for most female teens takes place within the family. The restrictions on girls are religiously and socially sanctioned.

As in all Arab and Muslim countries, premarital sex is forbidden. Premarital sexual relations are viewed as a disgrace to the family honor. Such behavior may result in extreme punishments. The society is more tolerant toward males in this regard. Males wear modern dress. While some females wear modern dress, a significant number wear the Islamic dress, or *hijab*, in various forms. However, teens from well-to-do backgrounds dress according to fashion, and females wear Western-style clothes. Most marriages were arranged in the past, but they are no longer the dominant form. There are at least three patterns of marriage today in Jordan: (1) the prearranged marriage, which is still practiced in nomadic, rural, and poor areas; (2) the semi-arranged marriage, in which the family helps to make contact and provide the forum for boys and girls to meet for compatibility under parental supervision (this process may take several meetings); and (3) the free type, where men and women meet and possibly date each other and then get married.

RECREATION

Sports in Jordan are very popular in all parts of the country and prevalent among all social groups. The main factor influencing participation in sports is gender. Soccer is the most popular sport in the country, but there is only a men's national league. However, both men and women follow the sport. There are national leagues for almost every other type of sport for both men and women. Basketball, volleyball, and table tennis are the most popular sports among females. In fact, there are youth leagues for most of these sports. Swimming is an elite sport in the country because there are no outlets to the sea or rivers. Those engaged in swimming use public or private pools.

Other forms of recreation are normally organized during the school year by various educational institutions. These include trips to tourist sites and archeological sites, or camping in favorite places. In recent years, different types of cultural festivals have been flourishing in Jordan. These are held at both the national and local levels, with increasing participation of artistic groups from abroad. Attending these festivals has become popular among youth of all backgrounds. In addition, there are several parks in the capital that are used for recreation by teens and families alike. Finally, the family in Jordan remains important to the recreation of youth. One form of family recreation is family picnics and trips. These take place in all seasons. Usually, family members go to parks or to rural areas during spring and summer and spend time together singing, playing sports, and barbecuing. Sometimes these gatherings extend to the early evenings. In winter, the same activity is carried out in different locations. The western and southern parts of the country, which are below sea level, are warm during winter and very hot in the summer. These warm areas represent an attraction for families during the winter season for picnicking and social activities. In other family gatherings at the homes of friends and relatives, many activities are carried out such as playing cards and eating favorite foods. But of late, the latter form of family social life is becoming less attractive to teens because these gatherings are restrictive; teens would rather be with other teens doing something else away from the family.

ENTERTAINMENT

Teenagers in Jordan opt for all types of entertainment. Like all teens around the world, Jordanian youth are attracted to music. They enjoy Western pop and rock-and-roll music as much they enjoy popular Arab music. Most popular among Jordanians is Lebanese and Egyptian pop music. They normally listen to music in public places such as malls and cafés. In addition, there are a lot of attractive places where teens meet and listen to music, especially during the summer. Restaurants and cafés with open space provide a venue for listening to music, smoking narghile (a water pipe used for smoking tobacco), and meeting friends. Teens also resort to private gatherings, at private homes or in leased public halls, for listening to music and dancing. In the capital city of Amman, some youth are able to go to nightclubs. Although the minimum age for entering these places is 18, the application of the law is not strict and many 16- to 18-year-olds visit these places for drinking, listening to music, dancing, and socializing with friends. Although the Islamic religion prohibits alcohol, the government allows its sale in specially licensed groceries, and all kinds of alcohol are manufactured in the country. Therefore, alcohol is available in nightclubs, restaurants, and hotels.

In other parts of the country mixed nightclubs are not available, and males do not have the chance to meet females as in Amman. Musical concerts and cultural festivals are other forms of entertainment available in Jordan. During the summer, a wide range of festivals takes place at both the national and local levels. The most important annual national festival is the Jerash festival. Every year, the most popular singers in the Arab world and international dancing groups participate in the month-long festival and attract thousands of teens. There are also many places known as "entertainment centers" where teens play video games, table tennis, snooker, and billiards. Only males go to these places, and they are more frequented in the summer and to a lesser extent during schooldays. Additionally, TV (especially satellite) is popular among teens for listening to music and watching movies. Some teens watch movies on video. More recently, youth have been enjoying the widespread availability of Internet service (either private or at cafés) and spending time surfing the Internet.

Jordanian boys at a video arcade. Courtesy of Ali Akbar Mahdi.

RELIGIOUS PRACTICES AND CULTURAL CEREMONIES

Most Jordanians are Muslims, but there is a significant and visible Arab Christian minority in the country. Both communities observe religious holidays and ceremonies. For Muslims, the most important occasion is the holy month of Ramadan, when people fast by refraining from eating, drinking, and smoking during daylight hours. The spiritual aspect of this month is to devote oneself to praying and reflection. It is also meant to serve as a reminder to Muslims of the suffering of the poor and the importance of the family and charity. Teens are expected to fast during this month and to engage in daily public prayers.

During Ramadan, the government adjusts working hours by reducing them to six hours. Restaurants are not allowed to serve food during fasting hours, but foreigners can eat at restaurants in hotels. All people are to refrain from eating, drinking, or smoking in public during this month; violators are subject to punishment (spending the remaining Ramadan days in prison). For youth in Amman, Ramadan has a special flavor socially.

Most restaurants hold "Ramadan Nights" by turning their premises into coffee shops where they offer special entertainment programs and special drinks and desserts. Ramadan Nights start about 9 o'clock in the evening and last until late at night. Most teens spend their time playing cards, chatting with friends, and listening to music. On other holidays, like Eid al-Adha, the country goes on a public holiday: family members and friends visit with each other, exchange gifts (especially for children) and enjoy themselves and each other.

Christians in Jordan are Arabs, and they are proud of their Christian and Arab heritage. They believe that they are the real descendants of the early Christians in the region and celebrate Christian holidays (Christmas, Easter, New Year's, and Palm Sunday) privately and publicly. In fact, Christians are given two days off for Christmas and Easter and one day off for Palm Sunday by the government and private business as well. In addition, Christmas and New Year's have become public holidays in Jordan since the year 2000. Christians celebrate their holidays in much the same way as Muslims: families and friends get together, offer gifts to their children, and eat special foods. Children and youth are at the heart of these celebrations because they are given gifts and greater attention. On Palm Sunday, Christian youth with their families celebrate by marching in the streets around the church. On New Year's Eve, special parties are organized publicly in hotels and restaurants or privately in homes. This occasion is increasingly celebrated by both Christian and Muslim teens in the country by dancing the night away. In addition, both communities share each other's religious holidays in a fraternal manner. The Western Christian community in Jordan is small and is composed of workers in embassies, international organizations, and companies. Their teens celebrate these holidays according to traditions in their country of origin and sometimes with Jordanian families and teens.

Religion is very much a part of the belief system of teenagers in the country, with a clear variation in the degree of observance. Many Muslim teens attend Friday prayers in mosques; other teens pray at work or at home during the week. Females normally do not go to the mosque, and teenagers pray at home or in school. However, not all Muslim teenagers strictly observe the Islamic teachings. For instance, drinking alcohol is prohibited according to Islamic teachings, but many teenagers drink in public. The same goes for dating before marriage. Strict application of Islam does not allow sexual relations before marriage, but teenagers do date before marriage. Finally, women are supposed to cover their heads, according to religious teachings, but many women see this as an issue of personal freedom. In short, Islam for some has become a spiritual and cultural identity rather than a strict code of conduct.

CONCLUSION

Teens in Jordan resemble teens in many parts of the world, including the United States, in their patterns of life, problems, and aspirations. They enjoy many of the things that teens elsewhere enjoy. They like pop music (Arabic and Western), and they have their own subculture that includes dress, issues of interest, values, and social life that separates them from the older generation. They also have their own frustrations. They are under pressure from school, family, and peers. They have to succeed in a more competitive world. They worry about their future in terms of finding a decent job and having a good life. They also complain that their voice is not being heard in society because there are not enough forums for expressing their views and opinions. They also aspire to have a good education, a rewarding job, and satisfactory social and emotional lives. However, class, gender, and region separate these commonalities. Male teens have more opportunities than female teens, teens of higher classes have more resources and more connections to the outside world and culture, and teens in the cities (especially in the capital) have more choices of jobs, education, and entertainment. Jordan has a youth and sports ministry that focuses more on sports and less on youth. Recently, the youth ministry and other governmental and nongovernmental institutions have begun to pay more attention to the youth and their concerns through various youth-targeted programs.

NOTE

1. Department of Statistics. *Employment and Unemployment in Jordan Survey*, Amman. 2001.

RESOURCE GUIDE

Books and Articles

Abu Nowar, Maan. *The History of the Hashemite Kingdom of Jordan*, vol. 1, *The Creation and Development of Transjordan: 1920–1929*. Oxford: Ithaca Press, 1989.

Abu-Odeh, Adnan. *Jordanians, Palestinians & the Hashemite Kingdom in the Middle East Peace Process*. Washington, D.C.: United States Institute of Peace, 1999.

Brand, Lairie A. *Women, the State, and Political Liberalization*. New York: Columbia University Press, 1998.

Dallas, Rolland. *King Hussein: A Life on the Edge*. New York: Fromm International, 1999.

Janson, Staffan. "Life and Health of Jordanian Children." In *Children in the Moslem Middle East*, edited by Elizabeth W. Fernea, 176–198. Austin: University of Texas Press, 1995.

Patai, Raphael. *The Kingdom of Jordan*. Westport, CT: Greenwood Publishing Group, 1984.

Salibi, Kamal. *The Modern History of Jordan*. London: I. B. Tauris, 1993.

Shami, Seteney, and Lucine Taminian. "Children of Amman: Childhood and Child Care in Squatter Areas of Amman, Jordan." In *Children in the Moslem Middle East*, edited by Elizabeth W. Fernea, 68–78. Austin: University of Texas Press, 1995.

South, Coleman. *Jordan (Cultures of the World)*. New York: Marshall Cavendish, 1997.

Fiction

Caulfield, Annie. *Kingdom of the Film Stars: Journey into Jordan*. Oakland, CA: Lonely Planet, 1997.

Saleh, Hajar. *Once upon the Jordan River*. Tucson, AZ: Hats Off Books, 2001.

Web Sites

http://www.jordanembassyus.org/new/index.shtml
Embassy

www.albawaba.com
Albawaba: The Middle East Gateway. Information about news and media, religion and philosophy, business and economy, culture and society, government, organizations.

www.hejleh.com/countries/jordan.html
The Country and People of Jordan. Links to sites in Jordan and related sites. General information about the country's politics, history, media, tourism, economy.

www.petra.gov.jo
Jordan News Agency. Information about Arabic news, English news, photos, links.

www.see-jordan.com
Jordan Tourism Board. Information about Jordan's tourism. The site's main goal is to promote Jordan's tourism product internationally.

www.dos.gov.jo
Department of Statistics, Amman. Statistics, brief history, publications, press releases.

www.youth.gov.jo

Hashemite Kingdom of Jordan. Information about Ministry of Youth and Sports
   departments and publications, as well as sports unions and sports sites.

www.jordantimes.com

Jordan Times. Links to news, economy, weather, and commentaries.

Pen Pal/Chat

http://www.baladna.com.jo

Chapter 5

KUWAIT

Taghreed Alqudsi-Ghabra

INTRODUCTION

Kuwait is a small Arab state on the western tip of the Persian Gulf. Its area is estimated at 6,880 square miles, which is slightly smaller than that of New Jersey. It is surrounded by Iraq, Saudi Arabia, and Iran. Kuwait's population is estimated at 2,270,000, including 45 percent Kuwaiti nationals, 35 percent non-Kuwaiti Arabs, 9 percent South Asians, 4 percent Iranians, 7 percent others.[1]

Kuwait is a Muslim country with a dominant Sunni population (60%), a large Shi'a minority (25%), and members of other faiths (15%, including Christian, Hindu, Farsi, and others). These religious minorities are free to observe their traditional religious practices provided that they do not conflict with public policy and morals.[2]

Kuwait is poor in natural resources other than oil and sea. It lacks water and has no arable land to develop agriculture. Except for fish, Kuwait depends completely on food imports. Prior to the discovery of oil, Kuwait depended mainly on the sea. Pearl diving and trading with Southeast Asia and Africa was the main business in the country. Men used to go to sea for months. Women were left to care for the family. As a result, political power was closely shared with the leading merchant families. However, after the discovery of oil and with the wealth acquired from the newly discovered "black gold (oil)," the Al Sabah family acquired a more prominent and powerful role in juxtaposition to the traditional merchant class.

The Al Sabah family has governed Kuwait since the mid-eighteenth century. As a modern monarchy, Kuwait gained its independence from Britain on June 19, 1961, and became a member of the United Nations on

May 14, 1963. As an Arab-Islamic sovereign monarchy, with an elected national assembly of 50 members, Kuwait is ruled by a government headed by a prime minister. The *Amir* (ruler) of Kuwait appoints the prime minister and exercises his executive power through the Council of Ministers. Elections for the national assembly are held every four years by selective male suffrage—men who are over twenty-one years old, non-members of the army or ministry of interior. In the 1999 election, women were neither allowed to vote nor to be candidates for election. A decree by the Amir, allowing women the right to vote and run for the Parliament is under review by the National Assembly. Both Sunnis and Shi'as serve as cabinet ministers, as members of the National Assembly, and in other influential positions. The legal system in Kuwait is based on the Constitution that was promulgated on November 11, 1962.

Oil has traditionally accounted for about 96 percent of the country's budget revenue. Until 1984–1985 it had always exceeded government expenditure, with the surplus being transferred to the State General Reserve. However, the situation changed drastically as a result of the August 1990 Iraqi invasion of Kuwait when the whole country was overrun by Iraq. A U.S.-led UN coalition began a four-day liberation attack of Kuwait, as a result of which Kuwait had to spend more than $5 billion to repair the oil infrastructure damaged during the 1990–1991 crisis. Huge deficits were incurred during the 1990–1992 fiscal years due to the costs of liberation and reconstruction at a time when oil production and its revenue were reduced sharply.

At present, and as a result of the oil revenues, "Kuwait is considered to be among the richest countries of the world in terms of per capita GNP [gross national product] or per capita income."[3] Since independence, the government of Kuwait has been committed to a program of social welfare financed mainly by oil revenues. While almost all Kuwaitis are employed in the government sector, most non-Kuwaitis work in the private sector. Working hours in the private sector are often longer than in the public sector. Kuwaiti society is very dependent on the non-Kuwaiti expatriate workforce working on contracts for the lucrative service economy. This expatriate population is divided between (1) professionals working for multinational corporations who most of the time choose to bring their families along, and (2) a class of paraprofessionals and housekeepers, drivers, cooks, and others on short-term contracts. Most of these helpers, who clean houses, cook, and chauffeur for Kuwaiti and non-Kuwaiti families, are from Southeast Asia.

According to a recent United Nations Development Program (UNDP) report, Kuwait's most important concerns today are the following: high defense expenditures as a result of the 1990 crisis with Iraq, high imports in consumer goods, the high burden of subsidies and salaries on government spending (84%), and the slow movement toward privatization. However, there are attempts to reform the fiscal system, reduce the budget deficit, and address public reform strategies. This is also accompanied by efforts to encourage the civil society and private sector to take on a developmental role, particularly with regard to the employment of nationals and the labor situation.

The border dispute between Kuwait and Iraq, which has existed since Kuwait's independence, resulted in the Iraqi invasion of Kuwait on August 2, 1990. This invasion was a big blow to the Kuwaiti people and government, coming from an Arab Muslim neighbor that had always been supported by Kuwait. The Iraqi occupation was ended when allied forces, led by the United States, liberated Kuwait on February 26, 1991. Since its liberation, Kuwait has opened its economy to all kinds of business for multinational corporations and has been forced to increase its defense and arms spending.

TYPICAL DAY

As it does for teens the world over, school life constitutes a major part of a teen's life in Kuwait. During weekdays, the typical day for a teenager starts with getting ready for school. Generally speaking, parents send their children to schools within their district. Students who attend private schools may commute a longer distance; these schools might be American, British, co-ed, segregated, or other. Students are driven to school by their parents, bus, or private chauffeur. Some parents carpool.

In a welfare state, where every Kuwaiti is guaranteed a job and most services are provided freely, almost every teenager goes to school. The dropout rate is insignificant, and it does not occur before 14 years of age. The school day generally starts between 7 and 7:30 A.M. and ends by 3 P.M. for private schools and 2 P.M. for public schools. At the end of the school day, families gather for lunch. Lunch is the main meal of the day in most Arab countries, and Kuwait is no exception.

People usually take an afternoon nap after lunch. In a country so hot and dry, this has been the norm for a long time. In the afternoon, teenagers do their homework and participate in social activities. Some teens visit the malls, go to a movie theater, or spend time in the gym.

In Kuwait, Thursday and Friday are considered weekend days, as opposed to Saturday and Sunday in Western countries. On Wednesday evening teens go out to restaurants, movies, malls, "carting," where they

Kuwaiti students at a private school. Courtesy of Taghreed Alqudsi-Ghabra.

experience driving miniature cars, or just hang out with friends. Since the liberation of the country from the Iraqi occupation in 1991, many American restaurant chains, like Friday's, Fuddrucker's, Chili's, Applebee's, and others have opened in Kuwait and have become popular hangout places for teenagers on Wednesday and Thursday nights. In addition, malls with food courts that house fast-food restaurants such as McDonald's, Hardee's, Burger King, and Kentucky Fried Chicken are usually crowded with teens during the weekends.

FAMILY LIFE

Because Kuwait is a welfare state, there is domestic help in many houses, often of non-Kuwaiti origin. This availability of foreign help at home has created some social problems for Kuwaiti teens: difficulties in language acquisition, confusion over values, and being spoiled. The situation can vary from family to family, but in general teens are rarely required to help with or take responsibility for family chores. Of course, more educated parents and those with a strong involvement in their children's affairs have been able to avoid the negative effects of this dependency on foreign help.

Kuwaiti women are either employees who go to work in the morning or housewives who tend to their homes. During the day, many housewives simply gather together or go out for morning coffee with friends. Women are mainly responsible for their children's homework and school affairs. Men are engaged with outside affairs. The Kuwaiti society, generally speaking, is a segregated one.

Although modern, Kuwait is still a paternalistic society. Men have a strong presence in public life. In the evening, there are meetings, informal gatherings (*deewaniyyas*) in which men discuss community affairs and engage in public debate and social exchange. This is the place where public opinion is formed in Kuwait. Male teens start attending the *deewaniyya* at an early age. *Deewaniyyas* are also the reception areas of every family, where people receive others to congratulate them for weddings or to pay condolences for deaths.

The legal driving age in Kuwait is 18. Almost all Kuwaitis get their driver's licenses, some even their cars, by age 18. This contributes to a widespread "show off" phenomenon in this diminishingly affluent society. In addition to cars, cellular phones, designer clothing, and traveling are popular among teens in Kuwait. Drunk driving by teenagers is a major source of accidents in the country, contributing to a disproportionately high rate of car accidents in relation to the overall population.

Drinking alcohol is illegal in Kuwait, yet there is a big black market for alcohol. Teens can acquire it through various means, ranging from buying it directly from sellers, finding it at their own home, and obtaining it from another family member or friend. In some cases, some teens bribe a driver or helper to obtain it for them. In general, it is not difficult to obtain alcohol.

Families maintain close relationships with their relatives. They often go to lunch with them on Thursdays, or to chalets (which are like beach houses) half an hour south of Kuwait City. They may also go to the desert during the spring. For the majority of the population, weekends are the time for family get-togethers.

Kuwait's liberation in 1990 opened the country to Western influences as never before. Kuwait was one of the first countries of the Middle East to permit Internet connections. Now Internet cafés, mostly visited by female and male teens, are spread all over the country. In these cafés, or at the computer in private homes, chatting has become a popular activity. There are chatting sites in English as well as Arabic on the Internet. Most teens in public schools use the English alphabet to write Arabic words while chatting on electronic boards. In other words, they use their own modified transliteration system. For example, the word *Ga3da* for the Arabic *ga'da* means "sitting in." Many of these Internet terms have become part of teens' language repertoire in Kuwait.

TRADITIONAL AND NONTRADITIONAL FOOD

Historically, Kuwaiti cuisine has depended on fish and seafood. Rice dishes with fish, shrimp, lamb, and poultry are eaten on a daily basis. *Machboos* is one of the most popular rice with saffron dishes. It is usually cooked with fish, lamb, or chicken.

While pizza, hamburger, and fried chicken are becoming popular, rice is still an important dish desired by young and old alike—particularly at lunch, the main meal of the day. With the expansion of all kinds of American and Western restaurant chains, the conflict between traditional healthy food and fast food is becoming an issue between parents and children of all ages whose food preferences differ.

With the availability of domestic help, female teens are not taught how to prepare traditional dishes at home. In public schools there are some home economics classes that include cooking and sewing; in private schools there are not.

SCHOOLING

In Kuwait, education until the age of 14 is compulsory. Different schools providing opportunities for all children to attend the school of their choice. During 1999–2000, there were 613 public schools in Kuwait, 336 private schools (187 of which are foreign schools), and 149 private Arabic schools.[4] Kuwaiti children predominantly attend public schools. Whereas the Ministry of Education finances Kuwaiti public schools, private schools are dependent on high tuitions. The Ministry of Education is responsible for the administration of all public schools.

Foreign schools teach the curriculum of their respective countries, yet they are also required to teach Arabic and religion to Muslim Arab students. The American school, for example, teaches an American curriculum, and the language of instruction is English. These schools started as a necessity for teaching the children of foreign professionals working in the country. In the aftermath of the liberation of Kuwait in 1991, these schools gained popularity.

The total enrollment of public schools is 308,560 students, who are predominantly Kuwaitis. However, the private school system has a population of 124,996 students, 50,221 (nearly 16% of the total student population in Kuwait) of which attend private foreign schools. The

Kuwaiti students at a private school. Courtesy of Taghreed Alqudsi-Ghabra.

remaining 74,775 are in private Arabic schools. The language of instruction is different in each school depending on its national affiliation. For
instance, Indian schools may teach in the Indian language. Still, English
is taught in all public schools. Bilingual and foreign education is becoming a popular choice for people who can afford it because it improves students' chances of succeeding in a competitive world.

Public schools are segregated. Boys' schools are taught by male teachers,
and girls' schools by female teachers. Among private schools, however,
one can find both segregated and co-ed schools. Almost all private school
students are (1) foreign expatriate children, (2) affluent Kuwaiti families'
children who belong to the upper middle and upper classes, or (3) the
children of professional, educated Kuwaitis. In private co-ed schools, the
school day is like that in an American school. In public schools and some
private ones, there are mandatory school uniforms. The school curriculum
in public schools is very dependent on textbooks and memorization.

A national high school examination administered for students in their
last year of secondary school is called the Tawjeehi exam. This is a very
competitive exam. Since the result of this test determines a student's
future, it is a very stressful exam. Scores earned in this national exam
determine students' opportunities for obtaining scholarships for study

abroad, admission to the most competitive majors and departments of Kuwait University, and taking advantage of better opportunities in society. Private foreign schools follow their own educational system, be they British or American or others.

The ultimate goal for every Kuwaiti teen is to hold a government job after college, with retirement benefits at the end. Consequently, very few teens seek summer jobs, a fact that puts pressure on both teens and parents who have to continue spending for "show off" purposes. Families are expected to provide for their children as long as they are unmarried. With resources diminishing due to high spending on defense and a lack of economic reform, these factors place an additional burden on every family in Kuwait.

SOCIAL LIFE

Kuwait is a closely knit society. As in other Middle Eastern countries, social life constitutes an important portion of daily life. In addition, Kuwait is a small society. Almost everyone knows someone from every family. So teens have several avenues to meet each other: familial relationships, friends' circles, and random coincidences.

The concept of dating is different in Kuwait. In Muslim societies, premarital sex is not allowed. As a result, when and if dating occurs, it simply means close friendship with intimate feelings for each other. In a closely knit and paternalistic society, reputation and chastity are very important for girls. Marriages in Kuwait are considered family marriages rather than person-to-person marriages. Early prearranged marriages are a norm in Kuwait. With people from a Bedouin background, who are very conservative, marriage becomes more of a tribal affair and consequently a more complex decision. As a result, caution is usually exerted before decisions are made about marriage. Despite all these precautions, the divorce rate is considered to be high by Kuwaiti standards.

In the public school system, where education is segregated, social activities are completely segregated as well. In the private schools, where education is mixed, social activities and parties occur; parents or teachers supervise these events. Even in hangout places for teens, public school students usually do not mingle with the opposite sex. There are exceptions, of course. The private school students who go through the whole day side by side in a mixed atmosphere do mingle with the opposite sex more comfortably. However, mingling in public is not an acceptable social act. Public displays of affection are not accepted and are considered shameful.

Kuwaiti teenagers celebrating Valentine's Day at a private school. Courtesy of Taghreed Alqudsi-Ghabra.

Teens, both boys and girls, are generally stylish and modern, yet conservative. For example, you would rarely see a teenage girl wearing shorts to the mall, but you would see her wearing tight stylish pants or skirt. Many female students in public and private schools cover their hair, especially in schools that are in areas outside the city limits. The percentage of conservative religious girls who cover their heads in the private schools is smaller generally.

Despite the conservative nature of Kuwaiti society, the number of segregated foreign private schools is increasing. The rationale behind this trend is to keep up with modern education yet to preserve the Kuwaiti identity and culture.

RECREATION

Soccer is the most popular sport practiced by Kuwaitis. There are both school and national teams for soccer. It is mainly a male sport, but some girls do play. Because Kuwait is located on the seashore, swimming, boating, jet skiing, and fishing are popular hobbies too. It is normal to see afflu-

Soccer match between two boys' teams at a Kuwait private school. Courtesy of Taghreed Alqudsi-Ghabra.

ent families leave on Wednesday afternoon to spend the weekend at their chalets (beach houses). Other people go to clubs where they pay an annual membership fee to spend their weekends. Teens participate in these clubs with their families. Activities vary from swimming, body building, and racing to riding buggies. There are mixed clubs and segregated clubs as well. In addition, there are public beaches that are open to all. Yet it is very rare to see girls, let alone women, with bathing suits at these beaches.

Once in a while teenagers go bowling, ice skating, or play billiards.

There are some traditional cafés where teenagers, both male and female, enjoy smoking hubble-bubble (a water pipe used for smoking tobacco) known as *sheesha*. This is more popular, and considered more appropriate, for boys.

ENTERTAINMENT

Conflicting images characterize the Middle East in general. Kuwaitis not only travel extensively but also encounter people from different cul-

Kuwaiti teen smoking a *shisha* (hubble-bubble) pipe. Courtesy of Taghreed Alqudsi-Ghabra.

tures working in Kuwait. This has given Kuwaitis the characteristic of being both modern and conservative. During the weekends, some teens like to hunt around for open parties, held at private homes or rented halls, to spend their time; however, given the conservative and closed nature of the society, most teens would be hesitant to participate in them.

In addition to malls, other places for teens to hang out include the movies, restaurants, public parks, and entertainment parks. Since Kuwait is a country exposed to other cultures, adults and teens alike enjoy listening to Arabic and Western music. Music is a major part of teen life in Kuwait. Public school teens usually listen to Arabic music, whereas private school teens listen to both Arabic and English. This is a result of the acculturation experienced in the dominant atmosphere of the school attended; it is augmented by the exposure to Western music and culture brought by the world of satellite dishes and the Internet. Rap, hip-hop, R&B, alternative, rock, and slow music are popular forms of Western music. Most teens like to watch the MTV channels, where video clips of their favorite songs can be viewed. There is an Arabic television channel modeled after MTV. Both Arabic and Western songs are enjoyed.[5] This channel can be received on Arab satellite and can be viewed in almost all Middle Eastern countries. Internet connections and satellite dishes are not unusual in most households.

RELIGIOUS PRACTICES AND CULTURAL CEREMONIES

Kuwait is a Muslim country where you see mosques in almost every street. The call for prayer (*Alsalat*), announced five times a day at the time of each prayer, is a very sacred commitment by most Kuwaitis. Second to *Alsalat*, the fasting (*Siyam*) during the holy month of Ramadan is a practice that changes the social atmosphere in which young and old interact. During the holy month of Ramadan, Muslims stop eating from dawn to sunset. Work and school hours are completely changed to accommodate the breaking of the fast time, which is at sunset. Teenagers are not exempted from this practice. Actually, some children start to practice fasting at the age of 7. Ramadan is a month of worship, yet by convention and practice it has come to constitute a month of socializing. Nuclear families rarely have their main meal at sunset alone. People gather in extended family homes to eat together or take turns in hosting the family themselves. Traditional special dishes and sweets are prepared for the occasion. Even though the spirit of Ramadan promotes worship and modesty, in a welfare society where everything is in abundance, this has come to be like having Christmas for a whole month.

During this month, people can stay out longer than usual. The country is in a festive mood, and it is safe to be out late more than usual. At the end of Ramadan, Muslims celebrate Eid al-Fitr, their first feast of the year. The celebrations continue for another three days before all details of life go back to normal. In another 70 days Muslims celebrate their second feast, which also ends the pilgrimage to Mecca season. This is called Eid al-Adha, a four-day annual celebration. Kuwait celebrates its national day on February 25 and its liberation from the Iraqi occupation on February 26 of each year.

CONCLUSION

In Kuwait, as in the whole Middle East, conflicting images are normal. It is not unusual to see conservative images in appearances or dress codes alongside the very stylish, modern teens all over Kuwait's newly expanding modern malls. Teens have come to accept and generally respect religious practices without considering them an infringement on their rights.

They still like to feel independent, free of limitations imposed by family and adults. Because family is a strong unit in Middle Eastern societies, teenagers perceive these practices and rituals as normal.

At the turn of the century and as the world enters the globalization era, Kuwait remains dependent on oil and foreign labor. It continues to be an expanding consumer society where consumer goods and food items are imported from the outside world. As a result, the main challenge that lies before Kuwait is how to use its oil resources in a more sustainable and productive capacity and develop its competitive edge in the regional and global economy. This seems to be the only measure that would guarantee and maintain a high standard of living for future generations of Kuwaiti.

Kuwaiti teens share the concerns of their society. Future security guaranteed by good education, a respectable job, and surviving in a competitive world are worries of teenagers and their families alike.

NOTES

1. CIA, *The World Factbook 2000—Kuwait* (2001) [on-line]. Available: http://www.odci.gov/cia/publications/factbook/goes/ku.html.

2. Kuwait Information Office (2001) [on-line]. Available: http://www.kuwait-info.org/home/fact_sheets/fact_sheets.html.

3. *Kuwait at the Threshold of a New Millennium: Education for the 21st century* Kuwait City (Kuwait: United Nations Development Program, 2000).

4. *Summary of Statistical Information about Education in the State of Kuwait for the year 1999/2000* Kuwait City (Kuwait: Ministry of Education, 2000).

5. A popular Kuwaiti site for downloading Arabic music is http://www.kubbar.com.

RESOURCE GUIDE

Books and Articles

Al-Dekhayel, Abdulkarim. *Kuwait: Oil, State, and Political Legitimation*. Ithaca, NY: Ithaca Press, 2000.

Al-Ghanem, Salwa. *The Reign of Mubarak Al-Sabah, Shaikh of Kuwait, 1896–1915*. London: I.B. Tauris, 1998.

Crystal, Jill. *Oil and Politics in the Gulf: rulers merchants in Kuwait and Qatar*. Cambridge: Cambridge University Press, 1990.

Lambert, Lee R., and Erin Lambert. *The Other Kuwait: An American Father and Daughter's Personal Impressions*. Worthington, Ohio: L.R. Lambert & Associates Publications, 1992.

McDonnell, Janet A. *After Desert Storm: The United States Army and the Reconstruction of Kuwait*. Washington, DC: U.S. Government Printing Office, 1999.

Rajab, Jehan S. *Invasion Kuwait An Englishwoman's Tale*. London: Palgrave, 1996.

Robinson, Gordon. *Bahrain, Kuwait & Qatar: Demystifying the Desert*. Oakland CA: Lonely Planet, 2000.

Salzman, Marian, and Ann O'Reilly, eds. *War and Peace in the Persian Gulf: What Teenagers Want to Know*. Princeton, N.J.: Peterson's Guides, 1991.

Vine, Peter, and Paula Casey. *Kuwait: A Nation's Story*. London: Immel, 1992.

Weller, M., ed. *Iraq and Kuwait: The Hostilities and Their Aftermath*. Cambridge: Grotius Publications, 1993.

Fiction

Alshalabi, Firyal. *Summer 1990: A Young Adult Novel*. Boulder: Aunt Strawberry Books, 1999.

Hays, Tony. *The Trouble with Patriots: A Novel*. Bridgehampton, N.Y.: Bridge Works, 2002.

Web sites

www.amideast.org

Amideast promotes understanding and cooperation between Americans and the people of the Middle East and North Africa through education, information, and development assistance programs.

www.alif.com/film

Information about the movie *Nahr El-Hayat*, a drama based partly on the lives of real people and real situations.

www.alif.com/mirror

Arab American mirror. Information about contemporary Arab American issues.

www.arab-aai.org

Arab American Institute. Information about the goals of the institute as well as Arab Americans, publications, events, and Arab students.

www.arabicnews.com

Information about Arab daily news, other countries in the Middle East, business, economics, politics, local news.

www.cafearabica.com

Arab-American Online Community Center. Information about organizations, people, cultures, politics, laws, and different perspectives on Arab-American Concerns.

www.lebnet.com

Lebanese Community Site. Information about Lebanon, business, media, news, music.

www.maktoob.com

Links to many different countries that give information about chats, fun and
   games, shopping, dictionary, jobs.

Pen Pal/Chat

www.candelightstories.com/ClassPenPalListings2.asp?Country-Kuwait
http://www.pen-friends.net/eslgroup/list1f.html

Chapter 6

LEBANON

Ali Akbar Mahdi

INTRODUCTION

A country smaller than the state of Connecticut, Lebanon consists of 4,015 square miles and is located on the eastern bank of the Mediterranean Sea. Bordering to the north and east is Syria, and Israel in the south. Lebanon has a population of nearly 4,200,000, plus 350,000 registered Palestinian refugees living in camps around the country. While ethnically homogeneous (95% Arabs, 4% Armenians, and 1% affiliated with other ethnic groups), Lebanon is religiously a divided Middle Eastern country (70% Muslim and 30% Christian). Muslims consist of five legally recognized traditions: Shi'a, Sunni, Druze, Isma'ilite, and Alawite. Eleven Christian traditions (four Orthodox, six Catholic, and one Protestant) and Judaism are officially recognized by the government. Very few Jews live in Lebanon. Numerous mosques and churches conduct services in Arabic, English, Latin, French, Armenian, and the Chaldean and Syriac languages. The official language is Arabic, although French and English are widely understood, especially in the capital, Beirut.

Lebanon is a remnant of the city-states known as Phoenicia. Historically, the area was governed by feudal states engaged in conflicts. For ethnic and religious minorities, the massive rugged mountain range dominating the country known as Mount Lebanon, served as a form of protection against invaders. The development of Lebanon began when Maronite Christians took refuge in Mount Lebanon from religious persecution. Later, Arabs brought Islam to the region but remained separated from the Maronites. After that, more and more religious sects, of both Christian and Muslim origin, took refuge in the area.

As a modern state, Lebanon was created from the lands controlled by the Ottomans. Under the control of the Ottomans, the diverse confessional (religious grouping) and ethnic communities maintained their own identities by paying tribute and taxes to the Ottomans. Following the collapse of the Ottoman Empire after World War I, the League of Nations designated the area as a French mandate. In 1926 a constitution was drafted recognizing the legal rights of the diverse communities in exercising their religions. In 1943, under pressure from the people of the country, Americans, and British, the French abdicated control over Lebanon, resulting in its independence.

Since its recognition as a sovereign state in 1943, Lebanon has been a confessional state whereby the state power is allocated to different religious groups. Although a constitution was drafted, it was the gentlemen's agreement known as the National Pact (al-mithaq al-watani), between leaders of the Maronite and Sunni Muslim communities, that laid ground for a "confessional democracy" and for unity between Muslim and Christian sects. According to this pact, Christians and Muslims share power proportionate to the size of their population in the 1932 census. According to this census, the Christians represented a larger percentage of the population than the Muslims: six for every five Muslims—a ratio mirrored in all other government offices. Muslims promised not to enter into a merger with another Arab Muslim country, and Christians agreed that they would not enter into an alliance with foreign nations. With slight modifications, especially in the number of seats available to each group in the parliament, this structure has remained constant. Traditionally, the president is a Maronite Christian, the prime minister a Sunni Muslim, the speaker of the parliament a Shi'a Muslim, and the commander of the army a Druze.

Although such an arrangement has unified people of different faiths and politics in a national government, on occasion it has been a source of tension among the religious communities. The establishment of Israel in 1948, the 1967 Six-Day War between Arabs and Israel, and the expulsion of the Palestinian Liberation Organization (PLO—a guerrilla organization formed to liberate Palestine from Israeli occupation) from Jordan in 1970 brought floods of Palestinian refugees to Lebanon. The increasing number of Muslims, both native Lebanese and Palestinian, contributed to the tensions among sectarian communities.

An added variable to internal tensions in Lebanon has been the influence of external powers, especially Israel and Syria. Expelled from Jordan in 1972, the PLO moved its headquarters to Beirut and expanded its activities into Lebanon. Soon it established a vast network of social services for Palestinian refugees and trained its militias in camps in Lebanon.

The PLO periodically launched attacks on the northern Israeli border, promoting severe counterattacks by Israel on Lebanese territory and civilians.

The Israeli-Palestinian conflict eventually spilled over to Lebanese forces. An attack on Christian forces on April 13, 1975, followed by a Palestinian counterattack, resulted in a series of battles between these forces for months to come. Unable to stop the fighting, the Lebanese government asked Syria for help. Continued fighting, increasing Palestinian attacks on Israeli forces and their Lebanese Christian allies, the Maronite Phalange Party, and the Syrian presence in Lebanon gave Israel an excuse to invade southern Lebanon in 1978. After three months of occupation, Israel established a self-proclaimed security zone, guarded by the friendly South Lebanon Army (mostly Christians), and pulled out its forces from Lebanon. To reduce the conflict and keep parties apart, the United Nations deployed forces in southern Lebanon.

Fighting among various forces continued and gave Israel another excuse to launch another invasion in 1982, chasing PLO forces north toward Beirut. International mediations resulted in the departure of Syrian troops and PLO forces preceding the arrival of a multinational force of American, French, British, and Italian troops. Soon thereafter Lebanon was engulfed in factional wars, bombings, kidnappings, and assassinations. A Lebanese president-elect was assassinated, many U.S. and French troops were killed, and a number of Westerners were taken hostage. To cut losses, multinational forces left the country. Violence among Lebanese forces, Palestinians, and Israelis continued. At this time a new force composed of Shi'a Muslims supported and trained in Iran became a major player in the conflict. In 1989, infighting spread to the Christian forces and led to deadly conflict in Beirut.

A 1989 meeting of members of the Lebanese parliament in Ta'if, Saudi Arabia, resulted in a National Reconstruction Charter and later the election of a new president, paving the way for a cease-fire. With Syrian help, the Lebanese government has made changes in the constitution, allowing for more seats in the parliament (currently 128 members), a more satisfactory representation of Muslims and Christians, and the recognition of Hezbollah (a Shi'a political group organized during the civil war) as a major political force in Lebanon. Despite the continued scattered violence, all militias were disarmed by 1993, except the Hezbollah. Continued Hezbollah attacks on Israeli forces in Lebanon throughout the 1990s resulted in Israeli withdrawal in 2000.

Although the 16-year civil war and 18-year intermittent Israeli occupation have devastated both the people and resources, Lebanon remains a strong and spirited country. It has recovered from the devastation of war much faster than societies afflicted with similar problems. Today, Beirut is a growing business center trying to regain its former status as a commercial center on the eastern shore of the Mediterranean. Construction is a 24-hour operation in the city, replacing old and damaged structures with modern and highly sophisticated buildings.

Still, Lebanon has not survived all effects of the war. Today, many teens find their families shattered by war; they have lost the peace and security they enjoyed in the past. The devastation of war has left a large segment of the population without employment and opportunity for career advancement. A quarter of the population has left the country, and another quarter lives in poverty. Young people find it economically hard to start a family, thus contributing to a decline in marriage rate. Forces of globalization, such as the Internet, fast food, and Western lifestyles, have left many parents unable to meet the demands these forces cause their children to make. Parental anxieties have left some teens wondering whether they will be able to chart their own future. Economic insecurity, political instability, and the inability to fight corruption are common concerns for both parents and teens.

SPECIAL CONSIDERATION: EFFECT OF CIVIL WAR AND REGIONAL DISPARITY

To understand Lebanon and the status of its teenagers, three important points must be addressed.

(1) One has to make a distinction between three periods: before, during, and after the civil war (1975–1990). It is almost as if Lebanon was three different countries during these three periods. Prior to the civil war, Lebanon had a booming economy with the most active commercial port in Beirut, a viable civil society with a free press, a government akin to Western countries', a relatively prosperous middle class, and a high standard of living in comparison to other Middle Eastern countries. To foreigners, especially rich Arab tourists, the country was known for its beautiful mountains, hills, long beaches on the Mediterranean Sea, and nightclubs. Yet, relying on its skilled labor force, dynamic entrepreneurial economy, and cheap foreign labor, Lebanese liberalism failed to pay adequate attention to the public sector, leading to a growing inequality among regions and populations. This imbalance had serious consequences for the quality of education available to teens of different religions and in different regions of the country. A decade later, uneducated and under-educated youth joined angry militias during the civil war.

During the war, the country was in chaos. No institution was unaffected by the violence. The economy came to a halt, and most of the previous achievements were lost. Between 1970 and 1990, 949 villages and towns were affected by the war, of which 174 were totally or partially destroyed.[1] Over 100,000 Lebanese died in the civil war. The country experienced its worst "brain drain" in decades. Those who had the means, mostly young males age 20 to 25, simply left the country, causing a distorted gender ratio. Most schools closed, and many teens joined the fighting. Most teens lived in a climate of fear, violence, and destruction. Many experienced the loss of parents, relatives, friends, home, and/or personal belongings. Many were displaced and had to move out of their old communities and towns. Mortars or bombs destroyed many schools. Students heard gunfire outside while sitting in class. A study of students who experienced a significantly larger number of war events found that they scored significantly higher in measures of anxiety, depression, and post-traumatic stress disorder.[2]

To many poor young teens whose parents could not provide any meaningful involvements for their children during the daytime, the streets were the way of life. Joining militias to fight the enemy had a strong emotional appeal. These teens yearned to be combat heroes and saunter through the streets of Beirut with Ak-47s and Kalashnikovs over their shoulders. It gave them a sense of power and adventure. A large portion of the Hezbollah militia is composed of Shi'a teenagers. Parents who could afford it sent their children outside the country for both continuing their education and remaining safe. Many also fled to villages away from Beirut and Tripoli. Some children attended schools in nearby cities, taking long-distance buses and shuttles. Thousands of teens lost their lives as bystanders caught in crossfire, participants in the war, or victims of blind bombings and shootings.[3]

One of the major effects of the war has been a form of depoliticization, often combined with cynicism and pessimism among some segments of the population, especially youth. Many students do not care about political issues. In a country where there is no popular magazine dedicated to youth and youth issues, it is not surprising that a large number of these teens are either indifferent toward politics or, due to bitter experiences of war and its effects, cynical about politics and politicians altogether. By and large, political activism among students has been declining in the past decade. Exceptions to this trend are several youth groups trying to engage youngsters in politics: Kuwwat and Kataeb among the Christians, Hezb Al-Ishtiraki among the Druze, Ahbash among Sunni Muslims, and Hezbollah among the Shi'a Muslims. The Hezbollah, the strongest of these groups, has developed a vast ideological machinery to educate their

Poster in Lebanon encouraging youths to get involved in the *Intifada* (resistance to Israeli invasion at the time). Courtesy of Ali Akbar Mahdi.

youth in their own Islamic educational forums and institutions. Given the rise of Hezbollah to power in Lebanon in the last two decades, it is not surprising to find many Shi'a youngsters motivated to join Hezbollah to improve their minority status in society, especially where the Shi'a community makes up a large part of the poor in Lebanon. Recently, some Lebanese youth have been waging a new campaign on war crimes on a new TV youth channel called Zain.

(2) By all standards, Lebanon is the most Europeanized environment in the Arab world. The geographical location of the country, its rich historical trading status, its diverse and long history, and the continued existence of the largest religious minority in the region have contributed to a degree of social liberalism rarely found in other Arab countries. The members of the Christian minority in this country always acted as a cultural mediator between Europe and the Middle East, Islamic and non-Islamic. They were also cultural agents bringing in ideas and views alien to traditional Muslim perception.

(3) Sociologically speaking, Beirut, as the capital and largest city, stands out from other cities in Lebanon. Although divided into a predominantly Muslim community in the west and a Christian community in the east, the degree of cosmopolitanism and heterogeneity in greater Beirut far exceeds that of other cities. Coastal Beirut and the eastern part of the city leave foreign observers with an impression that is hard to find in other parts of Lebanon. A strong multicultural atmosphere thrives in East Beirut, where fewer veiled women are found and Western cultural and business symbols are highly visible. Entrepreneurial individualism and Western lifestyle are the norm. Lebanon seems to be a highly capitalistic society with a business mentality rooted in centuries of trade.

This economic individualism has penetrated into other life domains, so much so that Beirut seems to be an exception to the rest of Lebanon. In terms of social attitudes, lifestyle, cultural orientation, and economic outlook, educated liberal Lebanese have more in common with Westerners than with religious conservative Lebanese. All cities and towns have acquired some of the basic elements of modern lifestyles, technology, and amenities; in fact, it is hard to drive around Lebanon and not see all the satellite dishes, even on the rooftops of poor families' homes.

Still, the Shi'a in south Beirut, the Lebanese peasants, and lower socioeconomic classes in smaller towns show greater conservatism, parochialism, and nativistic attitudes than can be found among the same socioeconomic groups in West Beirut. To the dislike of conservative, religious Lebanese, both Muslim and Christian, Beirut has acquired a cosmopolitan character beyond what is deemed tolerable and appropriate to them. Not only is teen life in Lebanon subject to class, urban-rural, and gender divisions, but it also is subject to a major distinction between teens in Beirut and the rest of Lebanon.

TYPICAL DAY

A typical day for a Lebanese teen varies depending on his or her location of residence, parent's occupation, social class, and religious background. For Muslims, the day starts with a call to prayer (*azaan*) over the mosques' loudspeakers—a recurring phenomenon all over the Muslim world. If their families are Muslim and follow their religious rituals rigorously, older teens might have to get up before sunrise to perform their morning prayer. Some parents find it hard to wake up their young ones that early in the morning.

In villages and rural areas, for teens not attending school the day is dominated by work. They get up very early, have breakfast, and go to work. Most of these teens are involved in their family business, especially if their parents are farmers. Some teens may work on construction jobs and vending operations. Some are involved in animal husbandry. Others may travel to the city to obtain food and farm supplies. An excursion in the middle of the day is a regular occurrence for these teens. Many teens take a rest by going for a swim in the rivers and visiting local cafés for a snack.

It is safe to say that for boys and girls going to school, the day begins around 6 A.M. Unlike in America, where most everyone takes a shower before breakfast, in Lebanon this depends on the families' social class and the facilities available in their homes. Poorer families living in shanty-towns and rural areas do not have running water at home and utilize public baths once or twice a week. Even some of the older urban homes lack such resources, and people visit public baths (*Hammaams*) regularly. Newer urban apartments in middle-class areas and single-family homes owned by wealthier parents have adequate water and shower facilities, and teens take showers on a regular basis. Living with the effects of the war, many homes in South Beirut do not have city water and have to manage access through local initiatives. Many still buy drinking water from stores.

Mothers often prepare breakfast for teens. In smaller towns and villages, teens might be asked to help in the preparation of breakfast: boys are sent out to buy fresh bread, milk, cheese, or whatever else might be needed for that morning. Girls are asked to help with preparation of tea, utensils, and so on. Breakfast used to include a combination of bread, feta cheese, *labneh* (fresh cheese made from yogurt), eggs, butter, jam, and tea. Nowadays, the menu in wealthier families also includes cereals, cakes, pop-tarts, bagels, and doughnuts.

Since most schools in urban areas are within walking distance, teens generally walk to school, especially those attending public schools. In villages, teens might have to walk longer distances to attend school because three or four nearby villages might share one school. In these cases, parents who use a car, truck, or tractor for their occupation might use it to transport their own as well as other kids to school. School buses are available in urban areas but are often run privately and used by teens in private schools. Most well-to-do parents who have a car drop their own kids at school, especially in private schools.

Once at school, teens are subject to the rhythm of activities in that environment. Like everywhere else in the world, recess and lunch times, are great opportunities for social interaction. In Lebanon, some female students may not have the chance to interact as easily outside of school as they wish. This is the only time to make friendships with teens from outside of their neighborhoods and family circles. Physical education hours also offer similar opportunities because they are not taken too seriously in schools and not all teens become seriously involved in sports. Depending on what kind of schools teens attend, they may have opportunities for participation in drama, journalism, and reading clubs.

When school is over, parents expect their teens back home on time. Walking to and from school, no matter what the distance, is an important opportunity for social interaction among teens, especially if the distance is long. Many times teens manage to plan some social activity before they get to school or home. On the way home many boys try to play a sport in the school courtyard or open fields, visit arcades for playing video games, and connect with friends to chat. Girls are under more pressure to be home on time since any delay will make parents worried. Concern with female public behavior, even by a middle- or high-school girl, is serious; any mischief by or harm to the teen could cause damage to her future or public humiliation for her parents. For parents who are devoted to maintaining the tradition of family lunch, being home on time is crucial for both boys and girls. Some richer and more liberal parents allow their older teens to go out for lunch with their friends before coming home.

Once at home, teens join the family for lunch. Most parents try (although some are unable due to their work requirements) to be home for this time, as lunchtime is regarded as an important family function. After lunch, teens are usually expected to do their homework. Watching TV is also on many teens' agenda. How they go about planning their homework and watching TV will vary. Stricter parents, who are home to monitor their children's activities, demand the completion of school assignments before allowing any other activity. More liberal parents trust their children with budgeting their time. Many boys get their daily playtime allowance between lunch and dinner and thus do their homework later in the evening. Most boys find opportunities to go out and visit friends, play games, and practice their favorite sports. Not all parents allow outside activity during the week. Still, many teens manage to go out and play some soccer or hang out with friends. To engage in outside activities, female teens have to observe more restrictions. Completing family chores is not unusual for teens in lower- and middle-class families. Boys are expected to do chores outside and girls inside the house. In devoted Muslim families, teens are expected to perform their five daily prayers.

Studying three to four hours a night is quite common, especially among highly motivated teens or those with close parental supervision. Schools generally give many assignments, and teens have little time for playing outside. Educated parents often spend a good deal of time helping their children with their studies. First-generation students often are deprived of any assistance from their parents or even private tutorials. Many wealthy parents hire private tutors to assist their children with studying.

Weekends offer teens a different routine. Schools are closed on Saturdays and Sundays. Because the weekend is a family time, most families try to visit each other. Teens are expected to go along with their parents to these family dinners or lunches. The big meals on Saturday or Sunday bring extended families together and provide an opportunity for all family members to be updated on family news, successes, concerns, and difficulties. Visiting mosques or churches is quite normal, and teens are expected to attend with parents. Going to theaters, visiting friends, playing sports, eating out, and hanging out are routine for teenagers on the weekend, and parents are more prone to approve of them than during the week.

FAMILY LIFE

As in other Middle Eastern countries, family is the cornerstone of Lebanese society. Lebanese society is composed of families and kin groups. While the concept of an individual, independent of a family, kinship, or tribe, is legally recognized and respected, it has not found a social place in all segments of Lebanese society. For those Lebanese still involved in agriculture, crafts, livestock, and business, family is still the unit of production and the center of socioeconomic activities. Family gives the individual his or her social identity and status in the neighborhood, community, and larger society. Lebanese do not see family solely as a nuclear unit sheltering parents and their children. Family takes on a broad meaning encompassing a host of values such as marriage, children, respect for parents and the elderly, obedience to authority, patience, loyalty, perseverance, spontaneity, cooperation, simplicity, hospitality, and neighborliness.

The Lebanese family is patriarchal, and relationships among family members are hierarchical and tightly knit. Older teens have control over younger ones. Males have control over females. The father is at the helm of the family and has the responsibility to provide for it. The mother is responsible for caring for all affairs inside the house, especially children's needs. Although the father has the final say in all matters related to the family, the mother's influence on the children's lives is extensive. Because she spends more time with the children than her husband does and makes most of the decisions related to their daily life, the mother is closer to her children than the father is. Mothers are known for their self-denial and continued sacrifice for their children and husband. Teens are supposed to be obedient to their parents and look up to them for direction. While such a strong support provides a solid basis for teens to grow, it restricts them in exploring new grounds and makes them dependent on their parents' will.

Although these traditions are still practiced in some families, especially in the more religious and conservative ones, it is becoming harder for men to practice traditional gender roles. Due to increased industrialization, urbanization, and education, women have become more assertive and involved in the public arena. The war economy and the increasing expectation for a better material life have forced many women to seek jobs outside the home in order to supplement family income. As more women work outside the home and participate in social activities alongside men, men relinquish more of their past privileges and share responsibilities with other members of the family. Migration and mobility are weakening extended families, contributing to the rise of nuclear families. Still, in conservative families in rural or poor urban areas, the majority of women are assigned a subordinate role, and female teens have less freedom of movement and interaction outside the home. Prevailing standards of morality define women's roles in terms of femininity, motherhood, and wifehood.

Rural areas and urban slums are tightly knit places where independence and privacy are hard to find and community control over the status of residents is widely practiced. This leaves teens with a great deal of community supervision and control. On the positive side, child abuse of the kind usually found in Western countries is rare. On the negative side, adult supervision and control, especially for female teens, become extensive and at times suffocating. Afraid of gossip and a bad reputation, parents go to great lengths to ensure their family honor and behavioral decency. For female teens living in rural and small-town communities, interactions outside the family are rare. Most often, women's fate and future are decided within the boundaries of their family because parental consent is a must for spousal selection. Relatives remain the most reliable vehicle of such a selection. By and large, marrying within one's kinship group is still the norm in Lebanese families. While the marriage age for females remains low in comparison to Western standards, male marriages during teen years (14–20) are becoming a thing of the past. Romantic love is playing a greater role in mate selection among educated people, and the age difference between husband and wife is decreasing—thus eliminating the unfortunate past practice of child brides who were married off to elderly men for economic reasons. Arranged marriage is still practiced among traditional families, both Muslim and Christian.

Lebanese culture demands parental control over children's lives. Teens are to obey their parents, respect their wishes, and receive their wisdom. Violating family rules and parental wishes will have consequences ranging from a disapproving look to serious physical punishment. While most parents try to command respect, fewer and fewer are succeeding in getting the result through physical punishment. Increasingly, educated families replace physical punishment by persuasion and reward as a better means of obtaining conformity. Whether effective or not, physical punishment is still used by some parents in religious, socially conservative, or rural families where the influence of modern education, media, and global forces have not been strong. It is much easier for parents to control their female teens than male ones. Societal norms support parents in restricting their daughters to the home environment while expecting boys to have some "learning experience" in the public domain for gaining maturity in social interactions outside the home.

TRADITIONAL AND NONTRADITIONAL FOOD

What is often offered as Middle Eastern food in America is usually Lebanese cuisine. While Lebanese food is very similar to food in other Arab countries, it has a unique feature of combining traditional Arab foods with French, Turkish, and Greek influences. It is this desire to combine the best of the Mediterranean foods and the beautiful Lebanese landscape that has given rise to a thriving tourist industry in Lebanon. Like Americans, Lebanese love to eat, and they eat with others in a collective setting. New restaurants open in Beirut on an average of one a week.

Most Lebanese dishes are a combination of meat and vegetables like greens and beans, rice, and nuts. Examples are spinach pies, stuffed grape leaves, mutton or fish stuffed with rice and nuts, deep-fried patties made of chickpeas and spices (falafel), salad of toasted croutons, cucumbers, tomatoes, and mint (fattoush), grilled shish kebabs, and roasted chicken. Traditional Arab appetizers (mezzeh) and salads like tabouleh (fresh vegetables with grains), hummus (puree of chickpeas, tahini, lemon, and garlic), baba ghanoush (grilled eggplant, tahini, olive oil, and lemon juice), and olive salad are served with most meals. Bread, in variety of forms, is a staple. Lamb is the desired meat, even though beef is served as well. Garlic, spices, and yogurt are commonly used in traditional foods. Dessert is also an important feature of the Lebanese meal. Given the French influence, Lebanese pastries represent a rich selection of items from Mediterranean, French, and Arab sweets. Baklava is the most well-known sweet.

It is also common to smoke *shisha* (hubble-bubble or water-pipe smoking) and drink Turkish coffee after a meal.

While local restaurants in small towns may offer more traditional food, no restaurant can be found without modern drinks like Coca-Cola, 7-Up, and Canada Dry. The traditional yogurt drink *ayran* is a favorite non-alcoholic drink, even among young people. Restaurant menus in major cities, especially Beirut and Tripoli, often include European items such as steaks and hamburgers. Ethnic restaurants offering foreign cuisine, like Italian, Chinese, Japanese, American, French, and Mexican, as well as fast-food restaurants like McDonald's, Burger King, Pizza Hut, and Kentucky Fried Chicken, have a strong presence in Beirut and other major cities. In Beirut, one can even find both the British and Canadian Hard Rock Cafés!

Mothers are in charge of food at home and bear most of the responsibility for preparing it. They often entice their young teens to eat local food by combining old and new, Western and Eastern—for example, making traditional meat cutlets that in fact are not too far off in taste and shape from hamburgers, or cheese and meat breads similar to Western pizzas. While Lebanese teens eat traditional foods at home, they have a strong tendency to eat foreign fast foods elsewhere. Snack bars are full of teenagers and young adults eating burgers, roasted chicken, *kebabs*, gyro-like chicken with vegetables (*shawarma* sandwiches), *falafel*, Arabic pizza (*lahma bi ajeen*), and thin bread baked on a domed dish over a fire (*marcook*) with soft drinks. Most international and foreign schools offer hamburgers, pizza, and other typical Western foods in their cafeterias.

SCHOOLING

In 1998 the Lebanese government passed a law making primary education free and compulsory for children below the age of 12. To encourage parents to cooperate with this law, the minimum age of child labor has been raised from 8 to 13 years. Still, there are parents who choose not to send their children to schools. In 1997, 4.5 percent of children age 5 to 9 were not in school. This number increased with children's age: 6 percent for children age 10 to 14, 35.7 percent for age 15 to 19, and 73.2 percent for age 20 to 24.[4] This shows that parental attitudes toward school as well as economic needs still determine access to basic education.

While the non-Muslim population shows no differential attitude toward male or female education, Muslim parents in rural regions are more likely to show a preference toward their boys, in terms of sending them to school and length of schooling. Even many of those parents who send their daughters to primary and middle school are anxious to find them a husband prior to college age. The sensitivity to female gender and concern for keeping their female teens away from free interaction with male teens cause many of these parents to prematurely end their daughters' education, marrying them off at an early age. To these conservative, lower-class, and often rural families, schools leave their daughters exposed to male students' or staffs' corrupting influences and possible abuse. Furthermore, to these parents the chance of a girl being labeled as immodest increases when she attends a co-ed school. However, all female schools provoke far less concern.

Given the multicultural and confessional nature of Lebanese society, the educational system can best be characterized as laissez faire. The Lebanese constitution allows "freedom of teaching" as long as it does not violate public order and remains respectful of various religions. This has allowed the establishment of numerous schools with denominational orientations, often founded by missionaries and run by administrators independent of the Lebanese government.

There are three types of schools in Lebanon: public, private, and semi-private. Making up 30 percent of the schools, private schools are of two types: local and foreign. Local private schools finance their operation through tuition, funds from private foundations, or a combination of both. Commercially organized local private schools are solely dependent on tuition and offer modern and secular education. While many local private schools are religious, most foreign schools are secular and avoid affiliation with religious sects.

Funded and run by the government, public schools constitute 55 percent of all schools in the country. The remaining 15 percent of schools are considered semi-private because the government subsidizes students' tuition. Public and private schools absorb about 80 percent of the students, leaving the remaining 20 percent to semi-private schools. Interestingly enough, and quite opposite of what is found in the United States, the ratio of teachers to students is higher in private and semi-private schools. Public vocational schools offer a diverse curriculum of two to four years to approximately 13,000 students and attract a higher number of students even though their number is smaller (31 public versus 208 private).

Derived from the French system and in existence from the early days of independence, pre-collegiate education in Lebanon is organized into three levels: five years of primary, four years of intermediate, and seven years of secondary education. While the curriculum in most primary public schools is taught in Arabic, private schools use English, French, Ger-

Lebanese youths studying in the hallway of their school. Courtesy of Ali Akbar Mahdi.

man, Italian, and other languages. Upon completion of the first five years, students automatically qualify to enter one of the two tracks at the next level: four years of the intermediate cycle or seven years of the secondary cycle. At the intermediate and secondary levels, failure to succeed results in repeating that level the following year. In the 1996–1997 school year, the repetition rate for different regions of the country was between 9.1 (Beirut) and 17.8 (the North).[5]

The intermediate level, or middle school, includes grades 6 to 9 for intermediate school and 1 to 4 for vocational school. The former prepares students for the baccalaureate examination and the second one for admission to teacher training institutes or vocational schools. Upon completion of the intermediate levels, students either enter high school (grades 10–12) or vocational institutions (1–3 levels). The latter prepare students for teaching in schools or gaining jobs in business, industry, and crafts. There are few opportunities for vocational training; it is little appreciated due to its association with low-status, low-pay jobs.

Traditionally, the high school academic track offered students three concentrations to choose from: humanities, experimental sciences, and

Band class in a Lebanese school. Courtesy of Ali Akbar Mahdi.

mathematics. Recently a new program was implemented in which four concentrations could be chosen: life sciences, general sciences, humanities, economics and sociology. Despite these changes, the emphasis continues to be on math and sciences. Most learning in public schools is by memorization. Analytical thinking is rarely emphasized or practiced. Overemphasis on mastery of content often suppresses creative and imaginative thinking in students. Students passing a final exam at the end of twelfth grade receive the Baccalaureate I and at the end of thirteenth grade the Baccalaureate II. The government administers this examination; its result determines the student's admission to a university. Private schools, which are free to establish their own curriculum and structure, have had to conform to the basic structure of the Baccalaureate II system and prepare their students for this exam.

Decision making in the Lebanese public schools is highly centralized in both administration and curricular structure. The stated goal of the educational system has always been to unify the country and promote a national identity among a heterogeneous population. Textbooks, schedules, and academic programs in public schools are uniform and controlled by the Ministry of Education. Despite the importance given to this issue and a strong state desire for control over national education, the educational sector receives less financial support from the government than does the educational sector in other countries in the region.[6]

The immediate concerns with postwar economic problems and attention to political issues arising from Israeli attacks, Syrian presence, and confessional politics have kept Lebanese politicians and educational leaders from paying adequate attention to educational reform and changes needed in modern society. Lebanon is entering the twenty-first century with an educational system designed for an earlier time and with inadequate resources. Most public schools do not meet the requirements of a modern educational system. They lack adequate space for classrooms and physical education, resources for laboratories, computers, and audiovisual resources, and in some cases even basic furniture. Textbooks are very expensive, and low-income parents find it difficult to send their children to public schools because of the high cost of books and school supplies. Most schools suffer from overcrowding and a recurrent shortage of teachers and staff, especially in rural and poorer urban areas. Shortages of teaching staff are harmful to high school students who have to prepare for national exams, especially in poorer areas where parents are unable to hire private tutors for their children. The teacher shortage is especially severe in foreign languages, mathematics, and sciences.

Due to budgetary concerns and lack of appreciation for counseling services, most public schools lack counselors, thus leaving students on their own in choosing careers and dealing with problems of adjustment between family and school life. There are no public schools for children with special needs. A number of orphanages take care of kids with special needs, but they are privately run. Many of the latter have expanded in recent years to include service to young war victims. Still, such services are limited to major cities and are not available to all disabled kids or those with special needs in rural and poorer regions. Kids with disabilities and special needs often find it difficult to stay in public schools where there is no adequate infrastructure for so-called "normal" students, let alone those with special needs. Lack of resources and a cultural misunderstanding of social disability have resulted in the marginalization of these kids. Some parents with disabled children associate disability with "shame" or are afraid of possible rumors that disability might run in their families. In order to avoid social ridicule and stigma, these parents keep their children away from schools and limit their chances of mainstreaming to their own private opportunities. Children with special needs from well-to-do families are often sent to private schools where special staff and facilities are dedicated to their needs and concerns.

While much of these problems were caused by the civil war and Israeli attacks on the Lebanese infrastructure, there are inherent biases in the Lebanese educational system contributing to such problems. Though the government does not allow for physical punishment in schools, it is still practiced by some teachers and principals in rural and poor urban areas. The discouraging effects of physical punishment and public humiliation in public schools, family financial hardships, and a high failure rate have resulted in a high dropout rate.

Although the majority of Lebanese youths find education an important means of achieving their life goals and would like to be able to continue their education beyond high school, they are confused by the educational system. On the one hand, for many teens the diversity of languages and educational systems used in Lebanon are a source of confusion. The language of instruction, the curriculum, and educational policies vary from school to school. While the official language is Arabic, French is widely used. Parents often speak Arabic in the home. Teens attending school in Beirut often speak to each other in English or French with a few Arabic words mixed in. Most graduating youths have difficulty making the transition from the educational system to the local economy and national institutions.

On the other hand, the confessional nature of the Lebanese political system has allowed different ethnic and religious groups to maintain their own identities, practice their own cultural ceremonies and rituals, and teach their value system to their children. As stated by Samir Khalaf a Lebanese sociologist, "a Christian is first a Christian, a member of a given family, and from a specific region before he is a Lebanese."[7] These forms of loyalties have undermined the national culture necessary for a modern state. Multiple loyalties of Lebanese youth can take different directions based on the political vicissitudes of political groups and their fortune in national and international arenas. Although education is a source of recognition in Lebanon, and historically it has served as a means of achieving high socioeconomic status, presently the correlation between high education and economic success is weakening. Commercialism and economic investment in postwar Lebanon require some education, but not a high degree. Business-oriented families with little education often encourage students to join the family businesses or pursue technical careers.

SOCIAL LIFE

Family interaction is the basis of most social relationships in Lebanon. Families visit each other daily or weekly, often without prior notice. It is not uncommon to knock on someone's door without prior notice. In certain cases it is welcomed and seen as a positive surprise, bringing joy to the person or family not expecting it. "Getting together for tea" is an old tradition of social interaction during which friendships are established, family problems discussed, financial deals made, marital proposals negotiated, political issues debated, and conflicts resolved.

Lebanese teens, like their parents, are very social and enjoy group activities, whether inside or outside of the family circle. There are numerous settings in which teens meet other teens, of either sex, such as: family parties, neighborhoods, schools, sports and cultural clubs, and mosques or churches. Teens base their association with others more on social class than on religion, place of residence, or other variables. Richer teens are often separated from poor teens by both school and neighborhood. This separation, and the status gap associated with it, encourages a form of arrogance among richer teens that leads to a "stuck-up attitude."

Family gatherings, marriage ceremonies, and funerals provide opportunities for interaction with friends of both sexes. Visiting Western-style cafés, where young men and women interact freely, is seen as a trendy behavior in Lebanon. Going to parties, picnics, and clubs are favored activities among teens of both sexes. For teens attending same-sex schools, the latter arenas are venues through which they interact with the opposite sex. For teens attending parties, it is important to inform their parents of the nature of the party and where it takes place—though not all teens do this and not all are honest about what goes on at those parties. For male teens, parental concerns are limited to the nature of the party and the character of its participants. For female teens, other considerations come into play. If it is an all-male party, female teens are often not allowed to go. If it is co-ed and teens can convince their parents of the necessity to attend, a chaperone most likely follows them. If it is an all-female party, then the nature of the party, its location, and the character of participants become determining factors for gaining permission to attend. It is not uncommon for the girl's parent to call up the host and make sure that everything is under control. Picnics are subject to the same sets of rules. While these rules apply to all Lebanese, a more liberal approach in implementing them can be observed as one moves from Muslim to Christian, poor to rich, uneducated to educated, and rural to urban populations.

Premarital sex is not expected to take place. Virginity is to be preserved until marriage. Loss of this "virtue" may result in family dishonor, social and psychological harm to the girl and her family, and reduced prospects for future marriage. Loss of virginity for a Muslim girl, if it does not result in some serious harm to her, is usually followed by a swift marriage to her lover without much publicity. Some high-class, liberal, Muslim girls may resort to corrective surgery of the clitoris to eliminate any sign of premarital sexual interaction. Still, premarital sexual interaction takes place among some teens, especially among those of the richer, liberal, and non-Muslim population. For most teens, however, sexual interaction with the opposite sex is limited to kissing, hugging, and flirtation. The attraction to sex is more subject to peer pressure than to cultural norms.

There are no sex education classes in or outside school in Lebanon. The discussion about sex remains a social taboo, not only among Muslims but also among most non-Muslim families. Such discussion is only possible among peers. In fact, among teens hanging out with each other a frequent topic of conversation is sex. Favorite topics of discussion among older male teens are girls, sex information, films, music, and sports. Computer and video games, movies, and sports are favorites of younger teens. Talking about sex is a lot easier for boys than for girls because of cultural norms surrounding the issue. That is why one finds boys speaking about sex among themselves in a more straightforward manner than girls, who approach the issue vaguely and indirectly. Sexual jokes are the most common vehicles through which views about sex are expressed.

Islam forbids drinking alcohol. However, given the multireligious and cosmopolitan features of Lebanon, alcohol has always been available and teens do not shy away from its consumption. There is no age limit for acquiring alcohol, and teens have no trouble purchasing it in the open market. Like sexual relationships with the opposite sex, drinking is more prevalent among richer, urban, Westernized, and non-Muslim teens. Rural and poorer teens have neither the money nor the opportunity to consume alcohol away from the eyes of parents or the community. The abundance of nightclubs, bars, and restaurants in Beirut that serve alcohol make it easy for rich urban teens to consume alcohol without getting caught by their parents. Legally, nightclubs should check for identification and do not allow in anyone below age 18. However, this is rarely enforced; when it is, using connections (*wasta*) to bypass the limitation is quite routine.

Drugs are around and some teens use them, but they have not caused as many problems as in the United States or Europe. Knowledge about drugs and their attraction often is brought to Lebanon by Lebanese teens who lived outside the country during the civil war and have now returned. Smoking is popular among some urban and rural high school teens; it is most often done without parents' knowledge or approval. To smoke in front of parents is both disrespectful and rebellious. When done away

from parents' eyes, teen smoking still receives disapproval from other
adults who see it as disrespectful, inappropriate, and intolerable behavior.

Even in the case of smoking, gender makes a difference. There is more
sensitivity to smoking by female teens than to male teens. Smoking parents are obviously more tolerant, if not less disapproving, of smoking
among teens. There are parents who are aware of their sons or daughters'
smoking but pretend otherwise for a variety of reasons, ranging from pow-
erlessness in changing their behavior, to permissive attitudes regarding
lifestyle.

Driving is very common among teens from wealthier families. Parents
who own a car often teach their sons to drive at an early age. Cars are generally cheap in Lebanon, and insurance is not legally required. Driving
cars around and cruising in front of female teens is a major hobby for
richer kids in major cities, especially Beirut. A car is a symbol of social status in Lebanon, and parents as well as teens use them to show off and
impress others. Attention to physical appearance and clothing is also very
important to teens in high schools. Most teens, of both sexes and all
classes, try to follow the latest fashions within their means. Much of teens'
attention focuses on how they appear in public and how they look upon
meeting members of the opposite sex on their way to school or other public places. Appearance serves as a necessary tool for gaining respect from
the opposite sex. At some neighborhood hangouts male teens stand
around and view girls passing by. Though inappropriate and regarded as
immoral, some male teens ogle female teens on the street as they pass
through the neighborhood.

Most interactions between teens, of any sex, are based on conversation.
Most conversations center around music, movies, and sports. The most
popular topics of discussion among female teens are boys, fashion, movies,
and books.[8] Attention to political and social issues increases with age and
educational level, though not with the intensity and enthusiasm shown
about entertainment issues. The exception is discussion about the Palestinian situation and Israeli attacks on Lebanon. Nationalist concern
about Lebanese sovereignty and Palestinian suffering generates passionate
debates among Lebanese of all faiths, especially Shi'as in southern
Lebanon.

Finally, there seems to be a widely held view among some Lebanese parents, as well as policy makers, that Lebanese youth are facing a crisis of
identity. The educational system in Lebanon, the multicultural character
of the population, Lebanese sectarian politics, and the effects of the civil
war have contributed to an identity problem for various segments of the
population. Christians like to think of Lebanon as a Christian country,

thus regarding Sunday as a day for going to church and renewing family vows. Muslims like to see it as a Muslim country, thus viewing Friday as a day of prayer and family union. Based on this view, youths have lost their sense of purpose and are alienated from Lebanese culture and values. The loss of a generation of adults in the war has left many of these youths without role models and a sense of confidence that there is a viable future for them.

This opinion, although widely held among intellectuals and parents, is hard to substantiate among young Lebanese all over the country because (1) few youths acknowledge that they experience this alienation; (2) those teens expressing feelings of nihilism, lack of loyalty to the country, and lack of direction in their life are few and mostly from upper and upper middle classes living in Beirut; and (3) those teens whose parents identify them as experiencing this crisis are often youths with life choices and ideals contradicting those of their parents. While there are teens who are confused in either choosing or prioritizing their loyalty and affiliation with their kin, their confessional community, and even their country, most teens have become pragmatists aspiring to become wealthy, have choices, travel, and possibly live abroad. Material possessions and freedom to choose their own lifestyle take priority over commitment to traditional values and practices expected by their parents. These teens express their ideals as becoming wealthy, wearing fashionable clothes, having unrestrained relations with the opposite sex, owning a car, and organizing their life without constraints from parents as well as society. This is a "crisis" for parents and the country, rather than for the youths. It reflects a failure to offer these youths more attractive local, national, and traditional choices acceptable to both generations.

RECREATION

Though not equally distributed in all segments of the society, Lebanese teens have a range of recreational opportunities available to them: basketball, volleyball, soccer, swimming, ping-pong, hunting, snow and water skiing, yachting, golf, and tennis. Beirut is especially blessed with all kinds of sports facilities. While some public schools are poor in outdoor and indoor sports facilities, some private schools offer state-of-the-art facilities as points of attraction to their prospective students. Among recreational activities, swimming, basketball, and soccer are the most popular with teens, male and female. Recently, rugby has been gaining popularity. Soccer and basketball are the focus of attention for all

Lebanese, young and old. Young people follow national teams and even international teams in these sports. Asked to name some of the most favorite foreign athletes, teens in a survey named: Kobe Bryant, Shaquille O'Neal, Pete Sampras, Andre Agassi, and Michael Jordan. When national teams are involved in international competitions, the whole country focuses on their performance; and at the time of their games, cities empty as people are glued to TV sets. Athletes on national teams are admired by teenagers and celebrated as national heroes.

Despite the fact that Lebanon is the most secular and Westernized country in the Middle East, gender and religion are two important factors determining teens' involvement in sports. Soccer is an overwhelmingly male sport in Lebanon. Although female students can play soccer at universities, there are no female soccer clubs or leagues for teenagers. Only in the most liberal environments do Muslim parents allow their daughters to engage in recreational soccer. Even in such situations, the team should be all female or, if mixed, in a private environment. Although Christian families do not have religious sensitivity to this issue, they live in an environment in which patriarchal values dominate, and many less educated Christians remain socially conservative. Female participation in sports was not on parents' agendas in the past. In recent years, parents have become more interested in seeing their daughters engage in physical education. Schools' programs of physical education have been an important factor in shaping this new attitude.

Given its long coastal beaches and wonderful climate, Lebanon offers six months of sunshine, allowing for the population to enjoy outdoor swimming half of the year. All boys can swim, if they wish and can afford to. Not all girls may do so. Swimming is available in a variety of contexts. Lebanon has beautiful beaches and many swimming clubs in major cities and in wealthy private homes. Male teens living in rural areas away from the seacoast have to be content with public swimming pools in smaller towns, or rivers and small ponds in the mountains. Teens in the cities are luckier because there are public swimming pools; if their parents have a car or are able to arrange public transportation, they may take them to public or private beaches. For Muslim female teens, the situation is quite different. Teens from educated liberal families, most of them of the upper and upper middle classes, have no problem with swimming. Their parents are comfortable with the idea and encourage them to do so. Religiously conservative parents, of both rich and poor families, in cities or villages, cannot fathom their daughters in a swimming suit at public pools or beaches. Some conservative richer parents allow swimming by their daughters and wives in all-female private clubs and in-house swimming pools.

ENTERTAINMENT

As a country with a vested interest in tourism, Lebanon is known for its entertainment.opportunities. Numerous nightclubs and discos, especially in Beirut along the coast road toward Maameltein, serve Lebanese and their foreign guests regularly. Theaters, cinemas, social clubs, and amusement parks are sources of entertainment for both adults and teenagers. All over Lebanon, there are numerous cinemas and theaters showing films and plays. Most cinemas show foreign films in their original language with Arabic or French subtitles and often without censoring adult scenes. Internet access is available in major cities through several different providers, especially in Beirut, where there are numerous Internet cafés. In these cafés teens play computer games and interact with other teens around the world in chat rooms.

By and large, entertainment in Lebanon is a matter of personal initiative and private industry. Civic organizations, confessional groups, and commercial clubs are the major agents providing cultural products to the country. The media is largely controlled by the private sector with an interest in promoting a business culture and interest in their commercial products. Beirut alone has six TV channels showing a range of Arabic, English, and French language news, movies, and sports. Lebanese shows are aired widely in the Arab world, and Lebanese TV channels are seen in all Arab countries in the Persian Gulf, Syria, Iraq, Turkey, Jordan, and Egypt. Both satellite and cable television are available, and many foreign channels like CNN, TNT, Star Movies, BBC World, and Start Sport in English, Euronews, TF1, and TV5 in French, and Arabic Movie are offered. There are also numerous radio stations that broadcast to the 2.85 million radios in Lebanon.

The affinity felt by Lebanese non-Muslims toward Western culture has always been an important catalyst in the spread of such culture throughout Lebanon. The high traffic in and out of Lebanon, by Lebanese and foreigners alike, has also contributed to the cosmopolitanization of Lebanese cultural taste. The lowbrow nature of American pop culture, reproduced and reinforced through movies, music, and television shows, allows it to spread easily among teens. Over half of television programming in Lebanon is foreign-imported. Given the multicultural nature of Lebanese society and the cosmopolitan nature of Beirut, it is not surprising to find a huge attraction to Western music of all types. Music shops in Beirut are filled with CDs by foreign artists. A survey of teens listed the following as the most favorite foreign artists: Bon Jovi, Bryan Adams, Andrea Bocelli, Eminem, Dr. Dre, Jay-Z, the Backstreet Boys, 'N Sync, Madonna, Whitney Houston, and Britney Spears—the latter being very popular with young Lebanese boys. Pop bands with both male and female performers, along with female dancers, are often shown on television. Widely available satellite dishes allow the population to watch the latest Western music videos on MTV. R&B, hip-hop, pop, and rap are listed by teens as their most favorite types of Western music.

An obvious, but important, factor in the attraction to Western music is familiarity with a foreign language—a reality much more natural to Lebanon as a multicultural society. The more familiar and competent in foreign languages a teen is, the more likely she or he will listen to foreign music. A survey of three class levels in the same high school showed that there is a positive correlation between (1) a student's age, foreign language competency, class level, and knowledge, and (2) the attraction to Western music. The higher the class level, the older in age, and the more proficient in English or French, the more knowledgeable about Western music and stars. Weaker, but still positive, correlations exist between ownership of CDs or tapes of Western music and a teen's age, notwithstanding the effect of social class.

While most Muslim countries in the region complain about the invasion of Western culture, particularly rock music, young Lebanese musicians have comfortably adopted Western pop and have made a successful industry out of it. This genre of music uses modern instruments to generate local songs by combining old and new, Arabic and Western. If Egypt is the center of traditional Arabic music, Lebanon is the center of Arabic pop music. Although successful in attracting Arab youth, this kind of music, especially when it is offered along with seductive female dancing, angers the conservative Muslims and older parents who see it as a corrupting influence on their youth.

By all standards, Lebanese parents are more liberal on social issues than parents in the other Arab countries. Lebanese teens also have more opportunities to experiment with various forms of entertainment than teens in other Arab countries. City youths are often attracted to foreign music available in music stores and international movies available through satellite dishes and theaters. Teens in rural areas are more likely to listen to Arabic music than teens in urban areas. Dancing to Arabic music is very popular among Lebanese teens, solo or mixed. However, mixed dancing to foreign music and in a low-light environment is clearly a Western import considered morally inappropriate by conservative religious parents. Aside from traditional folk dances, which are common among rural and urban lower classes, Western-style mixed dancing is quite common among upper- and upper-middle-class teens. Traditional dances like the *dabbke* and sword dances are often performed in rural areas as well as at cultural festivals.

Most Lebanese still view entertainment as a social activity to be enjoyed in the company of others. Going to coffeehouses, pastry shops, and restaurants with friends is very popular among both parents and teens. For richer and older teens in cities, going to bars, discos, and nightclubs is routine. The same teens also enjoy visiting restaurants and smoking narghile (hubble-bubble or water-pipe smoking). Upper- and upper-middle-class teens have more time and choices of entertainment than teens who have to work with their parents after school hours.

Lebanese teens also find many other ways of entertaining themselves. Playing cards is very popular, again more so for female teens, who may not get the chance to go out as much as their brothers. At schools, various clubs offer numerous extracurricular as well as entertainment activities. Art rooms, drama clubs, singing bands, and music clubs are common in many schools. Reading is another form of entertainment, though more attractive to girls than boys, and not as popular as other forms of entertainment. The survey of teens in Beirut shows that romance, mystery, and horror novels are top choices among female teens. Male teens show less attraction to books, and reading is not encouraged. When asked to name their favorite national writers, the survey used for this chapter produced only two names: Khalil Gibran and Emile Nasrala. Lebanon has no specialized magazine for teens. Adult magazines, especially related to entertainment, are the only venues of information for teens. There are not many public libraries in the country.

RELIGIOUS PRACTICES AND CULTURAL CEREMONIES

Being fully aware of their minority status, smaller religious minorities in Lebanon are generally more observant of rituals. Also, at least in the case of Christians, religious rituals do not involve as many daily rituals and practices as the Muslim rituals do. While the presence of mosques and clerics ensure the Muslim character of Muslim communities, the behavioral commitments of Muslim individuals are subject to age, gender, class, and ideology. Older Muslims are generally more committed to fulfilling their religious obligations, and they do this very rigorously. Females are also more committed than males, especially older ones, even though they are less expressive about it. The overall environment in a community is also a determining factor. It is very hard for a Muslim living in Daahieh (a predominantly Shi'a community in Beirut) not to be affected by communal religious practices. The same person may live in the richer part of Beirut and engage in activities contrary to his religion without repercussions.

While social class does not make a difference in religious beliefs and performances, it does correlate with ideological outlook and education. The more liberal, Westernized, and educated Muslim Lebanese are, the less likely they are to follow their religious practices as vigorously as are religiously conservative, educated Lebanese. These attitudes and outlooks are also good predictors of religious performance among teens of such parents.

By and large, these factors are relevant to teens' religious devotion and expression. Teens attending confessional schools are required to participate in their religious ceremonies and observe their obligations in private as well. Teens attending public or secular private schools may avoid any question or concern about their religious obligations but cannot ignore the watchful eyes of their communities. Rural teens have lesser chances of not abiding by the rules and practices of their religion.

Teens are not as observant of religious rituals as their parents would like. In a survey of a Beirut high school, Muslim teens were asked how many had done their five daily prayers in a week without missing one. Only 34 percent of Muslim teens responded. In general, Shi'a teens are more observant of their religious obligations than Sunni teens. At times in Shi'a areas, teens have to endure the Hezbollah militia's voluntary religious vigilantes who take it upon themselves to ensure that public behavior conforms with Islamic strictures—a remnant of the civil war period when the implementation of law and order was in the hands of various local militias. The focus of this vigilantism, aside from its political overtone, has often been the observance of Islamic dress codes by female teens, teens' interaction with the opposite sex, and the use of alcohol and drugs in public areas.

While most teens do not pray regularly, they do observe the fast in Ramadan with more devotion and enthusiasm. For Lebanese Muslims, as in other Arab countries, Ramadan has a communal and festive significance beyond religious obligations.[9] Christmas and Easter are two Christian holidays widely celebrated by Christians and enjoyed by Muslims as well. Among Shi'as, the Ashura commemoration, during which Imam Hossein's (the third of 12 religious leaders regarded and revered by the Shi'a Muslims as the successor to the Prophet Mohmmed) death is grieved, is widely attended by teens. Among national holidays, Independence Day (November 22), Liberation Day (May 25), and Flag Day receive special attention. General observances are also celebrated in varying degrees: Mother's Day, Teacher's Day, and Labor Day.

CONCLUSION

The uncertainty created by the presence of Syrian troops in the country, Israeli attacks on Hezbollah targets, and Iranian influence on Shi'a population, as well as the continued conflict between Palestinians and Israelis, make it very difficult for Lebanon to provide its teens with a secure sense of political stability. The economic challenges left from the civil war have left close to half the Lebanese population below the poverty line with little hope for prosperity. After the civil war in the early 1990s there was a widespread sense of relief that better days were ahead. However, that has turned out to be an illusion. Soon thereafter, the Israeli pressure forced Syrian fortification, and since then Lebanon has struggled to keep its balance and stability despite pressures from abroad. The combined effect of political and economic influences on the educational system and labor market has forced wealthy young Lebanese to look for a future outside their country. The attraction to study abroad, especially in North America, is very high among urban high school students, even though for the majority of Lebanese youth such a goal is not realistic.

Today's Lebanese teens carry the pains of the past and have no choice but to hope for a better future. Lebanon has been moving out of a state of war very quickly, and the politicians are doing their best to neutralize the conflicts and tensions imposed on Lebanon from within and without. In the face of increasing corruption in the political sphere, and the heavy influence of money in politics, many Lebanese, including youths, are becoming disenchanted with their own government and civil institutions. A number of studies carried out during 1990–1995 indicate that Lebanese teens are not generally satisfied with their lives. Unaware of the amount of influence the leaders have on their local municipalities, these teens see them as ineffective leaders and do not have high confidence in their ability to act in the teens' best interests.[10]

Lebanese political and intellectual leaders face the daunting challenges of simultaneously fighting this disillusion and responding to the real needs and concerns of their populations, especially young people. The success of these efforts will be a test of these teens' realism. Most teens show a keen awareness of the devastating effects of the war on their economy and environment, and they are energized by the speed at which the country has been able to overcome the effects of those turbulent years. However, their enthusiasm and energy are not matched with opportunities for fulfillment. There are not enough jobs for young graduates of universities and high schools; those who are employed suffer from low pay as well as a disparity between their education and employment.

Finally, Lebanese teens are concerned about the image of their country abroad. In their response to a survey conducted for this chapter, the majority expressed a desire that Western teens not view all Lebanese youth as terrorists and fanatics. They also expressed regret for what they see as the loss of respect for elders and family in Western countries. To Lebanese teens, a better future lies not only in use of the latest modern technologies and consumption of global goods, but also in maintaining healthy families and positive attitudes toward preservation of one's environment, cultural heritage, and national pride.

ACKNOWLEDGMENT

The author would like to thank Laila Hourani, Youmna Othman, and Maha Khani for their comments on this chapter; Ahmed Salkini for his personal assistance during the author's trip to Syria and Lebanon; Dr. Munir Bashshur and Dr. Maryam Ghandour of the American University of Beirut for sharing with me their views on Lebanese youths; and the TEW Fund at Ohio Wesleyan University for providing partial financial assistance for this research trip.

NOTES

1. United Nations Development Program, Country Profile, www.undp.org.lb.

2. M. B. Abu Saba, "War-Related Trauma and Stress Characteristics of American University of Beirut Students," *Journal of Traumatic Stress* 12, no. 1(1999): 201–207.

3. Although this chapter does not cover the life of teenagers during this period, it does recognize the devastating effects of these conflicts on a generation of current teens living in Lebanon—effects that have exacerbated the tensions and crises among Lebanese youth.

4. Source: CAS Survey, cited at http://www.bl.gov.lb.

5. Source: The Sustainable Human Development Data Base. See http://www.un.org.lb.

6. Based on data for the year 2000, Lebanon spends 2.5 percent of gross national product on education; Iran, 4.0 percent; Israel, 7.6 percent; Jordan, 6.8 percent; Kuwait, 5 percent; Oman, 4.5 percent; Saudi Arabia, 7.5 percent; Syria, 3.1 percent; Turkey, 2.2 percent; and UAE, 1.8 percent. See *World Development Indicators, 2000*. (Washington, D.C.: The World Bank, 2000).

7. Samir Khalaf, *Lebanon's Predicament* (New York: Columbia University Press, 1987), 119.

8. An earlier study found similar results some 20 years ago. See Faikah Kala-muni, "A Survey of the Interests of a Restricted Sample of Lebanese Adoles-cents," M.A. thesis, American University of Beirut, Lebanon, June 1972.

9. Richard T. Antoun, "The Social Significance of Ramadan in an Arab Vil-lage," *Moslem World* 58, no. 2 (1968): 95–104.

10. United Nations Development Program, 1997, www.undp.org.lb.

RESOURCE GUIDE

Books and Articles

Abodaher, David J. *Youth in the Middle East: Voices of Despair*. New York: Franklin Watts, 1990.

Barakat, Halim. *Lebanon in Strife: Student Preludes to the Civil War*. Austin; University of Texas Press, 1977.

Bashshur, Munir. "Education and the Secular/Religious Debate: Illustrations from Lebanon." Working Paper no. 19. Los Angeles; G. E. von Grunbaum Center Publications, 1992.

Berdal, Louise. "Children and War." In *Everyday Life in the Moslem Middle East*, edited by Donna Lee Bowen and Evelyn A. Early, 33–37. Bloomington; Indiana University Press, 1993.

Faour, Muhammad. *The Silent Revolution in Lebanon: Changing Values of the Youth*. Beirut: American University of Beirut, 1998.

Gilsenan, Michael. "Lying, Honor, and Contradiction." In *Everyday Life in the Moslem Middle East*, edited by Donna Lee Bowen and Evelyn A. Early, 33–37. Bloomington Indiana University Press, 1993.

Joseph, Saud. *Intimate Selving in Arab Families: Gender, Self, and Identity*. Syracuse, NY: Syracuse University Press, 1999.

Karame, Kari H. "Girls' Participation in Combat: A Case Study from Lebanon." In *Children in the Moslem Middle East*, edited by Elizabeth W. Fernea, 378–391. Austin: University of Texas Press, 1995.

Salibi, Kamal. *A House of Many Mansions: The History of Lebanon Reconsidered*. London: I. B. Tauris, 1993.

Shaabaan, Bouthaina. *Both Right and Left Handed: Arab Women Talk about Their Lives*. Bloomington: Indiana University Press, 1991.

Sharabi, Hisham. *Neopatriarchy: A Theory of Distorted Change in Arab Society*. New York: Oxford University Press, 1988.

Williams, Judith R. *The Youth of Haouch El Harimi, a Lebanese Village*. Cambridge, MA: Harvard University Press, 1968.

Novels

Alameddine, Rabih. *The Perv: Stories*. New York: Picador, 1999.

———. *I, The Divine: A Novel in First Chapters*. New York: Norton, 2001.

Awwad, Tawfiq Yusuf. *Death in Beirut*. Translated by Leslie McLaughlin. Boulder, Colorado: Lynne Rienner. 1995.

Ma'alouf, Amin. *The Rock of Tanios*. Translated by Dorothy S. Blair. New York: G. Braziller, 1994.

Nasrallah, Emily. *Flight Against Time*. Translated by Issa J. Boullata. Austin, Texas: Center for Middle Eastern Studies, University of Texas at Austin, 1997.

Shaykh, Hanān. *The Story of Zahra*. New York: Anchor Books, 1995.

———. *Beirut blues: a novel*. Translated by Catherine Cobham. New York: Anchor Books, ©1995.

Web Sites

http://www.lebanonembassy.org/
Lebanese Embassy in Washington, D.C.

http://www.arab.net/lebanon/lebanon_contents.html
Information about Lebanon: history, geography, business, culture, and government.

http://forum.dailystar.com.lb/cgi-bin/forum/dcboard.cgi
Information about the different conferences and the discussion forms for each conference. Topics range from Lebanese Hot Issues to the Lebanese-Israeli Conflict.

http://menic.utexas.edu/menic/countries/lebanon.html
Center for Middle Eastern Studies. Information about Middle Eastern countries such as Lebanon, its government, culture, education, as well as news and media. Links to other sites about Lebanon.

http://www.arabia.com/english/
News about the Arab world and various discussion topics.

http://tyros.leb.net/
General information about Lebanon, its major cities of Beirut and Tyre, and the old cedar trees representing the country.

http://www.undp.org.lb/
United Nations Development Program. Information about help that Lebanon is receiving from the United Nations. Information about United Nations Volunteers in Lebanon, United Nations Development Program, United Nations System in Lebanon.

Pen Pal/Chat

Chat@Lebanon.com
http://www.lebanonvoice.com/
http://libanis.com/libanischat/

Chapter 7

PALESTINIAN TERRITORIES

Rawan Damen and Dima Damen

INTRODUCTION

Historical Palestine lies on the western edge of Asia and the eastern extremity of the Mediterranean Sea. It is bordered by Lebanon, Syria, the Mediterranean Sea, Jordan, and Egypt. Though its borders have been fluid, Palestine is an ancient geographical entity with a rich history. Jesus was born in Bethlehem and lived in Nazareth and Jerusalem. Jericho is the oldest inhabited city dating back to the third millennium B.C. Palestine is called the Holy Land because it is a historically and religiously important site for followers of Christianity, Judaism, and Islam.

Although historically Palestine has been an important religious, political, and commercial region at the intersection of three continents, it has attracted most international attention since World War I. When the Allied Powers divided up the former Ottoman Empire, Palestine was assigned to the British Mandate. Incorporated to that was the 1917 British Balfour Declaration that promised the establishment in Palestine of a home for the Jews. Leaders of the World Zionist Organization had argued, at that time, that Palestine was a land without people for a people without a land. Yet, Palestine had then a population of more than one million.

In November 1947, the United Nations issued Resolution 181, which called for the partition of Palestine into two states: a Palestinian state (on 43% of the land) and a Jewish state (on 56%). In 1948, Israel was established far beyond the boundaries specified by the United Nations to include 78 percent of the land of Palestine. The establishment of Israel resulted in the demolition of 481 Palestinian villages. Over 750,000 Muslim and Christian Palestinians were forced to flee from their cities, towns, and villages.

Whereas Israelis consider May 14, 1948, their independence day, the Palestinians remember it as the Nakba (Catastrophe) that turned them into refugees in their own homeland as well as in neighboring countries. As a result, the UN established the United Nations Relief and Works Agency (UNRWA) to cater to the Palestinian refugees. The work of UNRWA covers the West Bank, Gaza Strip, Jordan, Syria, and Lebanon, where most Palestinian refugees' camps have been founded.

In 1967, Israel occupied the remaining 22 percent of the Palestinian land currently known as the West Bank and Gaza Strip. An additional 300,000 Palestinians became refugees. Currently the Palestinian political parties refer to the West Bank and Gaza Strip as "Palestine" and strive for an independent Palestinian state on 22 percent of the land of Palestine.

After more than 35 years of Israeli occupation, 4 million Palestinians are currently living in the Diaspora, (settlements away from their home-land) mostly in other Arab countries; 1 million Palestinians live in Israel and 3 million live in the occupied West Bank and Gaza Strip.

The West Bank and Gaza Strip include 16 main cities and towns, 470 villages, and 27 refugee camps. The biggest city, Gaza, has 200,000 inhab-itants. Located north of the Gaza Strip with 100,000 inhabitants, Jabalia is the biggest refugee camp. All camps lack infrastructure for water and sewerage. Half the population in the West Bank and Gaza Strip is under 14 years of age; teens comprise about 10 percent of the total Palestinian population. The Palestinians living in the West Bank and Gaza Strip are facing the hardship of military occupation in addition to the armed Jew-ish settlers in more than 200 settlements located strategically on top of the hills overlooking most Palestinian communities. Israel has already taken over 70 percent of the West Bank and Gaza Strip for building Jew-ish settlements and bypass roads, which connect the settlements with Israel through highways exclusively built for and used by Israeli settlers.

Every Palestinian aims at having a special identity and state. On December 9, 1987, after 20 years of occupation, the Palestinian Intifada (Uprising) erupted, calling for independence. This uprising received wide international attention and resulted in what has become known as the "peace process for resolving Palestinian-Israeli Conflict." On September 13, 1993, the Declaration of Principles was signed in Washington, D.C., between Palestinians and representatives of Israel. The agreement stipu-lated that negotiations would be conducted in two phases: transitional and final. Efforts have been made since 1993 for a settlement to ensure a just and lasting peace between Israelis and Palestinians. Yet no success has yet materialized. This failure has caused the eruption of the second Palestinian Uprising since September 2000.

TYPICAL DAY

Half the size of the Chicago metropolitan area, the West Bank is divided into 120 small territorial divisions, best known as sieged cantons, by Israeli military checkpoints and roadblocks. This configuration has affected the daily lives of all Palestinians, causing numerous social, psychological, economic, and political problems. Life under occupation is not normal for children or adults. Yet, in the face of the limiting and harsh consequences of this occupation, Palestinian teens, more than their parents, are determined to experience their teen years with hope and dignity.

The typical day for Palestinian teens varies according to social class and gender. Yet, generally speaking, most teens wake up at 6:30 A.M. and turn on their radios for the news. Given the constant clashes between Palestinians and Israeli soldiers at various checkpoints and roadblocks, to a great extent the news determines how a teen's daily routine will proceed. School schedules are determined not only by the educational calendar but also by intermittent "clashes" and "events" surrounding Palestinian life under occupation. Each year, schools and universities are closed for a month or two due to the Israeli policy of collective punishment, i.e., the demolition of Palestinian houses and public facilities in retaliation for each Palestinian attack on Israelis.

Breakfast is often served around 7:30 A.M. when schools are in session, whereas during holidays it is served around 11:00 A.M. After eating breakfast, most teens leave for school early, especially village teens who have to walk to distant schools. In cities, teens go to school either by bus or by their parents' car. For teens who attend private schools, parents are often involved in trasportation. Teens stay at school till around 2:00 P.M. After school they usually go home for lunch, which is the main meal of the day. Since female students have to wear a uniform in school, they change clothes as soon as they arrive home.

After lunch, teens do their homework. Wealthy teens usually receive private lessons at home for improving their educational skills. Although schools often assign a great deal of homework, thus leaving little time for other activities, most teens manage to spend a few hours watching TV— the cheapest and most available form of entertainment in the Territories. Some, particularly male teens, play soccer with their friends. Most teens in rural areas work on their family's land or in small shops helping their parents or gaining job experience for future employment.

Female teens usually help their mothers with housework. They also enjoy visiting their female friends or going shopping. Whereas in cities middle- and upper-class female teens visit cafés and restaurants, in villages and camps they spend a good portion of their time doing embroidery. Embroidery is a famous handicraft of Palestinian heritage. Each Palestinian area is famous for its own embroidered designs and embroidered cloth. Female teens often wear modern styles of embroidered jackets and vests for special occasions.

When schools are in session, teens, after having a light dinner, usually go to bed around 10 P.M. During holidays, the typical day changes. Teens wake up late, usually around 10 A.M., have breakfast, visit their friends, or spend the day with their siblings. Playing soccer or basketball is the main activity for males. They play in nearby schoolyards or in sports and youth clubs. Females spend most of the day at home watching TV, occasionally visiting their friends in the afternoon.

FAMILY LIFE

Family is the most important social institution in Palestinian society, and strong ties exist among family members. Though 73 percent of Palestinian families are nuclear (consisting of parents and children), extended family relations are still an essential part of social life. Teens do not leave their parents' home when they reach legal age. They continue to live with them until they get married. As social welfare programs are nonexistent in Palestinian society, elderly grandmothers and grandfathers live with the nuclear family and are financially supported by their son or daughter. Palestinian families are generally larger than Western families.

Most teens do not have their own bedrooms. In each family, brothers share one room to study and sleep in, and there is another room for sisters. Wealthy teens live in homes with all modern facilities. They often have their own private rooms decorated with posters of famous Western pop singers.

Parents often take full financial responsibility for their children's education, from elementary to university level. Those who can afford to, send their children abroad for education. After college, children come back and live with their parents in the same house. Independent residence often comes with marriage.

In terms of freedom of movement and travel, girls are subject to discrimination and numerous restrictions, especially in rural areas. The current political tension in the area has increased these restrictions for all female teens. Fear and worry have led parents to overprotection. This

well-intended but discriminatory practice has serious negative consequences for female teens, denying them the chance to gain a well-rounded
exposure to social life.

Given the cultural norm to provide full financial support for teens and
the dire economic conditions in the Territories, parents do their best to
support their children socially and financially. Fifteen percent of married
mothers with children work outside the home, either in the formal or the
informal sector. The majority of women in the formal sector work in services, especially education and health fields. They comprise over 22 percent of the employees in nongovernmental organizations. Most women
work to help the family in the midst of a difficult economic situation and
inflation. Over 10 percent of households are headed by women, including
families in which the husband has been either imprisoned or killed in the
conflict with Israel.[1] Widows work mostly in selling agricultural products
in cities and towns.

When it comes to lifestyle, educational issues, and social norms, there
is a gap between Palestinian teens and their parents. Teens often find their
parents too restrictive, too demanding, and old-fashioned. For instance,
they think it is unreasonable for parents to demand that teens not smoke
when they themselves are smokers. Parents also find it difficult to balance
(1) their desire for their children to develop indepedence, and (2) the
need to control their children's decisions. Overall, parents still have the
authority to monitor and advise their children in making important decisions. Strong ties still exist between parents and children.

TRADITIONAL AND NONTRADITIONAL FOOD

Palestinian cuisine depends heavily on bread and rice. All breakfast
dishes are eaten with bread. The Arabic loaf, called *ragheef*, which is flat
and round, is still homemade in most rural areas. Breakfast usually
includes one or more of the following: eggs, yogurt-based spread (*labaneh*),
white cheese, thyme, olive oil, and milk for young teens or tea for older
teens. Some teens try to imitate their parents in having Arabic coffee
instead of tea as a way of demonstrating maturity.

During holidays, a few other dishes are added such as chickpeas (*hummus*), smashed beans with olive oil (*foul*), and fried chickpeas (*falafel*).
Holiday breakfasts have a special ceremonial quality. All family members
gather for a longer breakfast during which chatting and teasing are quite
common.

Served anytime between 1 and 3 P.M., lunch is an important meal to
which Palestinians usually invite guests. Lunch is often started with a col-

lection of small dishes, including *hummus,* and salads of fresh aubergine, tomatoes, cucumbers, onions, and other vegetables. Olives are a mainstay of the Palestinian meal. (Palestine is sometimes referred to as the land of olives because olive trees are found almost everywhere—a tradition going back more than one thousand years.) The main lunch course contains lamb, vegetables, and Egyptian rice, which is smaller and bulkier than the American type. Fresh seasonal fruit or desserts usually follow the main lunch course.

Traditional dishes vary according to region. For example, in Gaza it is common to see a daily fresh catch of fish in the meal. In Hebron, one finds lamb and peppered rice casserole (*kidra*). Cities in the north, like Nablus, Tulkarem, and Jenin, are famous for their grilled chicken with onion and bread (*musakhan*), stuffed grape leaves (stuffed with meat and rice), rice, meat, and eggplant (*maqluba*), stuffed cabbage (*kusa mahshi*), and stuffed roast chicken with rice (*dajaj mahshi*). As for desserts, one of the most famous traditional Palestinain delicacies is *kunafa,* a combination of honey, melted white cheese, and a shredded wheat pastry topping. The old city of Nablus is known throughout the Arab world for its *kunafa.* Jerusalem's most delicious dessert is *mutabak,* a square dough with cheese covered in syrup and powdered with sugar. Milk pudding with honey and coconut (*muhalabiah*) is another famous dessert.

Dinner is usually light. It is served at about 8 P.M. It is not unusual for people to have a small sandwich for dinner. Teens like to stroll downtown with their friends to buy sandwiches made of sliced lamb with vegetables (*shwarma*) or fried chickpeas (*falafel*).

Some dishes are only served on special occasions such as during the holy month of Ramadan. *Qatayef,* a fried oriental pancake stuffed with sweetened white cheese and tossed in syrup, is a special dessert served merely in Ramadan. In addition, dried apricot (*qamardeen*) juice is the traditional drink for Ramadan. During Easter holy week, sweetened wheat kernel with nuts (*burbara*) is served. Rounded cakes made of semolina dough and nuts (*ka'ek* and *ma'moul*) are served at both Islamic and Christian feasts. Women usually prepare food whereas men are responsible for buying foodstuffs. Palestinians prefer to buy food from a marketplace. Each family has its reliable butcher and baker. Supermarkets are available in each neighborhood; thus teens are sometimes asked to buy the groceries.

Nowadays, fast-food restaurants, in addition to Chinese, Mexican, Italian, and Indian restaurants, are opening in the main cities. Teens have a growing appetite for pizza and hamburgers, especially when they are eating with their friends. Not all teens can afford to go to restaurants regularly, yet they try to go from time to time for fun.

SCHOOLING

Having become refugees since 1948, and having lost most of their homes and property, Palestinians view education as the most important investment they can make for their children. While most teens go to public schools, refugee teens go to the UNRWA schools. Public schools comprise 70 percent of all schools. In the West Bank there are a few schools, run by churches and charitable organizations, for students with speech, vision, or hearing difficulties. In the Gaza Strip the Blind Friends Association provides education for blind children. Also the UNRWA/Pontifical Mission Center for the Blind provides basic education and vocational training.

One-third of public schools are co-educational; the rest are segregated. In public schools the female students wear a special uniform, but males do not. UNRWA schools in refugee camps are mostly segregated, with uniforms for girls only. Rich and upper-middle-class teens go to private schools, where fees are around $2,000 annually. Each private school has its own uniform for both males and females, and the majority of these schools are co-educational.

According to June 2000 statistics, around 5 percent of teens work and do not attend school regularly. The vast majority of these teens are males. The literacy rate in the Palestinian society is about 85 percent.[2]

Schools open at 8:00 A.M. and finish around 2:30 P.M. The school year starts in the first week of September and ends by mid-July. It consists of two semesters divided by a winter holiday (Christmas and New Year holiday). The last two weeks of each semester are dedicated to written exams, followed by a certificate of completion.

The school system is organized in stages. For children age 6 to 12, the elementary stage offers six grades; for teens age 13 to 16, the preparatory stage offers four grades. Both stages are considered basic education. Basic education in public and UNRWA schools is compulsory and free.

The secondary stage is divided into two main streams: academic and vocational. Each stream has substreams: academic consists of arts (which includes human sciences) and science; vocational includes industrial, agricultural, and commercial. Teens at the age of 16 choose one of these streams on the basis of their grades. The science stream is a top choice because it gives teens the highest number of choices for selecting a major

Teenage boys read at a Gaza Strip educational center. (Trip/Ask Images)

for university admision. Vocational education is less popular; few, mostly males, choose it. Most females choose the commercial substream.

Preparation for the General Secondary Exam (Tawjihi examination), covering seven subjects and administered by the Ministry of Education in the last year of high school, is very stressful for teens and their families. Since the exam determines university admission, it is designed to be hard. Students must achieve satisfactory scores on all seven subjects. Only half the students pass the exam.

There are six universities in the West Bank and two in the Gaza Strip. Almost half of the undergraduate students are females. The oldest Palestinian university and the most competitive is Birzeit University, 10 miles north of Jerusalem. All universities are independent institutions, funded by donations and student fees. Universities' fees are affordable for middle-class families. There are also 21 post-secondary institutions known as colleges in Palestine. They, like community colleges in the United States, offer two-year diplomas. Also, several local charitable societies, like the YMCA and YWCA, run vocational courses covering secretarial education, computer skills, sewing, and other crafts fields. UNRWA training centers teach short-term courses for refugee teens such as mechanics, metalwork, welding, and electrical training.

It is clear that neither teens nor their parents are fully satisfied with the school system. Most public school buildings were built in the 1960s prior to the Israeli occupation. Most are overcrowded due to financial constraints. The average class size in public school is 34 in the West Bank and 42 in the Gaza Strip. Class facilities are rudimentary, including wooden desks (two students per desk), a blackboard, and a table and chair for the teacher. Class periods are 45 minutes long with a 5-minute break between each. Public and UNRWA schools have one main break (15–20 minutes) at 10:30 A.M., while most private schools have two breaks at 10:30 and 12:30. On rainy days teens stay in their classrooms, as most schools do not have closed multi-purpose halls. Most secondary schools have a laboratory with good facilities. The majority of girls' schools have a room for home economics. Very few schools have computer labs, music halls, or theater halls.

Teaching methods are still based on lecturing, memorizing, and lots of homework. Teens carry very heavy schoolbags, as they have to carry the textbooks for the seven daily periods together with their notebooks. Financial and political constraints have affected teachers' salaries and status negatively. They are underpaid, overworked, and unappreciated. This in itself has contributed to a lessening of the quality of education.

SOCIAL LIFE

Friendship is an important social tie among Palestinian teens. Friends are mainly one's schoolmates or neighbors. Teens, whether boys or girls, exchange visits, play together, and go downtown. It is also common for friends to exchange long telephone calls after school. Palestinian teens like to talk about the latest games, jokes, favorite pop singers, and TV series.

At private schools mingling is common. However, since most public schools are sex-segregated, boys and girls have to find other venues for interaction with each other. Palestinian teens rarely select their own dates. Only very few teens in larger cities, like Jerusalem and Ramallah, select dates. Traditional and religious values make teen dating almost impossible in smaller cities, villages, and refugee camps. This does not mean that dating does not take place in Palestinian society. Some teens meet each other after school without the knowledge of their parents. Many boys and girls walk together on their way home from school or go to cafés for a drink. Drinking, dancing, and premarital sex are all subject to tradition and religious restrictions. Most teens don't drink, and bars are very few. Cultural traditions discourage drinking, especially among teens. Mixed dancing also is not common in Palestinian society. If it does take place, it is at special festivals or private weddings. Private parties also provide an opportunity for rich and poor teens, of different sexes, to mingle or even dance together. Premarital sex is forbidden and strictly prohibited among both Muslims and Christians.

While prearranged marriages still take place in rural areas, they are rare in cities. Yet parents prefer the marriage of girls and boys at an early age, if they can afford it. Around 30 percent of girls marry at the age of 18. Teens think, in general, that a suitable marriage age for girls is around 20, while for boys it is around 30.

The legal driving age is 18, and driving lessons are offered in special schools. Some richer teens use their parents' cars and drive around, with or without their permission. At times, this has resulted in tragedies for the teens themselves and other innocent people. As for clothing, Palestinian teens, try to follow the fashion as much as they can afford. They prefer to wear jeans, T-shirts, and other casual clothes. They also like to wear their hair in fashionable styles. Teens usually imitate Western and Arab singers and actors in their style. Yet, most teens cannot afford to buy stylish clothes. In general, Palestinian teens experience a considerable level of independence in choosing their clothing.

RECREATION

After school, teens tend to spend a considerable portion of their time playing. This depends on their homework. During holidays, teens spend most of the day playing outdoors. It should be noted that the summer holiday lasts from mid-June until the first of September.

Palestinian teens do not enjoy most of the recreational activities that teens in other parts of the world do. Due to curfews and checkpoints imposed by Israel, teens cannot enjoy nature outside their residential locations. Sports clubs, if they exist, provide only basic facilities. To enjoy their leisure time, most teens walk downtown with their friends. Older teens spend evenings in cafés and restaurants. In urban areas teens use the school playground for their recreational activities, while in rural areas they usually use unpaved playgrounds. Whereas boys and girls play together in urban clubs, they rarely play outdoors together in rural areas. This activity is restricted to larger cities.

The most popular sport for boys is soccer. They organize local teams at schools and in neighborhoods. Boys do not miss watching important soccer matches; they know all the popular local and international athletes. At times, when an important match is to be broadcast, teens gather in groups to watch it in homes or cafés. Although no other sport can compete with the popularity of soccer, boys also like basketball. Some local communities organize basketball teams. Another popular sport in Palestine is bicycle riding. Most boys who can afford a bike ride it downtown in the afternoons. In addition, billiards and bowling have become increasingly popular among teens. Some halls for playing these sports are being opened in cities and towns. As for girls, they have less interest in sports than boys. In general they prefer volleyball, tennis, and jogging.

The seashore is only available in the Gaza Strip, which overlooks the Mediterranean Sea. Since Israeli authorities do not allow Palestinians living in the West Bank to go to the Gaza Strip, teens in the West Bank are denied swimming in the sea, canoeing, or other aquatic sports. Only rich teens can afford to swim in the pools of private clubs. Other sports that need special equipment, like golf and horseback riding, are not available at all. Because of the political situation in Palestine and the lack of security, parents do not permit their children to go camping, hunting, or go on other outdoor activities.

In 1996, a Palestinian team participated in the Olympic Games in Atlanta, Georgia. In 1998, the national Palestinian soccer team ranked fourth among the Arab teams in Amman, Jordan. Since then, interest in a wide range of sports has increased, and teens now work for participation in their favorite national sport teams with the hopes of becoming heroes and heroines. Annual sports competitions are held at schools for common sports like soccer, basketball, and tennis.

ENTERTAINMENT

Entertainment in the Occupied Territories is also a victim of political conflicts. Due to curfews and restrictions of movement by Israel, teens can only enjoy visiting their friends, walking together downtown, and talking on the phone with each other. Teens spend most of their leisure time watching TV.

Palestinian teens like movies, serials, music, and contest shows, whether Arabic or Western. They like all types of movies, yet most boys prefer action movies and most girls prefer dramas. Teens like Mexican soap operas, as well as Western and Arabic ones. In the Arab world, it is Egypt and Syria that produce the best and largest number of serials.

Since the early 1990s, satellite dishes have become popular in Palestine. Many Palestinian families are keen to own satellite dishes and receivers, as TV is the most common form of entertainment. The wide range of Arabic satellite channels provides a great choice of programs. Teens are mainly interested in music videos and interviews with famous singers. They also love to watch contest shows, mainly because of their competitive nature.

Palestinian teens spend a considerable portion of their time watching news on more than one channel. This is definitely due to the political situation. Most of the time, the Palestinian situation is in the headines on Arabic channels. On the other hand, teens also enjoy borrowing videocassettes, particularly during holidays. Listening to music is an entertainment that most teens enjoy. They either listen to local music on FM channels or play their own favorite cassettes or CDs. They like Arabic and Western pop music. Most teens use headphones and spend hours listening. Teens who can afford computers at home enjoy playing computer games. Game Boy and similar digital games are popular. These games provide an opportunity for teens to engage in healthy competition and spend time with each other.

At present, only a small percentage of the Palestinian community has an Internet connection at home. Teens enjoy surfing the Internet and spending hours in chat rooms. Most teens enjoy the Internet through Internet cafés, which are found in cities and some towns. Yet they are expensive. The Internet in Palestine is still developing.

Palestinian teens like to read, particularly about arts and history. They have their favorite poets and novel writers who discuss teen aspirations for freedom. Teens also enjoy romantic poems and novels, whether Arabic or translated from famous Western writers. A high percentage of teens keep diaries, particularly girls. They also write short stories, poems, and notes to reflect their feelings and longings for their future, homeland, and loved ones.

Theaters and cinemas are only found in Jerusalem, Ramallah, and Bethlehem. A large number of Palestinian teens have never attended theaters or cinemas.

RELIGIOUS PRACTICES AND CULTURAL CEREMONIES

Muslims and Christians have lived together in Palestine for more than 1,400 years. They are used to celebrating each other's feasts and festivals. Although not all Muslim and Christian teens strictly follow religious practices, all of them enjoy celebrating feasts with traditional ceremonies. In Palestine, both Fridays and Sundays are holidays. Muslims close their shops on Fridays; Christians close on Sundays. This enables people to have access to shops all week. Whereas public schools close on Fridays only, private and community schools close on both Fridays and Sundays.

Teens have the freedom to practice their own religion. Muslim teens may go to mosques on Fridays, and Christian teens may go to church on Sundays. Both Muslim and Christian holidays are considered national holidays. They include the Eid al-Fitr and Eid al-Adha feasts, Easter, Christmas, and New Year's. During these feasts, Muslims and Christians prepare sweets and cookies, and exchange visits.

In addition, both Christians and Muslims fast. Muslims fast during the holy month of Ramadan, and Christians fast 40 days before the holy feast of Easter. During their fast, Christians avoid all dairy products; Muslims avoid any food from sunrise to sunset. In other Arab countries, the month of Ramadan is accompanied by special ceremonies. Yet in Palestine such ceremonies are not practiced due to political conflicts between Palestinians and Israel. Both Muslims and Christians end their fasting with celeberations: Eid (feast) al-Fitr for Muslims and Easter for Christians.

The second Islamic feast, Eid al-Adha, celebrates the season of the pilgrimage to Mecca during which Muslims from around the world gather in Saudi Arabia for performing a set of religious rituals. It takes place about 70 days after Al-fitr. Christmas is celebrated in Palestine as in other parts of the world. Yet here it has a special quality because Christians do not only celebrate Christmas Eve at home, but they also celebrate it at Manger Square, near the Church of the Nativity where Jesus was born in Bethlehem. Christmas is celebrated three times a year in Bethlehem. Catholics and Western denominations celebrate Christmas on December 25, Greek Orthodox followers celebrate it on January 6, and Armenians celebrate it on January 18.

The Christmas tree came to Palestine in the late nineteenth century. Although until then it had played no part in the traditional celebrations of Christ's nativity, the German-inspired custom of decorating a tree for Christmas was enthusiastically adopted by Palestinian Christians. Palestinian teens love to carry the Christmas tree home and decorate it. Decorations include gossamer balls and bells, miniature birds in full plumage, a tinsel star at the top, and real candles that are lit on Christmas Eve. Whereas in the West it is Christmas that is celebrated the most, Easter is the most important feast in the Eastern Christian calendar. Many Easter features that are common in the East are not familiar in the West.

During Easter Holy Week, Christians from all over the world gather in Jerusalem to celebrate Easter week. They walk along the Via Dolorosa, the road that Jesus took carrying the cross, and visit the Church of the Holy Sepulchre to get a flame of light from candles at the Church. It is believed that this holy light blesses their homes.

In addition, children and teens enjoy coloring eggs at Easter—a tradition whereby extended family members meet to color the eggs. Palestinian Christians have often been forbidden by Israeli forces to enter Jerusalem on such occasions.

All Palestinians celebrate New Year's, whether Christians or Muslims. All teens celebrate December 31 for the whole night. They go to restaurants or have parties at home and hope for a better year to come.

CONCLUSION

When we speak of Palestinian teens, we need to remember that a large segment of this population, as refugees, is scattered around the world. Some of them have acquired the identity of the country they live in; others, particularly those living in Syria, Lebanon, and Jordan, are refugees living under the auspices of the United Nations. Almost half the Palestinian teens in the West Bank and Gaza Strip, without an identity or state, are eager to have this basic human right.

Although most Palestinian teens have only minimum basic requirements and lack recreation and entertainment facilities, they try their best to live a normal life within their communities.

As the West Bank and Gaza Strip embrace many important religious and historical sites, Palestinians have hosted tourists for hundreds of years. This is clear in the friendly attitudes of Palestinians toward strangers—particularly on the part of teens, who like to meet people from other parts of the world.

Two more characteristics are noted among Palestinian teens. First, they follow international and local political news more than other teens. This is due to the political situation they live in. Second, they are keen to pursue their education to the highest level possible, because they remember that their grandfathers and grandmothers lost their houses and property and became refugees. Therefore, they believe that an investment in education is the most important one. Palestinian teens are known worldwide for rejecting the Israeli occupation by throwing stones at Israeli soldiers. This act symbolizes the Palestinian struggle for independence, especially since the Palestinian Uprising of 1987. On the other hand, Palestinian teens are like all teens: they look forward to a better, modern, and happy life.

NOTES

1. *Gender Statistics*, Ramallah, West Bank: the Palestinian Central Bureau of Statistics (PCBS), 1999.

2. *Labor Force Survey Report Series*, no. 17, Ramallah, West Bank: The Palestinian Central Bureau of Statistics (PCBS), April–June, 2000; Also, *Child Statistics Series*, no. 3, Ramallah, West Bank: The Palestinian Central Bureau of Statistics (PCBS), April 2000.

RESOURCE GUIDE

Nonfiction

Diwan, Ishac, and R. A. Shaban, eds. *Development under Adversity: The Palestinian economy in transition.* Washington, DC: World Bank, 1999.

Khalidi, Rashid. *Palestinian Identity: The Construction of Modern National Consciousness.* New York: Columbia University Press, 1997.

Khalidi, Walid. *Before the Diaspora: A Photographic History of the Palestinians 1876–1948.* Washington, DC: Institute for Palestinian Studies, 1984.

Lynd, Staughton, et al., eds. *Homeland: Oral Histories of Palestine and Palestinians.* New York: Olive Branch Press, 1994.

Matar, Ibrahim. *Jewish Settlements, Palestinian Rights, and Peace.* Washington, DC: Center for Policy Analysis on Palestine, 1996.

Said, Edward. *The Politics of Dispossession: The Struggle for Palestinian Self-Determination 1964–94.* London: Vintage, 1994.

———. *The Question of Palestine.* New York: Vintage Books, 1992.

Sayigh, Rosemary. *Palestinians from Peasants to Revolutionaries.* London: Zed Press, 1979.

Zuriek, Elia. *Palestinian Refugees and the Peace Process.* Washington, DC: Institute for Palestinian Studies, 1996.

Fiction and Poetry

Antonius, Soraya. *The Lord.* London: Hamish Hamilton, 1986.

———. *Where the Jinn Consult.* London: Hamish Hamilton, 1987.

Darwish, Mahmud. *The Adam of Two Edens: Selected Poems.* Edited by Munir Akash and Daniel Moore. Syracuse, N.Y.: Syracuse University Press, 2000.

Darwish, Mahmoud, Samih al-Qasim, and Adonis. *Victims of a Map.* Translated by Adullah al-Udhari. London: Al-Saqi Books, Zed Press, 1984.

Elmessiri, N., and A. Elmessir, eds. *A Land of Stone and Thyme: An Anthology of Palestinian Short Stories.* London: Quartet Books, 1996.

Habiby, Emile. *The Secret Life of Saeed: The Pessoptimist.* Northhampton, MA: Interlink Publishers, 2001.

Web Sites

http://www.dci-pal.org

Defense for Children International—Palestine Section. Statistics, reports, petitions, press releases.

http://www.passia.org

Palestinian Academic Society for the Study of International Affairs. Facts and figures, historical chronology, personalities, maps, photography archive.

http://www.fmep.org

Foundation for Middle East Peace. Information about the Israeli-Palestinian conflict and Israeli settlements in the Occupied Territories.

http://www.pcbs.org

Palestinian Central Bureau of Statistics. Statistical information on demographic, social, economic, and environmental issues and trends.

http://www.un.org/unrwa/refugees/me.html

United Nations Relief and Works Agency for Palestine Refugees in the Near East. Information on refugees, projects, photos.

http://al-awda.org

Al-Awda: The Palestine Right to Return Coalition aims to educate the international community to fulfill its legal and moral obligations vis-à-vis the Palestinian people.

http://www.lawsociety.org

The Palestinian Society for the Protection of Human Rights and the Environment is a nongovernmental organization dedicated to preserving human rights through legal advocacy.

http://www.hdip.org

Health, Development, Information and Policy Institute (HDIP). Fact sheet and press releases about current life in the West Bank and Gaza Strip.

http://www.addameer.org

Focus on Palestinian Prisoners. Prisoners Support and Human Rights Association is a Palestinian nongovernmental, civil institution that focuses on human rights issues.

Pen Pal/Chat

http://www.safara.com/voice/palestine.htm

http://Jerusalem.indymedia.org/irc/

Chapter 8

SAUDI ARABIA

M. A. Nezami

"And (remember) when Luqman said unto his son, when he was exhorting him: O my dear son.... Turn not thy cheek in scorn toward folk, nor walk with pertness.... Be modest in thy bearing and subdue thy voice."

The Koran, XXXI: 13–19.

Socrates: "In youth good men often appear to be simple, and are easily practiced upon by the dishonest, because they have no examples of what evil is in their own souls."

Plato, *Republic*, III, 409A

INTRODUCTION

In its modern history, Saudi Arabia was founded in 1932 when King Abdulaziz bin Abdur-Rahman Al Saud (1880–1953) joined two regions, hitherto administered separately, into a single political entity and called it Saudi Arabia. The two regions were Najd and Hejaz, and each had its own distinct historical and cultural characteristics.

Najd—currently divided into four provinces—was a vast region bordering the Persian Gulf and situated at the center and east of the Arabian Peninsula. As mainly a desert land, it had for centuries been divided among, and ruled by, warring tribes; inhabitants lived a very simple Bedouin (nomadic) life almost completely isolated from the rest of the world.

Hejaz, on the other hand, was located at the west of the Peninsula along the Red Sea shores. As the birthplace of Islam housing its two most sacred sites and cities, Mecca and Medina, it had for centuries been one of the world's most revered and most visited religious sites—hence, one of the most diverse international and intercultural crossroads. For the same reasons, it had always been the focus of attention and rivalry among Muslim rulers and dynasties, among them the Ottoman Empire, which ruled it for four centuries until 1916.

Abdulaziz came from the ruling family of a well-known tribe of Najd. After more than two decades of successful military campaigns in his native region, he turned his attention to Hejaz, then a semi-independent kingdom. On October 16, 1924, his forces occupied the holy city of Mecca, the capital of Hejaz, and thus brought to a climax two historically interrelated and allied movements, namely, a long military-political campaign aimed at unifying the strife-ridden Arabian Peninsula, and a revivalist religious movement that began two centuries earlier by a Najadian clergyman of the Hanbali School,[1] Sheykh Mohammad Ibn Abdilwahab (1703–1792), who aimed at ridding Islam of what he thought were huetical influences, and hence return it to its pristine state as practiced by the Prophet Mohammad.

With an area of about 830, 000 square miles, the country occupies over 70 percent of the Arabian Peninsula; as such, it is the largest country in the Middle East, larger than England, Spain, France, Germany, Italy, Austria, the former Czechoslovakia, and Hungary combined. This vast land mass is mostly uninhabited desert. Estimates of the native Saudi population vary widely. The last census, taken in 1992, indicated an indigenous population of 12.3 million people and a growth rate of 3.3 percent; based on this rate of growth, the Saudi native population for the year 1999 was projected by the government to reach 21.4 million.[2]

In addition to the native population, there are large numbers of foreigners who have come to the country mainly for work. While some of these foreigners are from Western countries, most are from Arabic-speaking countries, chiefly Egypt; followed by Yemen, Jordan, Syria, and Kuwait; then Pakistan, India, the Philippines, Sri Lanka, and South Korea. In 1985 the number of foreigners in the country was estimated at 4,563,000, with a total foreign workforce of 3,522,700. In 1990 this number increased to 5,300,000, with foreign workers constituting 79 percent of the country's total workforce. The 1992 census gave the number of resident foreigners as 4.6 million. In recent years, although the process of "Saudization" has been pursued with a faster pace, it is common knowledge that each year between $15 and $20 billion of the country's revenues are taken out by foreign workers.[3]

The influx of such a huge foreign workforce into the country had nothing to do with Abdulaziz's nation-building genius or his conservative approach to Islam. Instead, it was the consequence of an event that he did not even dream of in the beginning of his career: the discovery of petroleum.

Oil was discovered in Saudi Arabia in the early 1930s, and its commercial production started in 1938. For almost 35 years, oil revenues did not amount to more than meager royalties; then in the early 1970s came a more than fivefold jump in oil prices, from about $2.50 per barrel to about $12.00, and the trend continued, bringing Saudi Arabia's total revenue to $113.2 billion in 1981.

With such sudden and fantastic wealth, the country embarked on a massive process of development that came to be unprecedented, not only in its scope and magnitude but also in terms of its speed. Having none of the prerequisites for such an ambitious undertaking except the money, the country had to import everything—from screwdrivers to jet fighters, from garbage collectors to sophisticated radar specialists.

Nevertheless, Saudi Arabia adopted a policy unique among the Islamic and developing nations: its avowed pledge to move into the modern age with strict adherence to its ideological foundation, namely, the canons of Islam as it was preached and practiced by Mohammad Ibn Abdilwahab— hence the term *Wahabism*, to "modernize" without being a "modernist."[4] In practice, this meant that Saudi Arabia wanted to import and adopt all the material-technological goods and products of the West, but, unlike its neighbors—Egypt, Iran, Turkey, etc.—avoid and reject all aspects and manifestations of its nonmaterial culture.

Thus, within a period of less than three decades starting in the early 1970s, Cadillacs replaced camels, Toyota pickups and Mercedes-driven trailers became normal means of farmers' livestock transportation, super-highways cut across the vast sandy deserts, and ultra-modern buildings and supermarkets mushroomed in cities and towns. All these material changes took place in a context whereby a ceaseless campaign, open or indirect, against secularism and all manifestations of Western values and way of life was the cornerstone of the country's mass communication and educational systems. Also, young religious guards—known as *motawwa'a*—with portable loudspeakers at hand and regular police alongside, roamed the streets and shopping malls, enforcing the most conservative codes of morality and behavior and thereby safeguarding a set of religious/traditional norms and values that they regarded as sacred and fundamental.

Of these values, the one with most visible effect on Saudi social life is the separation of sexes. Except in the privacy of family, it is resolutely enforced in all areas of social life: in schools, universities, banks, business establishments, and restaurants. When open contact between the two sexes is unavoidable, special remedial measures are taken that vary from case to case. For example, in public places like shopping malls, wearing the complete veil (for women) is strongly enforced. In schools, when lack of female instructors necessitates the assignment of male professors to female students, they are seated in separate places, sometimes very far apart, and instruction is carried out through closed-circuit television so that no physical contact or face-to-face interaction can take place.

These efforts notwithstanding, the changes had inevitable consequences. First, they meant a cultural lag, which, given the country's stated policy, was very evident. Second, in view of the speed with which the changes took place, they created a degree of anomie: a state of social vacuum or uncertainty whereby old and established norms and values lose their meaning and applicability without time for their replacements to emerge and get established. Third, in view of the millions of foreigners these changes brought into the country, they meant potential cultural conflicts and social problems.

Of those foreigners, one group that needs special mention, because of its relevance to our subject, is foreign servants—maids, cooks, and drivers, which have become indispensable parts of Saudi family life. Whereas foreign drivers are, in most cases, necessitated by the fact that women are barred from driving and men are too busy outside the home, maids are a phenomenon of luxury and a mark of conspicuous consumption. These domestic aides, especially maids, are the cause of many social and psychological problems, of which their influence on children has been a source of great concern and debate.

In such an environment Saudi teenagers are born and brought up, and within it they study, work, live, and interact with the world. This activity takes place in the context of two additional rules that define teens' position in society, especially in relation to adults: parental/adult authoritarianism, and adolescent/youth submissiveness. In fact, there is no term in the Arabic language referring to teenagers as such, and they are not recognized as a distinct social or age group. In view of the separation of sexes, these rules are far more pronounced for female teenagers and youth than for their male counterparts.

The most salient features of being a teenager in Saudi Arabia is addressed in the following sections. Given the heterogeneity of contemporary Saudi society, the discussion reflects the experience of a group of

Saudi teenagers that could be considered the country's largest and most conspicuous sector. These teens' main characteristics could be summed up as (1) living in major urban areas, (2) belonging to middle-class traditional Saudi families, and (3) attending governmental or private Saudi schools.

TYPICAL DAY

For many reasons, it would be an overgeneralization to talk of a "typical day" in Saudi Arabia, not only for teenagers but for other age groups as well. As in other so-called developing countries, the modernization process has not been carried out uniformly in all parts of the country. Although there are glittering ultra-modern cities such as Riyadh and Jeddah with skyscrapers and floodlighted houses, there are also rural communities that are still inhabited by migratory tribes living in tents.

Furthermore, even within urban areas, it is the cultural-behavioral diversity—not uniformity of lifestyle—that is the dominant feature of life. One unmistakable reason for this is the attitude toward the Westernization of lifestyle. Whereas some vehemently reject, as heretical and sacrilegious, such things as birthday parties and Christmas greetings, and bar from their homes even such simple things as radios and televisions (let alone satellite dishes), others stand at the opposite end of the continuum, living in "little Londons and New Yorks" inside their homes or within their gated housing complexes generally referred to as "compounds." Added to this dichotomy is the separation of sexes, which is generally maintained by all and across all lines; this makes teenagers—and adults— of the two sexes each live in a separate sphere with its own lifestyle, types of activity, and social entertainment.

For an onlooker, the most salient feature of life in the country is the fact that each day is divided into five unequal periods, and every responsible (*mokallaf*) Muslim has the obligation to perform a prayer—one of the five pillars of Islam—in each period, preferably at its beginning and in congregation. The first of the five periods starts with dawn and ends with sunrise. During these prayer times all activities stop; all public places—shops, restaurants, schools, offices, and the like—are closed; and, except for non-Muslim foreigners, all bystanders on streets are reprimanded, and sometimes even arrested, by the religious guards, the *motawwa'a*, for not having gone to mosque for prayer.

The typical school day for a Saudi teenager starts with prayer. Whether required or encouraged—depending on his or her age—a teenager wakes up for the morning prayer, by means of an alarm clock or parents, and starts the day. After going through the ritual of ablution,[5] he, alone or with other members of the family, goes to the mosque and performs the morning prayer, the shortest of all five daily prayers.

From the morning prayer to going to school there is a short period of about one hour or more. During this time some students, like adult members of the family, go back to sleep; others stay awake to complete their homework. Between 6:00 and 6:30 A.M. they take off for school, which usually is not very far away. But what they do immediately before going to school and how they go vary. In most cases they are helped in preparation for school by maids and eat breakfast, sometimes at home and sometimes individually. Some walk to school with their neighboring schoolmates; many boys drive their own cars; some, like all the girls, are taken to school by male members of the family, by their family drivers, or by school vans.

FAMILY LIFE

As in all traditional/tribal societies, family has always had a pivotal place in Saudi social and political life. Certain basic characteristics and values have always been fundamental features of the Saudi family. Well known among them are: extended family structure, separation of sexes, male dominance with an excessively protective attitude toward women, strong internal solidarity and in-group feeling, in-group marriage, and youth submissiveness.

Due to rapid changes and modernization that have been sweeping the country in the recent decades, all these values have come under pressure and are changing. One manifestation of these changes is a significant increase in divorce rate—currently one of the highest in the world. Other changes include an increasing deferral of marriage by youth, one reason being their general refusal to go along with the traditional norms of marriage, in-group and in-family marriage in particular.

Although the extended family is disappearing in the rapidly changing Saudi society, the psychology and values associated with it are still dominant. One of these values is tribal affiliation: one is either a *qabili* ("tribal"), belonging to a tribe, or a *Khedhairi* (from *hadhari*, meaning "urban"); thus, if a *Khedhairi* young man requests to marry a *qabili* young girl, his request, in most cases, is rejected, no matter how high his status in terms of, say, wealth and education. A similar example is the role of aging: the elderly of the family still command a very high degree of respect and devotion, wield a tremendous degree of influence, and, in many areas of family life, such as marriage of youngsters, have the final say.

This respect and influence are not shared equally by both sexes. From pre-Islamic days, when female infanticide was a common practice in the Arabian Peninsula, the region as a whole has come a long way, due, (1) to Islamic teachings, including its strict banning of female infanticide, and (2) to the developments in education and the sociopolitical condition of the society. Yet women in the region, and in Saudi Arabia in particular, are far from being treated equally in terms of rights, status, and opportunities; this is so not only in comparison with the men in their own societies, but also with women in Western societies. For example, it is a well-known fact that women in Saudi Arabia are not allowed to drive; they also are not allowed to associate with men, other than their husbands and close kin, in any public activity such as weddings, academic conferences, sports stadiums, classrooms, and the like. Whether women should be allowed to work or not is a great public issue in Saudi Arabia. In areas of public life where women are allowed to take part, such as banks and educational institutions, their business is conducted in separate and strictly all-female buildings. In fact, a book entitled *Safeguarding of the Virtue* (*Herasatol-Fadhilah*) was published recently by a top religious pontiff, making it a religious and moral duty of all men to safeguard and protect their wives, daughters, and sisters from falling into the trap of modern Westernized ways of life.

These societal norms have domestic echoes as well. Generally, female members of the house live, dine, entertain guests, and do their things apart from the male members. When a Saudi couple visits another couple, the visiting husband and wife are separated at the entrance; each is led to a separate guest room of his or her own sex, and as a rule men have priority over women.

Teenagers, girls and boys alike, usually have little to do with the daily functions of the family. Depending on the wealth and social position of the family (and hence the availability of domestic aides), the situation may vary; but as a rule Saudi teenagers enjoy a very high degree of after-school free time, and they spend it mainly socializing with peers of their own sex. Boys enjoy greater freedom and privileges than girls; in fact, they begin practicing male dominance very early in life. Hence, it is not unusual to see a young boy exercising authority and approval or disapproval over the behavior not only of his older sisters but also of his mother.

TRADITIONAL AND NONTRADITIONAL FOOD

Saudi Arabia was made up of the tribes who, from time immemorial, lived a simple Bedouin life on the harsh desert of the Arabian Peninsula.

This simplicity was reflected in its food, not only in terms of ingredients but also in terms of the way it was prepared and served. Each of these three aspects has an interesting story and together they make up Saudi traditional food.

Today, this food is generally known as *kabsah* (most probably meaning "filled with meat"). The *kabsah* is made up of rice and meat plus some other ingredients. To prepare it, a whole sheep (or young camel) is boiled in a large pot and placed whole on a large, usually aluminum, round dish. Then, a large amount of rice is boiled with the juicy water of the cooked meat. After adding the secondary ingredients—boiled eggs, spices, raisins, and the like—to the rice, it is poured onto the cooked meat so that it is fully covered and then served.

In its strictly traditional way, the *kabsah* is served on the floor (no dinner table) and is eaten by hand directly from the main dish, that is, without plates or spoons and forks. It is a sign of respect and hospitality that the host or the men of higher status rip off a chunk of meat and hand it to another person on the same dish.

Although the *kabsah* remains the nation's national/traditional dish, it is no longer the main food served or consumed. Until two decades ago, a visitor to Saudi Arabia would have a very hard time to find a decent restaurant even in the big cities. But not any longer. Today, as a part of the country's phenomenal development, foods of all types and nationalities are served in restaurants of all sorts and levels. Included among these are fast-food places, which range from such international names as McDonald's and Burger King to many local varieties serving Middle Eastern dishes. Of the latter, perhaps the most popular is a dish of mainly chicken or meat (*shwarma*), prepared similarly to Greek gyros but served with vegetables rolled into a thin loaf of bread. Saudi teenagers are more inclined toward the fast foods, and the most chaotic double/triple parking and traffic jams always take place in front of fast-food restaurants.

SCHOOLING

A well-known political event during the reign of King Faisal (1964–1975), the third king of Saudi Arabia, was a mass demonstration against his attempt to introduce modern education into the country. The protest is said to have been motivated by the fear that such a policy would eventually lead to girls going to school—a prediction that came true.

Currently, there are three types of primary and high schools. First, the public or governmental (*hokumi*) schools constitute the main body of the country's pre-college education. These are fully financed by the government and administered by the Ministry of Education.

Second, there are an increasing number of private (*ahli*) schools that charge tuition, sometimes as high as $15,000 or more a year, and that are owned and managed by private individuals. Although both of these two types are regulated by the government and Arabic is the language of instruction in both, the private schools generally offer a better education. They are also allowed a greater degree of flexibility, especially in teaching foreign languages, which they emphasize, and which is one of the main reasons for their increasing popularity, especially among well-to-do middle-class Saudis.

Third, the international (*dowali*) schools are mostly attached to the foreign embassies—American, British, Pakistani, Philippine, etc.—and are established mainly for the children of their respective citizens. Some of these schools, the American in particular, are very popular among other nationalities, mainly non-Europeans, and in spite of the very high tuition there is always a long waiting list of applicants. This does not include Saudi families, who, except under very special circumstances requiring special permission, are banned from sending their children to these schools.

For both sexes, life and activity in school are closely supervised and highly regimented. Special care is taken not to allow the students, especially the girls, any free time between classes. Some years ago the university curricula in the entire country was changed from the credit-hour system—common in the United States—to the old "package" system in which all students are given a uniform set of courses, all taught in a period of continuous hours, and all starting and ending at the same time. It was widely believed that the reason was to prevent female students from having free time between classes in which they could slip out of school.

The school day commences at 6:45 A.M. with a ritualistic chore (*taabur*) that lasts for 5 minutes. The chore consists of reciting, by one of the students, a few verses from the holy Koran, followed by reading some of the sayings (*hadithes*) of the Prophet Mohammad and/or some words of wisdom. Then classes convene at 6:50, go through 7 sessions of 45 minutes each, and continue till about 1:00 P.M. During these 6-plus hours there are only two breaks. The first is after the third class, when the students are released and allowed to freely go to the school yard; the second is after the sixth class, when students and teachers congregate for noon prayer (the second of the five daily prayers). The rest of the morning classes are continuous, with only a few minutes between them to allow students to go

Saudi girls in language school in Riyadh, 1999. Trip Photo Library.

from one room to another. After the noon prayer the students assemble for their seventh and last class; after that they are released to go home, and the school gets closed.

The curriculum is strictly packaged, with a set number of subjects taught throughout the country almost in the same format and sequence: beginning with "hard" subjects such as mathematics and physics and ending with "soft" ones such as the arts.

For years after its foundation, Saudi Arabia's limited educational system—like that of most other countries in the Arab world—was almost entirely staffed and managed by the government of Egypt due to lack of manpower. After the income boom of the 1970s, although the trend toward "Saudiazation" was pursued at a much faster pace and with noticeable successes, the process, as far as pre-college education is concerned, rarely went beyond replacing some foreign teachers with native Saudis. As far as content and method are concerned, much remains to be done. And one of the main problems of the educational system, is its heavy emphasis on memorization and its lack of attention to comprehension, problem solving, and creative thinking.

Not all high school students graduate, although the percentage of dropouts is far lower than that in the United States. Of those who do graduate, not all enter colleges or universities. With the high rate of population growth and the increasing demand for higher and better education, the shortage of educational facilities is increasingly being felt; getting one's sons or daughters admitted to a college is becoming one of the biggest problems for Saudi families. Yet there is no college entrance examination in Saudi Arabia (as there is, for example, in neighboring Iran); in one way or another, all those who desire a college education do get admitted. Officially, the sole criterion for admission is high school grade point average, but, as in many other areas of life in Saudi Arabia (and most of the Middle East, for that matter), favoritism and nepotism (*wasetah*) play a decisive role.

Through its ministries of Education and Higher Education, the government finances and administers all educational institutions and activities in the country. Under the umbrella of the Ministry of Education, a huge and semi-autonomous organization closely supervised by religious authorities is set up exclusively for the pre-college education of girls.

In terms of facilities—computers, libraries, modern buildings—Saudi Arabia's educational system is second to none in the Middle East. College students not only do not pay any tuition or fee, but they even receive monthly pocket money from the government. Lately there has been a great deal of talk about allowing private colleges and universities, but not much has materialized yet.

SOCIAL LIFE

Two dominant features characterize Saudi society. The first is the degree of its religiosity, at least on the formal and official levels: Islam, in its most pristine and conservative form, permeates and overshadows everything else in the country, be it family life, gender relationships, education, mass communication, or the like. Related to the first feature is a second one, namely, the separation of sexes: literally all social activities—from simple outings in the desert and informal socializing to formal wedding ceremonies and academic conferences—are carried out by each gender, adults and teenagers alike, in complete isolation from the other.

Given these restrictions, dating, as understood and practiced in the West, does not exist in Saudi Arabia. The only time an unmarried young girl and boy are allowed to meet is in the presence of their parents, usually in the informal (pre)-betrothal ceremony that takes place when the boy's parents visit the girl's to request their consent for having their daughter marry their son.

This is the formal and ideal norm. What actually goes on in real life is different. One of the most common practices nowadays is that young boys, and sometimes even young girls too, write their telephone numbers on pieces of paper and, in a variety of ways, pass them on to their opposites when they come across each other in public places like supermarkets. In this way they start a process that could be called dating.

Finally, there is one interesting feature in the social life of the Saudi male youth that deserves mentioning. Although foreign domestic aides—drivers, cooks, and so on—play a vital role in managing the daily affairs of the Saudi family, there is a tendency to minimize dependence on foreign drivers, either for economic reasons or, most important, on the grounds of a socio-religious contradiction.[6] As a result, there is always a strong demand and a "golden opportunity" for young boys, from a very early age, to become the sole or part-time driver for the family, transporting "sis" and "mom" to and from school and work, taking them around for shopping, and whenever possible, cruising the streets just for fun.

RECREATION

Recreation has always been among the top priorities in developmental plans of the Saudi government. Over the past 25 years, numerous national parks, sports facilities, beach areas, hotels, tourist resorts, camping grounds, and other recreational facilities have been built throughout the country. Moreover, in recent years, a campaign has been under way for the encouragement and expansion of internal tourism. Although the facilities are increasingly being used by both teenagers and adults, and modern recreational activities are increasingly becoming a part of life in Saudi Arabia, the phenomenon is still very limited. Even traditional recreational activities like the annual camel and horse races are in decline, though they are still performed in the Jenadriyah, or National Culture and Heritage Festival.

As in other countries of the Middle East, soccer is the most popular sport in Saudi Arabia. It is an all-men sport not only in playing but also—except perhaps in the privacy of homes—in watching. There are a good number of soccer teams of varying popularity among teenagers; the Saudi soccer team is one of the best in the Middle East. In high schools there is practically no extracurricular activity, but among some universities soccer matches are held, though they are irregular and informal.

Important national and international soccer matches are always big events for Saudi teenagers. When their favorite team wins, they crowd the streets in their cars and indulge in such a frenzied merrymaking that traffic comes to a standstill for hours. In fact, cruising the streets in cars is one of the most popular pastimes for Saudi male teenagers. They start driving at a young age, and it is common to see young boys roaming the streets well after midnight.

ENTERTAINMENT

Entertainment, in the sense that it is understood in Western societies, does not exist in Saudi Arabia. For example, there are no theaters, movies, music halls, discos, dance parties, or nightclubs in the country. Considered as sources of social problems and moral degradation, or even contrary to the teaching of Islam, these activities are strictly banned.

This does not mean that there is no entertainment at all. For example, the rooftops of houses, especially in cities and towns, are crowded with satellite dishes that bring to the Saudis in the privacy of their homes the news and entertainment of all sorts from every corner of the planet. According to a religious edict (*fatwa*) issued some years ago, the use of these dishes is forbidden; but so far the government has cast a tolerant eye on the issue, and no attempt has been made to enforce the edict (as is done, for instance, in neighboring Iran).

On the other hand, in recent years many coffeehouse-like places, or public resorts (*esterahas*), have been allowed to mushroom in the big cities. In these increasingly popular resorts, which play the role of nightclubs in the West, groups of young men, teenagers in particular, spend their nights in such "safe" activities as chatting, dining, smoking water pipes, and watching TV, especially when there are important national or international soccer games.

These facilities are strictly for men; no woman is allowed in them. Outside the haven of home and family, the only occasion when women could have recreation is a wedding ceremony. These ceremonies usually start late in the evening and continue well into the next morning. Since the increase of oil wealth in the country, the wedding phenomenon has evolved into a lavish extravagance that is virtually an all-female function. On this occasion, men maintain their own all-male party, which is often more subdued than those of women.

RELIGIOUS PRACTICES AND CULTURAL CEREMONIES

Whereas social activities for Saudi men are much freer, wider in scope, and relatively more diverse than those practiced by Saudi women, they are limited in comparison with other Arab and/or Islamic societies. Thus, except for the two Islamic holy celebrations, namely, Eid al-Fitr and Eid al-Adha (the festivals, respectively, of the end of Ramadan, the fasting month, and of Hajj, or the pilgrimage to Mecca), no occasion is considered worth celebrating. For example, the celebrations of Prophet Mohammad's birthday, of New Year's Eve, of national days, of personal anniversaries and birthdays, and many similar occasions that are observed with pomp and ceremony in Egypt, Syria, Iran, and many other Islamic countries, are all considered heretical, that is, contaminants of the original Islam, and strictly banned.

Emphasis is placed instead on the two Islamic festivals. Whereas they are observed as a one- or two-day holiday in most of the Islamic world, in Saudi Arabia they are considered the most important national events, and each is celebrated for a full 10 days. In the Hajj season in particular, when millions of Muslim pilgrims from around the world pour into the country, literally the whole country mobilizes to provide generous services to the pilgrims, generally referred to as guests of God (*dhoyuforrahman*).

CONCLUSION

The Saudi teenager is a product of a unique set of circumstances. Born in a country originally made up of warring Bedouin tribes, Saudi teens have been raised in a society of tremendous wealth and luxury on the one hand, and traditional religious conservatism on the other. Today, while enjoying one of the world's highest standards of living, these teens go to school, marry, work, and spend their time in a world where religious duties have priority over all others, open interaction with the opposite sex is considered unacceptable, and social life outside the family is limited.

NOTES

1. Founded by Ahmad Ibn Hanbal (A.D. 780–855), the Hanbali School is the last of the four Sunni schools of Islamic jurisprudence and the most conservative of all—in the sense of taking Islamic canons literally and rejecting any attempt to subject them to rational interpretation. The other three schools are the Maleki, Hanafi, and Shafi'i; these, along with the Shi'a school of Ja'afari, constitute the whole of the Islamic world.

2. Saudi Arabian Information Resources, *Fact Files*. At http://www.saudinf.com/main/010.htm.

3. Ibid.

4. Joseph Schacht, "Islamic Law in Contemporary States," *American Journal of Contemporary Law* 8 (1959): 133–147.

5. It consists of the following sequential actions: (1) expressing, verbally or by heart, the intention of making ablution, (2) washing the face, (3) washing both

hands and arms, (4) wetting a part of the head, and finally (5) washing (or wetting, according to some schools) both feet.

6. The contradiction is as follows: (1) women are not permitted to drive a car; (2) by Islam, they are forbidden from association—let alone being alone—with men other than their husbands and close relatives; (3) to attend to the daily needs of life—shopping, socializing, going to work or school—they are constantly on the move outside the household; and (4) because the men of the family are also busy with their own affairs, the only alternative for the women is reliance on foreign drivers.

RESOURCE GUIDE

Books and Articles

Alghofaily, Ibrahim Fahad. "Saudi Youth Attitudes towards Work and Vocational Education: A Constraint on Economic Development." Ph.D. thesis, Florida State University, 1980.

Almofadda, Omar A. "Age and Sex Differences in Spontaneous Self-Concept in Saudi Arabia: Preadolescents, Adolescents, and Youth Adults." Ph.D. thesis, Ohio State University, 1985.

Al-Oofy, Abdellatif, and Drew O. McDaniel. "Home VCR Viewing among Adolescents in Rural Saudi Arabia." *Journal of Broadcasting & Electronic Media* 36, no. 1 (Winter 1992): 217–223.

Bird, Jerine B. "Revolution for Children in Saudi Arabia." In *Children in the Moslem Middle East*, edited by Elizabeth W. Fernea. Austin: University of Texas Press, 1995.

Boyd, Douglas A., and Ali M. Najai. "Adolescent Viewing in Saudi Arabia." *Journalism Quarterly* 61 (1984): 295–301.

El Mallakh, Ragaei. *Saudi Arabia: Rush to Development: Profile of an energy economy and investment.* Baltimore: Johns Hopkins University Press, 1982.

Kay, Shirley. "Social Change in Modern Saudi Arabia." In *State, Society and Economy in Saudi Arabia*, edited by Tim Niblock, 171–185. New York: St. Martin's Press, 1982.

Lancaster, William. *The Rwala Bedouin Today.* Prospect Heights, IL: Waveland Press, 1997.

Long, David E. *The Kingdom of Saudi Arabia.* Gainesville, FL: University Press of Florida, 1997.

Nasser Ibrahim, Rashid, and Shaheen Esber Ibrahim. *King Fahd and Saudi Arabia's Great Evolution.* Joplin, MO: International Institute of Technology, 1987.

Peters, F. E. *The Hajj: The Muslim Pilgrimage to Mecca and the Holy Places.* Princeton, NJ: Princeton University Press, 1994.

Vasilev, A. M., and Alexei Vassiliev. *The History of Saudi Arabia.* New York: New York University Press, 2000.

Wolfe, Michael. *The Hadj: An American's Pilgrimage to Mecca.* New York: Atlantic Monthly, 1993.

Yamani, Mai. "Children of Oil." *The World Today*, March 2000, 20–22.

———. "The New Generation in Saudi Arabia: Cultural Change, Political Identity, and Regime Security." In *Security in the Persian Gulf; Origins, Obstacles, and the Search for Consensus.* Edited by Lawrence G. Potter and Gary G. Sick. New York: Palgrave, 2002.

Fiction

Bagader, Abu Bakr, Ava M. Heinrichsdorff, and Deborah Akers. *Voices of Change: Short Stories by Saudi Arabian Women Writers.* Boulder, CO: Lynne Rienner Publishers, 1998.

Khashoggi, Soheir. *Mirage.* New York: Forge, 1996.

Wilkinson, David Marion. *The Empty Quarter.* Albany, CA: Boaz Publications, 1998.

Web Sites

http://www.saudiembassy.net/
Saudi Embassy. Information about media, current news, publications.

http://www.saudinf.com
Saudi Arabia Ministry of Information. Information about Islam, history, culture, government, communications, agriculture, industrial development.

http://www.saudi-un-ny.org/
Permanent Mission of Kingdom of Saudi Arabia to the United Nations, New York. Information about political, economic, developmental issues.

http://www.arabnews.com/
Information about Arab news and links to other sources on Islam, business, and the Kingdom of Saudi Arabia.

http://lexicorient.com/e.o/saudi.htm
Information about the Saudi Arabian Kingdom; articles on the political situation, economy, health, education, religions, peoples, history.

http://www.lonelyplanet.com/destinations/middle_east/saudi_arabia/
Information about Saudi Arabia, its culture, statistics in economy, history, culture, environment.

http://www.sinsal.com/Saudi/index.asp
Information about airlines, hospitals, book reviews, newspapers.

http://www.arab.net/saudi/saudi_contents.html
Saudi Arabia Contents. Information about history, geography, business, culture, government, transportation, links to Saudi Arabia–related sites.

http://www.odci.gov/cia/publications/factbook/geos/sa.html
General information about Saudi Arabia, its people, government, economy, transportation, military.

http://www.mideasttravelnet.com/mideastsite/saudiarabia/bh.htm
Information about Saudi government, cities, sights, travel information, accom-
    modations.
http://www.arabia.com/
News, business information, sports, links for search and discussion.
http://saudicities.com/
Saudi Cities, The Saudi Experience. Information about the cities of Saudi Arabia
    as well as informational segments that reflect the diverse land and culture.
http://www.geocities.com/TheTropics/Resort/2389/
Provides traditional photos of women with costumes in Muslim countries,
    including Saudi Arabia.
http://www.saudi-un-ny.org/
Permanent Mission of Kingdom of Saudi Arabia to the United Nations, New
    York. Information about political, economic, developmental issues.

Pen Pal/Chat

http://www.wsu.edu:8080/~i9248809/saudia.html
http://www.arabchat.org/acn.htm (chat)

Chapter 9

SYRIA

Ali Akbar Mahdi and Laila Hourani

INTRODUCTION

About the size of North Dakota, Syria lies between the Tigris and Euphrates Rivers, extending over 71,500 square miles in area. It is bounded on the west by the Mediterranean Sea and Lebanon, on the east by Iraq, on the south by Jordan and Israel, and on the north by Turkey. Syria has a population of 17,938,000, of which 53 percent live in urban areas. The majority of Syrians are Arab (90.3%). Ethnic minorities include Kurds, Armenians, Circassians, and Turks. This predominantly Sunni Muslim country (74%) also has several other religions and religious sects: Alawite (12%); Druze and Shiite (6%); Orthodox, Catholic, Protestant, and other Christian sects (8%); and a tiny Jewish community. There are also 367,945 Palestinian refugees currently living in Syria.[2] Though they are a minority in number, Druze and Alawites have impacted Syrian society far beyond their numbers. Today, Alawites occupy the most important political posts in the country. The official and dominant language is Arabic. Respective ethnic groups use Kurdish, Armenian, Aramaic, and Circassian languages.

It has often been said that Syria is the cradle of civilization. The land upon which stands the Syrian Arab Republic today has been home to numerous cultures, civilizations, and populations throughout history. Its history goes back 12,000 years when agriculture began. Sumerians, Amorites, Akkadians, Hittites, Pharaohs, Assyrians, Canaanites, Phoenicians, Aramaeans, Persians, Greeks, Seleucids, Ptolemies, Romans, Nabateans, Byzantines, Gassanids, and Muslim Arabs have all either lived on or governed this land at some time in history. Modern Syria represents a small portion of what it once was. At the time of Christ, ancient Syria covered an area including Palestine (currently Israel), Jordan, Lebanon, Iraq, and southern Turkey. Even today, given its diverse history and cultures, Syria serves as a bridge between Mediterranean and West Asian cultures. Damascus, the current capital, and Aleppo, another major city, are the oldest continually inhabited cities in the world.

The latest nonnative people governing Syrian land were the Ottoman Turks (1516–1918) and the French (1920–1946). World War I saw a rise in Arab nationalism and European opposition to the Ottomans. The French and British helped Emir Faisal, a member of the Hashemite family serving as Protector of the Holy Shrines of Islam, to defeat the Ottomans in 1918. In 1920, Faisal proclaimed himself the king of Syria but was opposed by both the French and British, who had a secret agreement to divide the defeated Ottoman territories. As a result, Faisal was defeated and the Europeans divided the area known as Natural Syria into Lebanon, Palestine, Jordan, and Syria. The new Syria became part of the French Mandate. Resistance by local people and pressure by Allied nations, especially the United States, the Soviet Union, and Britain, forced France to evacuate Syria in 1946. On April 17, 1946, Syria became an independent state.

Syrian independence was followed by a series of destabilizing events in the next three decades: numerous military coups beginning in 1949 and ending in 1970; the establishment of Israel in 1948 in Palestine; the rivalries among the Druze, Alawites, and Sunni majority; inexperienced and weak leadership; and a war with Israel in 1973. The Ba'th Party (meaning "resurrection" in Arabic) has been the dominant force in the political life of the country since independence. The party, originally founded by a Christian and a Sunni Muslim with the aim of Arab unity, merged with the Arab Socialist Party in 1953. The new party called for freedom, socialism, and Arab unity. The latter idea led to the formation of party branches in Iraq and Lebanon and also resulted in a brief union between Syria and Egypt (1958–1961). While the Ba'th Party became the dominant force in the country, the real power changed hands among military and civilian party leaders several times until the rise of Hafez al-Assad to power.

In 1970, Lieutenant General Hafez al-Assad, a former defense minister, succeeded in a bloodless coup and managed to be elected and re-elected as the president five times from 1971 to 1999. In 1973 a constitution was adopted, according to which the president was given broad control over political and military affairs, including appointing ministers, heading the army, and directing national policies. Political parties were to exist and the economy was to be pre-planned. The Ba'th Party has remained the dominant force ruling Syria since 1963. The constant fear of a war with Israel and the political structure imposed on Syria distorted local politics, directed much of Syrian political energy toward controlling dissent, and reduced political education to an exercise in absolute loyalty to the ruling party—tendencies that have left a mark on the Syrian society and its people, especially teens.

Upon Assad's death in June 2000, his son Bashar Hafiz al-Assad was elected both as the head of the Ba'th Party and then as the new president of the country. The new president is so young and so new to his position that it remains to be seen what kind of legacy he will establish. However, he inherits a country that is ripe with political dissent, faces opposition to its official secularism by rising Islamic fundamentalists, and has fallen behind economic trends of the time. During the 1970s and 1980s, Syria became a close ally of the Soviet Union, and the Syrian economy was guided by semi-socialist policies. Since the collapse of the Soviet Union, the Syrian economy has suffered more setbacks and failed to effectively integrate with the post-Soviet global economic structure. Efforts were made to reform the economic system in the 1980s, then in the 1990s, and as recently as 2001. In the absence of broad and meaningful political reforms, Syria seems to continue to reinvent wheels that do not find a trail to move on. The Syrian economy suffers from an outdated economic infrastructure, poor industrial management, over-regulation, bureaucratic and political interference, an outdated educational system, widespread corruption, high population growth, lack of appropriate technology, and inadequate financial and natural resources, especially water. Many skilled Syrians are migrating to other countries, and the youth do not see a prosperous future for themselves.[1]

TYPICAL DAY

Despite the variety among Syrian teenagers in terms of gender, family background, social class, and religious affiliation, one can still speak of a typical day for most teenagers, be it in cities or villages. During the school year, such a day would start at around 6:30 A.M. when mothers wake their kids up to have breakfast and get ready to go to school. Public schools are normally located not far from the teens' residence and can be reached by walking. There are no buses for public schools. Teens who attend private schools in cities are usually driven to school by a school bus or by their parents, with the exception being a few students who own their own cars.

After school, family members gather for lunch. Lunch is an important event in daily life in Syria since it brings the family together, ends the workday for many, and allows for a transition from formal activities in public into informal ones at home and in the neighborhood. After lunch, teens take a short rest and then spend most of the afternoon doing their homework. The few hours left between finishing their homework and going to bed are usually spent watching TV, playing for a short time with friends in the neighborhood, and helping parents with family chores. An increasing number of teenagers, especially those from rich and middle-class families, are taking private lessons in the afternoons to help them cope with the school curricula and exams. Some of these teenagers also take afternoon language and computer courses in private institutes, which have spread widely in all parts of the country in recent years. Big cities provide a wider option of such institutes. Teenagers from poor families not only cannot afford such institutes or private tutoring but are sometimes obliged to work in the afternoon, or drop out of school, to support their families.

Whereas during the school year the pattern of teen life is more or less the same for all teenagers (with the exception of lower-class teens who work), in summer the gap between rich and poor teenagers widens. Naturally the rich can afford a wide variety of entertainment and educational activities, while most of the poor spend the summer working. Almost 7 percent of Syrian teens between the ages of 12 and 14 work. This figure rises to 19 percent for teens between the ages of 15 and 17. The percentage of working teens (15–17 years) is higher in rural areas (21%) as compared to urban areas (17%) and considerably higher among boys (33%) than girls (3%).[3] The latest economic downturn has aggravated this problem, increasing the number of Syrian boys carrying a shoe-shining toolbox and begging for customers in major cities.

A typical day for non-working teenagers in summer would start at 11 or 12, depending on how late they stayed up watching TV or returned from an evening out with friends. For working teens the day starts much earlier and may involve working till the evening. Although the law prohibits the labor of teens below age 15 for more than 6 hours, 98 percent of working children exceed this limit. While some work with no breaks or on weekends, others work overnight. Teens do all types of work, some of which is inappropriate for their age and safety. A survey shows that 44 percent of teens are engaged in industrial and craft work as opposed to 6 percent in agriculture and pasturing. A considerably higher percentage of girls (29%) are involved in agricultural work than boys (5%). Boys are usually engaged in car maintenance (12%) and construction work (16%). In addition to agriculture and industry, girls are also engaged in sales (12%) and services (4%), especially household services.[4]

While most working teenagers come from poor families, some rich and upper-middle-class families also send their male children to work in order to "learn a craft" or "appreciate the value of money." These are normally traditional merchant families, particularly in big industrial cities like Damascus and Aleppo, who believe that education in itself does not provide their children with all the necessary tools they need to face life and become "men."

FAMILY LIFE

The traditional patriarchal family is still the core of social life in Syria. An average family with kids in their teens would consist of five children in addition to the parents. It is quite common for the grandparents to live with their sons' families. The elders still hold high status in the family and are looked up to and respected by the teens. With a high fertility rate of 6.7 percent, extended families with up to eight children are still common in Syria, especially in rural areas and religious families. Modern family planning methods are still unaccepted by some of these families. According to official government statistics, the rate of family planning implementation stands at only 30 percent.[5] It is not surprising therefore that in 1998 Syria had a population growth rate of 3.4 percent.[6]

This traditional family structure may be a source of security and balanced emotional life for teenagers, but it may also be a source of restriction to their freedom, individualism, and natural desire to break the rules and traditions. It all depends on how strict the family is in implementing traditions and customs. As a rule, children are required to respect their elders and obey their wishes. In families where traditions are strictly followed, the father is the most respected authority who generates income, makes major decisions, serves as a role model for his sons, and guards the integrity and honor of the family. This authority figure is not only respected but also feared. The mother is usually the source of love, care, and in-house service. In cases of conflict between family members, especially teens and their father, she serves as a mediator. In such families, physical punishment is quite common and sometimes is applied to children, and in some cases even to the mother.

Gender discrimination is another common phenomenon in Syrian families, especially traditional ones. Sometimes the very birth of a baby girl may be considered an unfortunate event, especially if it has not been preceded by the delivery of a boy. Emphasis on female chastity and family honor has made parents very cautious about their daughters. Female teens generally face more restrictions and regulations regarding their clothing, interaction with people outside of the family and with teens of the opposite sex, and time spent outside of the house, whether with friends and relatives or in public places like parks, restaurants, and libraries.

More liberal relations are allowed among urban educated middle-class families, where both parents are involved in earning income and raising the children. In such families, teens are given more freedom to express themselves and question their parents' decisions. But even in these families, the traditional male and female chores still hold in many ways: cooking, cleaning, and washing are tasks carried out primarily by the female members of the family, be it the daughter, the sister, or the mother. Shopping, garbage disposal, and paying household bills are primarily male tasks, be it the father or sons. In families with teens, a good deal of daily shopping is done by male teens.

Compared to other Arab countries in the region, Syrian women have a high public profile. Women work in farms, factories, schools, beauty salons, hospitals, private corporations, and government offices. In fact, women run both the Ministry of Higher Education and the Ministry of Culture. Whereas in recent years more men have been obliged to work longer hours or two shifts to support their families, women often work only one shift in order to be available to their children in the afternoon.

Since lunch is still a sacred time for most families, even in families where both parents work, the mother still remains responsible for preparing the meal. Lunch is normally served at around 2 or 3 and is followed by a short nap, especially on hot summer days. The weekend, Friday as per the Islamic week, is also still to a large extent a time for the family. Breakfast is the main meal on this day, unless the whole family is invited for lunch at the aunts', uncles', or grandparents' house. Generally, teenagers spend more time with their parents in Syria than teenagers do in the United States.

A huge gap exists between the lifestyles of teenagers in rich and influential families and those in poorer or less privileged families. Although the legal driving age is 18, many rich teens at younger ages are seen driving expensive cars. These are usually the children of influential government or military officials, for whom driving fast, showing off car models, and breaking driving rules are a favorite form of entertainment. Attempts have been made in recent years to curb this phenomenon, which has caused several accidents.

Another gap exists between liberal educated families and traditional families, both Muslim and non-Muslim. Whereas for the former drinking alcohol and a certain level of mingling between the two sexes are acceptable, for the latter such behaviors are strictly prohibited. To many Muslim families, such practices do not necessarily conflict with today's Islam as they see it. For non-Muslims, such practices may not conflict with their religious beliefs at all. Given the secular nature of the government and its policy of promoting religious harmony, one observes a form of tolerance and harmonious coexistence between Muslims and non-Muslims. One consequence of such coexistence is frequent interaction among teens of various religious communities. For instance, in Aleppo, every Sunday afternoon a large number of Armenian youths gather in a neighborhood called Azizieh. It is not uncommon for Muslim youths to join these Armenians, socialize, and go to restaurants and bars with them.

In cities where there are sizable religious minorities, they are free to have their own schools. Interactions between Muslim and non-Muslim teens are quite common in big cities and multi-religious villages. Where there are intimate interactions between Muslim and non-Muslim teens, they do not go too far because parents discourage them from getting too involved. Since the marriage of a Muslim man to a non-Muslim woman requires the conversion of the woman to Islam, non-Muslim parents are particularly afraid that their daughter's religion might be sacrificed for the sake of youthful passion.

TRADITIONAL AND NONTRADITIONAL FOOD

Syria has a very rich cuisine. Eating is an important factor in social life. Friends and relatives usually meet over lunch or dinner tables, mainly at home but sometimes also in restaurants for those who can afford it. Cooking is predominantly a woman's task. Some men cook, but more as a hobby than a duty. In preparation for marriage, most girls learn how to cook from their mothers. Men usually do the shopping, although many women, especially in poorer families, share the task. Children, especially boys, are usually asked to share small shopping chores.

Most Syrian dishes consist of rice with meat and vegetables. In most villages rice is replaced by wheat, which is also a main component of many dishes. In addition to the vegetable and meat dishes known in all parts of

Syria, each region has its own main traditional dish, which is usually served at weddings and on other important social occasions. Syrian cuisine, like Lebanese, is famous for its appetizers: hummus, (puree of chickpeas, *tahina*, lemon, and garlic served as a dip with bread) *baba ghanoush*, (grilled eggplant, *tahina*, olive oil, lemon juice, and garlic puree served as a dip) and different types of salads. However, what Syrians consider appetizers are actually main dishes by Western standards.

Though more and more teens show interest in Western foods, Syrian dishes with meats like ones featuring a mixture of yogurt and meat (*shakreeyeh*), eggplant, zucchini, and other vegetables stuffed with meat and rice (*mahashi*), and barbecued chicken, lamb, or beef generally known as *kebab* or *kabob* in other countries (*mashawi*) are the most popular ones. Pizza-like bread in various forms (*manakeech* with olive oil, *fatayer bejebneh* with cheese, and *sifiha* with meat) is a favorite food served in most school and university cafeterias. The choice between local and Western food is also dependent on the teen's age. As teens enter high school, they become more interested in Western-style food and show less interest in regularly eating local food at home.

The fact that Syrian cuisine is very rich and tasty has made it hard for Western dishes to overtake traditional ones. However, European, Chinese, and recently Thai foods have become popular among wealthy families. While most teenagers like the local dishes, almost all of them also enjoy Western-style fast food: hamburgers, hot dogs, pizza, and so on. Parents often complain that their teenage children generally prefer fast food like french fries, pastas, and local and Western-style sandwiches with lots of ketchup and mayonnaise (two alien elements in the Syrian cuisine) more than the traditional dishes, which take a longer time to prepare but are more nutritious and less expensive. It is perhaps not so much the taste that attracts teens but the ritual of going out to a Western-style café or to a fast-food place, to have a pizza or a hamburger and drink Coke or beer. Teens often insist on eating outside because it serves as an additional occasion for socialization with their friends. In some cases, such a demand is part of a scheme by a boy and a girl who like to direct their families to the same restaurant in order to create an opportunity for visual, and possibly verbal, interactions.

Eating out is a ritual affordable only by wealthy and upper-middle-class teens. Their fellow teens from lower classes can afford such a luxury from time to time but are more likely to replace it by a *falafel* or *hummus* sandwich, which are much cheaper than Western-style sandwiches. Syria is one of the few countries that have not licensed the opening of Western fast-food chains like McDonald's, Burger King, and Pizza Hut—restaurants readily found in other Middle Eastern countries. In Syria, Western fast food is only served in locally owned cafés.

SCHOOLING

Primary education is compulsory by Syrian law. It consists of 6 grades and covers ages 6 to 12. This period is followed by a 3-level preparatory period (age 13–16) and another 3-level secondary period (age 16–18). These are the equivalents of middle and high school in the United States. In urban areas, some private schools and all public schools are sexually segregated as of the preparatory period. In rural areas, mixed schools exist wherever they are socially accepted or where there are not enough schools to apply segregation.

Public schools in Syria are free and usually within walking distance in both rural and urban areas. Most schools begin between 7:45 and 8:00 A.M. and end between 12 and 2:30 P.M., depending on the level, type, and location of the school. In some villages and overpopulated urban suburbs, schools operate in two shifts: morning from 7:45 A.M. to 11:45 A.M., and afternoon from 12:00 to 5:00 P.M. Students for the second shift arrive shortly after those for the first shift leave. In rural areas, some schools have to even combine classes due to the small number of students, the shortage of teachers, and the lack of facilities and resources.

While the majority of Syrian teens attend public schools (94.5% of middle and high schools in 1999), there are a sizable number who go to local private schools found mainly in major cities (4.5%).[7] There are two types of private schools: local (77 middle and high schools in 1999) and foreign (49 schools). Wealthy families often send their children to local private schools, which offer a better education, more upgraded facilities, and an environment compatible with these parents' social and economic class. The Ministry of Education controls the curriculum in these schools and recognizes their diplomas for employment and further studies at universities. Foreign private schools are free of the Syrian educational framework and operate more or less according to the educational system of their respective countries. The Syrian government does not recognize their diplomas; if students from these schools wish to transfer to public schools, they have to pass special exams qualifying them for the officially recognized diplomas. Despite high tuition in these schools, some influential Syrian families, who want their children to pursue higher education abroad later, send their children to these schools.

The curriculum in Syria is uniform in all schools: public, private, and United Nations Relief and Works Agency sponsored (with the exception of foreign private schools). The only difference in curriculum between public schools and local private ones is related to the teaching of foreign languages: public schools teach French or English only at the fifth grade of primary level, whereas private schools provide better foreign language teaching and offer it as of first grade. This is the main reason why many rich and upper-middle-class families prefer to send their children to private schools, although they are sometimes more crowded than public schools.

Until the mid-1990s, teens could move to secondary school regardless of how good their grades were at the end of the preparatory period. In an attempt to encourage vocational training and reduce the enormous pressure on universities, the system was changed. Now, students can only continue their secondary education if they score high on their final preparatory school exams, known as the Brueve. New vocational institutes have been opened to absorb the increasing number of students who fail to move to the secondary level. The final secondary school exams, known as the Baccalaureate, are crucial to those who manage to get to the secondary level. They determine students' admission to college and their major. Increasingly higher grades are required for popular disciplines such as medicine and engineering. While the use of a universal grade standard equalizes access to higher education, it reduces the chance of poorer teens graduating from schools with poor facilities and limited resources. Once they are unsuccessful at university admission, many teens from poor rural areas join the army in the hope of securing a better future.

The availability of schools, and the fact that primary schooling is compulsory, do not necessarily mean that all teens continue going to school in Syria. According to UNICEF reports, the 98 percent male enrollment rate in primary school drops to only 45 percent in secondary school. The rates are even lower for females: 95 percent in primary school as opposed to 40 percent in secondary school.[8] Far fewer rural children attend secondary school than their urban counterparts: dropout rates in the rural northeast stand at between 31 percent and 46 percent for girls compared to between 19 percent and 28 percent for boys.[9]

These figures are actually a significant achievement when compared to the educational situation in the 1960s and early 1970s when primary enrollment rates were between 50 percent and 80 percent and illiteracy was widespread. In 1970, the illiteracy rate for females over age 10 was 73 percent, against 34 percent for males. In 1990 these figures dropped to 39 percent and 11 percent, respectively.[10] This drop was the result of a government strategy actively launched in 1982 and aimed at creating literacy classes in all regions, with a special focus on highly illiterate rural areas.

Despite these achievements, the educational system in Syria still faces many challenges: increasing enrollment and retention, improving facilities and the quality of teaching, and integrating various aspects of the curriculum into a meaningful and relevant education.

Public school buildings are unattractive, cement complexes with black iron bars on the windows. In contrast to private schools, which generally have better facilities and more resources, classrooms in public schools are equipped with only the very basic teaching facilities: old-fashioned wooden desks that fit up to 4 students each, the traditional blackboard and white chalk, a wooden table in the center of the room for the teacher. Computers, audiovisual facilities, and labs are nonexistent in Syrian schools. Some schools lack even basic facilities like functioning heaters and bathrooms. The lack of latrines in rural Syrian schools has been found to be a significant factor in parents keeping their girls home from school despite severe legal penalties for preventing children from attending primary schools.

But the lack of latrines is not the only reason for girls dropping out of school. The other reasons are mainly cultural. Some families, especially in rural communities, do not value the importance of education for girls. When daughters reach puberty, many conservative parents tend to protect them from any exposure to the other sex and thus find mixed-sex classrooms and male teachers undesirable. Early marriage is another major reason for this phenomenon. Parents who believe that a woman's destiny is in her husband's house would give priority to a marriage opportunity over keeping their daughter in school.

Child labor is another phenomenon related to school dropout, among both males and females. A survey conducted by the Ministry of Labor and UNICEF in 1998 revealed that an unwillingness to study (not poverty, as commonly believed) is the primary incentive for child labor. The second incentive, according to the survey, is failure in school. Only 6 percent of the surveyed working children (age 6–17) said they were working to support their families.[11] A more important, but less frequent, factor is the disciplinary environment in the schools, where children are punished or defamed for the slightest violations by their teachers as well as their classmates. Physical punishment, though strictly prohibited by law, is still practiced in many schools, especially at the primary level.

Schools generally operate with strict discipline. Students have to wear a green military-style uniform, with stripes on the shoulder indicating grade level. No make-up or fancy accessories are allowed. In some areas, even shoes have to be the same color: black. The uniform, no matter how much disliked by students, is a relief for many parents who cannot afford

Two Syrian teens in their school uniforms. Courtesy of Ali Akbar Mahdi.

to buy different sets of clothes for their children to wear over a whole school year. The cost of the school uniform itself is a burden to many poor families.

All schools begin the day by assembling all students in rows in the schoolyard in order to sing the national anthem and pay respect to the government. Teens are expected to respect a traditional, teacher-centered educational system. School curricula are generally heavily theoretical, outdated, and exam-focused, leaving very little room for developing ana- lytical or critical thinking skills and almost no room for creativity on either the teacher's or the student's part. Information flows from top to bottom in lecture and rote memorization forms, leaving little room for active participation in class. Teachers have to put up with an increasingly larger number of students (up to 50 in a class), low wages, scarcity of train- ing, and few incentives. Many teachers, especially men, are obliged to do other afternoon jobs to make a living. While teaching was a highly regarded and well-paid job in the 1960s and 1970s, today with the rise in inflation it is a low-paid, poorly respected position. This situation has led to a low teaching morale and deteriorating teaching quality. Attempts have been made in recent years to reform the educational system and modernize the outdated curricula. This came in response to the pressing need for an educational system that meets the challenges of the modern-day world and equips students with real-life skills. So far the change in the curricula has not been accompanied by a change in teaching methods, due to the lack of sufficient teacher training.

More parents are obliged to spend hours teaching their kids and helping them with the increasing load of homework. However, the change in school curricula has made this task impossible for most parents, who sometimes have no other option but to hire private tutors. Some parents claim that the need for private tutors is an artificial one created by both "spoiled teens" and "greedy teachers" for whom private tutoring provides an additional income.

In addition to the basic subjects of reading, writing, math, science, and so on, students are taught subjects known as national education and military education. These are aimed at raising students' awareness on national issues, the Ba'th ruling party values, and speeches by the president of the republic. Islamic religion is another subject taught in schools, but the focus on religion in Syrian schools is not as strong as it is in other Islamic countries in the region. Christian students are free not to attend these lessons or are offered alternative lessons on Christianity. The general government trend is for schools to be nonreligious, secular institutions. Other supplementary subjects such as art, music, and sports exist theoretically but are greatly undermined in practice, considering the exam- and grade-oriented educational system and culture. Educated parents who are aware of the importance of such subjects send their children to private afternoon institutes.

Social activities in public schools are restricted to picnics and trips to historical sites, which take place twice in the school year. Preparatory and secondary school students are obliged to attend so-called youth camps in the summer. These camps are run by the state-controlled Youth Organization and involve different types of voluntary work, like cleaning streets or planting trees. They also involve some light military training and political education. When students reach the preparatory school level, they automatically become members of the Youth Organization. Prior to that they have all been members of the Pioneer Organization, which covers the primary school period. Teens are also encouraged to enroll in the Ba'th Party; but unlike the Pioneer and Youth Organizations, party membership is optional.

Students who finish school and fail to attend a university, or do not wish to do so, are called to the army for a 30-month period of compulsory service. The official enrollment age in the army is 18; however, university students have the right to postpone their service for as long as they are studying.

SOCIAL LIFE

The variety of social behaviors strikes most foreigners who visit Syria. In cities, it is common to see a veiled female teenager walking together with a non-veiled fellow teenager. In some districts, teenagers are dressed in the latest Western fashions: girls in mini-skirts and boys in shorts and T-shirts. In other districts, the traditional Islamic veil for girls and white plain gown for boys are predominant. Even the veil takes different forms in Syria: a black veil and gown that cover the whole face and body, or a colorful veil that covers the face alone while the body is in tight jeans and fashionable shirt. Some girls have even chosen to replace the veil with fashionable veil hats that serve the purpose of covering the hair while preserving a modern and fashionable look. Some city cafés can be full of boys and girls drinking Coke, eating pizza, and smoking hubble-bubbles (water pipes used for smoking tobacco and known in Syria as *argile*), while other cafés in a nearby street are full of men alone, drinking strong tea and smoking the traditional hubble-bubbles. In some villages, it is common to see teen couples taking afternoon strolls or dancing together at weddings. In other villages, such behavior is unacceptable.

This variety reflects a society rich in religious and ethnic backgrounds and a political regime that has managed to hold a delicate but steady balance among all these backgrounds. While the whole society is guided by certain traditions and customs in a Muslim cultural context, each family is to a large extent free to choose the social behavior that suits its beliefs and interpretations of this heritage. Like parents everywhere, Syrian parents try to exert influence on teens' clothing. This control has a reverse correlation with parents' social class: the lower the social class, the more control exerted by parents; the higher the social class, the more freedom and choice afforded to the teens. Living in a Muslim society, female teens experience more supervision and restrictions on their choice of clothing.

Social life for teens in Syria is generally family-centered; but the more liberal the family is, the more likely the teens are to mingle with other teens from the opposite sex outside the family circle. Generally, but not necessarily, nouveau-riche and middle-class families are more liberal in their social attitudes than the traditionally rich and poor families. School is the main place where rich and poor teens socialize. But social activities

Syrian girls socializing. Courtesy of Ali Akbar Mahdi.

are very limited in these sex-segregated schools. Therefore teens, especially from opposite sexes, have to look for other places to meet each other. A visit to the entrance of the nearby girls' school on the way back home from school is a daily ritual for many male students. Parks are another place where teen couples meet if they manage to escape their parents' monitoring. Wedding parties, especially in villages, are another major meeting place. Much communication between teens of the opposite sex takes place on the phone while parents are away from home. Teens are often very creative in escaping their parents' supervision and meeting their friends of the opposite sex.

Teens from wealthy and middle-class educated families can usually invite their friends, from both sexes, to their houses, have mixed parties, and go out to restaurants and cafés. Discos are available only in 4- and 5-star hotels in major cities. Modern Western-style cafés and fast-food centers are more likely to be filled with teenagers than these discos. Smoking is more widespread among teens than drinking. Teens usually smoke in secret, since most parents do not allow them to do so. Hubble-bubble is another form of smoking that has recently become very popular among teens. Drugs are still not common due to the strict government security control. Certain over-the-counter pills obtained from pharmacies are more accessible to teens with addiction tendencies than are illegal drugs.

Girls are generally expected to behave and dress "decently" and avoid staying out late in the evening unless accompanied by their brothers or cousins. In some families, mingling between the sexes is allowed only among relatives. This explains why many girls end up marrying their cousins, which is an accepted and even encouraged practice in Islamic cultures.

Teen social activities in conservative Muslim families are strictly sex-segregated. When a girl reaches puberty in such families, her parents start preparing her for marriage and do everything to protect her from having any contact with the other sex. They make sure that she only attends all-women parties, weddings, and other social gatherings. This discipline is strictly monitored by the parents or by the older brother. Boys from such families enjoy more liberty than girls but are often also confined to strict discipline when it comes to mingling with the other sex. Both boys and girls from such strict families usually end up with an arranged marriage to a person they have never met.

Mingling between the sexes is more acceptable in Christian communities than in Muslim ones. However, whether Christian or Muslim, conservative or liberal, rural or urban, the vast majority of Syrian parents cannot tolerate premarital sex. A woman's virginity is still believed to be a symbol of honor and dignity. Many men, even educated and supposedly enlightened ones, would refuse to marry a woman if they were to find out that she was not a virgin. Girls who fail to curb their sexual desires sometimes undergo a special surgical operation to retain proof of their virginity. This is often done with the approval, or even under the pressure, of the parents, who are ready to do anything to save their family honor.

Sex is still one of the major social taboos in Syria. While some educated parents may discuss sexual issues with their children, most parents are either unwilling or unable to tackle the subject, finding it too complex and embarrassing. There is no sex education in the school curricula. Most teachers still dread the chapter on reproduction in the science book and are unlikely to be of any help to teens when it comes to this subject. The lack of sex education, both at home and in the school, forces teens to find their own, often unhealthy, ways to learn about sex: smuggled pornographic video tapes, CDs, magazines, and pictures. Television has recently become another source of such knowledge after the widespread availability of satellite dishes, which bring in some foreign erotic channels.

While teen social life is in many ways more liberal in Syria than in other countries in the region, this liberty ends where the sexual issue begins, leaving Syrian society with yet another challenge to face in the coming years.

RECREATION

There are several public parks, playgrounds, and sports complexes, especially in big cities, where kids can play or exercise at a nominal fee or for free. However, there are not enough of these places to cover the growing number of Syrian teens. Only wealthy kids can afford to have fun in the few private Luna parks (amusement parks) and sports clubs that exist in big cities. The majority of kids have fun in the streets or alleys near their homes. The scarcity of parks and playgrounds has enabled these kids to turn the streets and alleys into playgrounds for soccer, cycling, or imaginary battlefields. Girls are usually allowed to join boys in their street games only until the age of 9 or 10. Once a girl reaches puberty, she is supposed to start behaving like a young lady, avoid public places unless for a definite purpose, and stay home helping her mother with the household chores.

There is hardly any area, be it in the city or village, where you do not see kids playing outdoors. Even rich kids cannot resist the temptation of a casual outdoor soccer match. In rich and upper-middle-class areas, however, most buildings have a fenced area for kids to play. Kids in these areas do not have to rely only on their imagination to play, since their parents can afford to buy them: roller skates, scooters, fancy bicycles, and many other new gadgets. They also enjoy a variety of games that can be played indoors such as Atari, Nintendo, and computer games.

Within the school system, physical education classes are greatly undermined. Girls have the option to attend so-called Household Management lessons instead of sports classes. Soccer is the most popular sport among both teens and adults, but it is a strictly male game. Most teens either play it or watch it on television. As the weekend holiday, Friday is devoted to soccer games among clubs, leagues, and neighborhood teams. Each city has its own teams and fans. Boys in some city districts and villages form their own teams and create their own matches and competitions. Some schools organize soccer matches, others do not; it all depends on how active the physical education teacher is.

Other sports, like basketball, volleyball, handball, tennis, and badminton, are also followed by teens. Basketball is probably the second, and volleyball the third, most favorite sports for which there are leagues, teams, and clubs. Most schools have a basketball court (or at least a hoop) and a volleyball net, allowing students to play in the schoolyard during free times. Badminton, tennis, and handball are sports of wealthier kids who have access to private clubs with special courts. They are also costlier sports in comparison to soccer, basketball, and volleyball.

Swimming is more popular in cities, especially seaside ones, than in villages. This is mainly due to the lack of swimming pools in most villages. All government sports complexes have swimming pools that can be used by teens at nominal fees. Although not too many parents allow their daughters to swim with boys, boys and girls have the choice to swim together during mixed-sex hours, or to swim separately during the hours specified for each sex. Teens who do not manage to get into these overcrowded complexes and cannot afford to go to private swimming pools have to simply forget about swimming. In summer, many families travel to seaside areas for short or long vacations, depending on their income. Some rich families own private villas in these areas or can afford to stay at expensive seaside hotels. Less privileged families share the rent of seaside bungalows, often at a density of up to several families in a single two-room bungalow.

Billiards has recently become anther extremely popular and relatively affordable game. An increasing number of billiard centers are opening in different districts, in both rural and urban areas, but billiards is again a boy's game. Girls are more into all sorts of fitness exercises; however, only upper-middle-class and wealthy girls can afford to go to private fitness clubs. Strolling in shopping areas is a more affordable activity and a favorite one for most girls, especially those who can afford to shop while strolling. Whereas girls stroll to shop, boys stroll to flirt with girls.

Playing cards is another affordable and popular game among both girls and boys. Girls usually play it within the family, while boys are freer to have late-night card games with friends in summer. There are also some traditional indoor games that girls play, especially those from strictly conservative families. The most common one is a game called Bargeece that originated in Turkey.

Finally, parks are the most popular sites for most recreational activities in Syria. Syrians miss no opportunity to visit parks or find shaded areas where they can spread a blanket, barbecue their favorite meat, and drink tea or coffee. These outings are always welcomed by teens in the family, especially females, who get a chance to be with their friends and relatives outdoors. In the summer, going to parks and public greeneries at night is also a way of beating the heat.

ENTERTAINMENT

How teens entertain themselves in Syria depends to a large extent on four factors: social class, family social outlook, gender, and locale. Entertainment is generally family-centered; but the wealthier and more open-minded the family is, the more likely the teens are to entertain themselves outside the family boundaries. All teens join their parents on visits to relatives, lunch invitations, and wedding parties. But teens from wealthy and middle-class families also go to cafés, pizza houses, birthday parties, dancing and music classes, and movies and theaters. Teens who go to these places are allowed to socialize and dance with the opposite sex as long as this mingling does not go too far in sexual terms. Parents usually monitor teen parties, and brothers or male relatives normally accompany girls. In urban areas, teens have easier access to these forms of entertainment, regardless of their economic status. Male teens are also given more freedom of movement for seeking entertainment in public facilities. Reading is another form of entertainment for some female teens who may have fewer opportunities for spending time outside of the home.

In the past few years, computers have become another source of entertainment to many wealthy and upper-middle-class kids who have private PCs at home. Internet access is controlled and monitored by the government. So far, the Internet has not been opened to the public at large and remains restricted to university graduates and professionals. A few Internet cafés have opened up in big cities like Damascus and Aleppo, but their number is small and their appeal limited mostly to high school and university students from the middle classes. Even with limited access to the Internet, teens still exchange computer games, chats, and Web site addresses. More and more parents are complaining about their kids spending long hours in front of the computer screen. Many teens are developing an interest in computer technology and programming.

While computerized entertainment is limited to those who can afford access to PCs, watching television is a common form of entertainment for all teens, regardless of their class or social background. Until five years ago, TV watching was limited to only two local channels, with the exception of some rural, borderline villages and cities, where locally installed antennas gave access to some Lebanese and Jordanian channels. Today, with a satellite dish at home, the average Syrian can flip through many Arab and foreign channels. The policy of making satellite dishes cheaply available to the population, even in most rural areas, has had its strongest influence on teens—a group more open than their parents to new values and attitudes.

Most teens like to watch contest shows that allow telephone participation and promise expensive rewards. Sports programs are also popular, especially among boys. Girls like to watch Mexican soap operas and local drama series. Everybody likes music programs, which show video clips and interviews with Arab and Western pop stars. Western pop music in all its types has always been popular among Syrian teens. Parents' influence to encourage native music essentially ends with middle school.

In the last decade, contemporary Arab singers have managed to attract teens to their songs by introducing Western instruments and rhythms to traditional melodies. Live concerts by these singers attract thousands of teen fans, especially on special occasions when entrance is free. As the production of local films and TV shows, especially those featuring native pop singers, increased in the 1990s, their popularity increased among young people as well. The gap between the type of music that teens and their parents listen to is growing larger by the day. To many parents, these contemporary singers are loud, noisy, and lacking the basics of good-quality singing. To teens, the traditional music that their parents listen to is slow and boring. Still, it is not uncommon to see rural teens listening to tapes of popular local singing or watching a traditional group dance such as the *dabkeh*.

Whereas traditional Arabic music remains a choice of parents, contemporary pop music, both Arabic and Western, is the choice of teenagers. This conflict of tastes shows itself in numerous settings. Family clubs and modern restaurants tend to put on Arabic music, while cafés and discos play Western music. This conflict of tastes reaches its peak in villages, where there is a continuing argument between the older and younger generations on whether or not to allow cassette players at wedding parties. These villages have a rich heritage of folk songs and dances, and the elders' concern is that this heritage is fading away. The younger generation, on the other hand, is fed up with traditional songs and dances and is eager to hear new rhythms. One can tell who is winning in this argument by the simple fact that fully traditional village weddings do not exist anymore, even in the most remote villages.

RELIGIOUS PRACTICES AND CULTURAL CEREMONIES

Although a secular government governs Syria, Islam is the dominant religion and is followed by most Syrians. The state views the practice of religion as a personal or family matter and, therefore, does not interfere. The state also expects religious authorities to leave the politics to the state and to not interfere with the governance of the country. While all Muslims are free to practice their ceremonies, the state keeps an open eye on all Muslim activities to monitor and control the development of any possible fundamentalist movements. Unlike other Islamic countries in the region, religious practices like prayer and fasting are not compulsory by law. It is not so much the law that defines a Syrian people's commitment to religious practices, but social norms.

Neither teens nor their parents necessarily follow all religious practices. Practicing religion depends on family background, degree of religiosity, education, social class, and a host of other factors. Some teens join their parents at Friday prayers in mosques; others pray at home or do not pray at all. Some orthodox Muslims send their children to Koranic schools to learn verses from the holy book and get some religious education. Others prefer to engage their kids in more secular activities like playing a musical instrument or studying a foreign language. Attendance in mosques, collective prayers, and religious ceremonies are as much expressions of loyalty and devotion as a venue for social interactions. These settings are often a place where teens meet their friends, hang out, and look for social interactions outside of their family circle.

Fasting in the month of Ramadan is perhaps the most followed practice, among both teens and adults. In fact, it has turned to a large extent into a social ritual rather than a religious practice. Even some of the most Westernized kids, who form rock bands and rap groups, fast during Ramadan. Fasting involves refraining from eating, drinking, and smoking from sunrise to sunset and is particularly difficult to do during summer months because of the heat. Originally, Ramadan was meant to be a time for spiritual reflection away from the physical needs of the body and for more sympathy with the poor. Today, Ramadan is a time when relatives and friends meet over extended breakfast tables, when families spend hours chatting in the mosque after long prayers, and when merchants fill the markets with all sorts of delicacies and sweets, irresistible to hungry fasters, commercially exploiting the occasion to the fullest.

Two major Islamic annual feasts are celebrated in Syria: Eid al-Fitr at the end of the month of Ramadan, and Eid al-Adha (sacrifice feast). These two feasts, like all other major Islamic and Christian celebrations, are official holidays in Syria. During the feasts the streets, especially in cities, fill up with different types of rides for children: swings, roller coasters, merry-go-rounds, and Ferris wheels. It is a fun time for children, who in addition to getting away from school for a few days enjoy other privileges like buying new clothes and shoes, playing, and buying fireworks with the money given to them by adults on this special occasion. Eid al-Adha is also a time when lambs are slaughtered and offered to the poor. Teens are especially fond of this holiday because it is an occasion for receiving gifts and money from parents and relatives.

In addition to these Islamic feasts, Christmas, Easter, and New Year's Eve are also well known to Syrians through their Christian community. Christian teens go to church either every Sunday or only on special occasions like weddings and baptisms. Some Christian teens also travel with their parents to monasteries in different parts of the country to celebrate the days of certain saints. Teens are also involved in activities organized by local Christian Associations, which are very active in Syria. These activities include: charity work, trips to Christian sites around Syria, exhibitions, social gatherings, and parties. Christian and Muslim Syrians share each other's celebrations. It is very common for Christians to visit their Muslim friends during the annual feast and for Muslims to visit Christians on Christmas or Easter. A village with a population of only 5,000 people may be a home to two or three religions or religious sects, co-existing peacefully in a predominantly Muslim country. Although these religious minorities may have their own separate quarter in the neighborhood, they are still well integrated into the overall community.

As most celebrated social occasions are of either religious or national origin (Independence Day, Correctionist's Movement Day, for celebration of President Hafez Assad's coming to power in 1970, etc.), teens tend to look for celebrations of another character. This is why in the past five years Valentine's Day has become a widely celebrated occasion, especially by teens belonging to wealthy and middle-class families. They use this occasion to exchange flowers, presents, and cards, which are available in a market eager to exploit such profitable occasions. While some liberal parents encourage such innocent expressions of love, other, more conservative parents disregard the occasion as alien to Syrian and Arab culture.

CONCLUSION

For Syrian teens, life may be not as privileged and liberal as for their fellow teens in the United States. Nevertheless, Syrian teens, probably like American teens, are often described by the older generation as being spoiled, irresponsible, and lost: spoiled because everything has been given to them on a "golden plate," unlike their parents, who had to struggle for the very basics; irresponsible because they do not value what they have and do not plan for the future; lost because they are not guided by any values or beliefs, unlike their parents, who might have fought for certain causes and values.

Teens, on the other hand, feel that the "golden plate" is not as shiny and full as it looks to their parents. As the country is opening up more to the world, they are realizing that what their parents and country have given them is not enough to help them face the challenges of a rapidly changing world. Their "irresponsible" reaction to education, for instance, probably stems from a realization that even if they manage to finish school and university, a low-paid job or unemployment is all that awaits them. They seem "lost" and lacking values because they have suddenly been exposed, through the Internet and satellite TV, to totally different values from those of their parents. Whereas family and national values have often been conveyed to them through rhetoric or an oppressive manner, these new values are "screened" to them in very attractive images. Satellite TV has certainly opened their eyes to the world, but it has also reinforced their belief that a better life exists elsewhere in the world. What makes this belief a dangerous myth is the fact that many of them think that obtaining this "better life" can be as simple as pressing the remote control button to turn to another channel!

NOTES

1. The introduction was written solely by Ali Akbar Mahdi.

2. See Central Bureau of Statistics, *Statistical Abstract* (Syrian Arab Republic: Office of Prime Minister, 2000).

3. UNICEF, Ministry of Labor, *Child Labor Survey* (Syria: 1998).

4. UNICEF, Ministry of Labor, *Child Labor Survey* (Syria, 1998).

5. UNICEF, *The National Plan of Action for Child Survival, Protection and Development* (Syria: 1997).

6. In 2000, the population growth rate decreased to 1.81 percent.

7. Central Bureau of Statistics, *Statistical Abstract.*

8. UNICEF, *The State of the World's Children* (New York: 2001).

9. May Rihani, *Learning for the 21st Century: Strategies for Female Education in the Middle East and North Africa*, Amman Jordan: (UNICEF MENARO, 1993).

10. UNICEF, *The National Plan of Action for Child Survival.*

11. UNICEF, *Child Labor Survey.*

RESOURCE GUIDE

Books and Articles

Barakat, Halim. *The Arab World: Society, Culture, and State.* Berkeley: University of California Press, 1993.

Dodd, Peter C. "Family Honor and the Forces of Change in Arab Society." *International Journal of Middle East Studies* 4 (January 1973): 40–54.

Early, Evelyn. "Poetry and Pageants: Growing Up in the Syrian Vanguard." In *Children in the Moslem Middle East*, edited by Elizabeth W. Fernea, 410–419. Austin: University of Texas Press, 1995.

Goodrich-Freer, Adela. *Arabs in Tent and Town: An Intimate Account*. New York: AMS Press, 1995.

Jenkins, Siona. *The Arab Child: Challenges for a Brighter Future*. Amman, Jordan: UNICEF MENARO, 1993.

Joris, Lieve. *The Gates of Damascus: Travel Literature*, trans. Sam Garrett. Oakland, CA: Lonely Planet Publications, 1996.

Perthes, Volker. *The Political Economy of Syria under Asad*. London: I. B. Tauris, 1998.

Rihani, May. *Learning for the 21st Century: Strategies for Female Education in the Middle East and North Africa*. Amman, Jordan: UNICEF MENARO, 1993.

Roberts, David. *The Ba'th and the Creation of Modern Syria*. New York: St. Martin's Press, 1987.

Rugh, Andrea B. *Within the Circle: Parents and Children in an Arab Village*. New York: Columbia University Press, 1997.

South, Coleman. *Culture Shock! Syria.*: New York: Marshall Cavendish, 1995.

UNICEF. *The Progress of Nations*. New York: UNICEF, 2000.

Fiction

Ali, Tariq. *The Book of Saladin*. London: Verso Books, 1998.

Bell, Gertrude. *The Desert and the Sown: The Syrian Adventures of the Female Lawrence of Arabia*. New York: Cooper Square Press, 2001.

Lindisfarne, Nancy. *Dancing in Damascus: Stories*. Albany, NY: State University of New York Press, 2000.

Web Sites

http://www.syrianobles.com/index-e.html
Information about the Syrian embassy, Ministry of Economy, Ministry of Education, and other Arab organiztions.

http://lcweb2.loc.gov/frd/cs/sytoc.html
General information about Syria and its history, society, environment, economy, government, politics, national security.

http://www.odci.gov/cia/publications/factbook/geos/sy.html
Information about Syria, its geography, people, government, economy, communications, transportation, military.

http://www.arabia.com/syria/english/
News and businesses in Syria.

http://www.arab.net/syria/syria;llcontents.html
General information about Syria, its history, geography, business, culture, links to Syria-oriented Web sites.

http://almashriq.hiof.no/base/syria.html

Information about the general history of Syria as well as its external resources, such as tourism and Syria-net.

http://leb.net/iss/

Internet Society of Syria. Information about links to Arabic organizations, personal Arabic home pages.

http://www.golan-syria.org/

This site is designed to explain how the occupied Golan is part of the Syrian homeland, seized by Israel.

http://www.medea.be/en/index174.htm

Information about the European Institute for Research on Mediterranean and Euro-Arab Cooperation.

http://www.algonet.se/~sfol/

Information about the Syrian people's civil rights. Arabic links and women's links.

http://www.cafe-syria.com/

General information about Syrian economy, travel, statistics, geography, government.

http://syria-online.com/

Information about Syrian news, business, culture, tourism.

http://www.syriatoday.com/

Information about Syria today as well as government, geography, history, tourism.

http://www.thawra.com/english/english.htm

The *Al-Thawra* newspaper has an English section containing major editorials. *Al-Thawra* is an authoritative voice in the Arab world.

http://ramijarjour.8m.com/

General geographical information about Syria, links to cities in Syria, links to sites with Arabic music and newspapers.

http://www.sesrtcic.org/members/syr/syrhome.shtml

General information about the Syrian Arab Republic, its geography, economy, demography.

http://www.4arabs.com/links

Countries/Syria/

Links to Arab countries, including Syria, and information on Syrian business, economy, government, education, culture.

http://www.arabicnet.com/main.asp

Arabic Net provides information on education, science, health, recreation as sports, society and culture, and arts and humanities in Arab countries, including Syria. It also offer free Arabic e-mail as greeting cards for Islamic occasions.

Pen Pal/Chat

http://www.visit-syria.com/frameang.html

Chapter 10

TURKEY

Meral Kaya

INTRODUCTION

Turkey covers an area of 301,400 square miles, slightly larger than the state of Texas. It is bordered by Greece and Bulgaria to the west; Georgia, Armenia, and Azerbaijan to the north; Iran to the east; and Iraq and Syria to the south. The Black Sea sits to its north, the Mediterranean to its south, and the Aegean Sea to the west. The Sea of Marmara separates the land of Turkey into two unequal parts, leaving 3 percent of the country's landmass on the European side and 97 percent on the Asian, or Eastern, side. The country is divided into seven diverse geographical and administrative units offering different opportunities and obstacles to its people. For example, the eastern part of Turkey has a poorer economy whereas the western part of the country has better economic and social conditions.

The population of Turkey is approximately 70 million. Young people in the 12 to 24 age group constitute 31 percent of the population. The population growth rate is 1.4 percent per year. Sixty-five percent of the population live in urban areas. Turkey's population is predominantly ethnic Turkish, but it also hosts a significant Kurdish minority as well as small numbers of Armenians, Greeks, and Jews. Ninety-eight percent of the population is Muslim, while 2 percent belong to Eastern Orthodox, Jewish, Catholic, Protestant, and other Christian sects. The official language is Turkish, yet Kurdish, Armenian, and Greek languages are used by the various ethnic minorities.

Although the Republic of Turkey was founded in 1923, the history of the people of this land goes back many civilizations. The story of Central Anatolia starts as early as 10,000 B.C. The Hittite Empire was one of the first known settlements in this area, now called Anatolia. After the Hittites, kingdoms such as Phrygian, Ionian, Lycian, Carian, and Urartu left their mark on Central and East Anatolia. The Byzantine and the Eastern Roman Empires flourished in Anatolia until the arrival of nomadic Turkish warriors. Following the wars between Seljuk Turks and Byzantines, the era of the Ottoman Empire began.

Starting in the 1300s, the Ottomans began to make incursions into the territory of the Byzantine Empire, expanding their realm until they reached their height of power in the sixteenth century. During this "golden age," the Ottoman Empire ruled not only in Anatolia but also in parts of Eastern Europe and the Middle East. By the end of the nineteenth century, the Ottoman Empire had lost most of its territories and a nationalist movement began the task of building modern Turkey.

By abandoning Ottoman traditions, Mustafa Kemal Ataturk, the founder and the first president of the Republic of Turkey, led a successful opposition that liberated Anatolia from foreign occupation and established the Republic of Turkey on April 23, 1923. Ataturk initiated important civil, social, and political changes. He founded the Grand National Assembly and was elected its president. He modernized the state by building democratic institutions and introducing secular policies. He created a multiparty system, institutionalized a modern legal system, and gave rights to women to vote and appear in public without the veil. He brought significant reforms to education by replacing the Arabic script with Latin characters and opening public schools, making education accessible to both men and women.

Although Turkey maintained neutrality during World War II, the postwar developments changed Turkish politics, economy, and social life and gave way to contemporary problems that Turkey now faces. By the 1950s Turkey had begun to experience poverty, high unemployment, and social repression. Turkish politics began to be characterized by conflicts. In the 1970s anti-government organizations and groups appeared, and political turmoil reached its peak in 1980. In 1983 a new government, led by the Motherland Party, started new economic policies of privatization and free market. In the mid-1980s, as a result of the detrimental minority policies of the government, an armed struggle led by the Kurdistan Party (PKK) claimed thousands of lives in a long civil war in eastern Turkey, where a greater number of Kurds live (among them the Kurdish nationalists).

For more than two decades Turkey has tried to join the European Union in an effort to improve its economic prospects and enhance its political fortune. Turkey's application, however, has been rejected because of inadequate human rights conditions in the country. Currently, Turkey is struggling with Islamic fundamentalism, Kurdish nationalist concerns, and a significant economic crisis in which the Turkish unit of money (*Lira*) has lost much of its value. Moreover, earthquakes in 1999 had a devastating effect on the economy.

TYPICAL DAY

A typical day for a teenager in Turkey varies according to where the teenager lives, which schools she or he goes to, and what type of family she or he belongs to. Typically, most teenagers who attend schools do so in shifts so that more students can be served in the same school building. Those who attend the morning shift get up early, have their breakfast (which is usually prepared by their mothers), and go to school until noon. When they come back from school they have lunch (also usually prepared by their mother if she is a housewife). After school they spend time studying, socializing with their friends, or joining some activities in their schools or neighborhood. If the school shift is in the afternoon, they spend the afternoon at school and do their homework in the morning or evening. For teenagers in private schools, their typical day starts later in the morning and ends in the late afternoon since their schools do not have shifts.

The size and features of the town or city where a teen resides greatly affect the opportunities available. In rural areas, especially in small towns and villages, a teenager whose family engages in farming is expected to help with the farm work, even though she or he attends school. While the majority of Turkish villages have elementary schools, some have no middle schools or high schools. Where there are no such schools, teens must attend schools in the closest towns. They either reside with relatives, stay in dormitories if available, or commute by any means possible, including walking or riding a bus, depending on the distance between the two towns. Teenagers in urban areas have access to a larger number and better quality of schools and jobs.

Most of the teen population attending school in Turkey live predominantly in the western, northern, and southern regions, where there are better socioeconomic conditions. There are, however, a small percentage of teenagers from low economic levels who do not attend secondary or high schools. These teens may work full-time in order to contribute to the household income. In small towns or villages, working teens engage in farming or other agricultural activities with their elders and relatives. In cities, working teenagers either join the family business or take other jobs to earn money. Jobs are available mostly in factories or in places with

Turkish teens hanging out. Courtesy of Ali Akbar Mahdi.

apprenticeship opportunities so that teenagers can gain skills for finding better employment in the future. Due to the poor economic conditions in eastern Turkey, there are more working teenagers there than in western Turkey.

The typical day for working teenagers, in both urban or rural areas, starts in early morning and ends late in the evening. After work, these teenagers may spend their time at home watching TV, socializing with the household, or interacting with friends in the neighborhood or in coffee-houses, which are more common in small towns. In larger cities, working teenagers may spend evenings at home, at the movies, or in another locale where they can socialize with peers, such as bars.

Gender has a distinct impact on teens' social lives and determines how they go about their typical day. As do boys, girls who attend school get up early, have breakfast prepared for them by their mothers, and then go to school. However, since female teenagers have more familial and social pressures and constraints on them than do their male counterparts, they observe stricter rules during the school day. After school, girls study, do their homework, or spend time with their family, peers, or friends at home. If leaving home, female teens have to observe stricter curfew hours

Teen vendors in Turkey carry household goods for sale in baskets strapped to their backs. They walk through neighborhoods, loudly announcing their offerings, and deliver to customers at home. Courtesy of Ali Akbar Mahdi.

while also adhering to culturally and socially appropriate behaviors. Only moving away to attend a university may relieve familial pressure and give girls more freedom, though never as much as is afforded to boys. Those girls who must stay at home instead of going to school or work, merely because of their gender, sociocultural, or economic status, have more traditional daily routines than their peers. They help their mothers with chores, do errands, watch TV, and visit friends. It is more common to see them knitting and doing lace work for their hope chest, which is traditionally required for marriage.

It is a cultural tradition for the family to take responsibility for providing financial help to their children. The number of teenagers who work part-time while also attending school is low. Although in most cases the parents provide educational expenses, state schools do accept students of low economic status and provide financial support for their education. Some teenagers of low economic status work during the summer break and fund their own education. There are also some teenagers, primarily boys, who work part-time or during school breaks for spending money or

Turkish teens hanging out on Ankara's shopping strip. Courtesy of Ali Akbar Mahdi.

social experience, even though their parents financially support their education.

FAMILY LIFE

The family is a very valued component of Turkish society. Blood relatives play a significant role in the family structure even though socioeconomic changes might affect the dynamics of the family unit. Typical family life is represented in both extended and nuclear forms. The well-known extended family includes more than one parent and the siblings. The closeness of such relatives can still be seen in both rural and urban areas, but it is most often observed in rural areas where land ownership survives. Due to economic and social changes, the traditional extended family is fading away.[1] However, a tightly knit relationship within the family and kinship, coming from traditional extended family life in the past, is still observed even in relations with neighbors.

The relationship among family members varies according to the hierarchal status of each member within the family. Turkey still exhibits the pattern of male dominance in which the father has the role of financial provider and protector of the household, and the mother is homemaker and caretaker of the children. This traditional structure is modified in urban and industrialized areas, where many mothers work. Working mothers take the role of financial provider in addition to their traditional roles. In more educated liberal families where the wife works outside the home, the husband also shares the household responsibilities.

Children are at the center of the family structure. The father keeps his authoritarian role toward them while the mother meets their emotional needs. Children are expected to obey the rules of the house and to respect the parents and their elders. Despite the disciplinary nature of family relationships, the bond between parents and children is strong and characterized by love and affection. Family closeness and interaction are most readily observed at family gatherings. It is very common to see a Turkish family having meals together on a daily basis. Attending breakfast and lunch gatherings depends on who is working and who is available at that hour. Dinners are the most common gathering time for members of the family.

Children and teenagers live with their parents until they marry or go to college in a different city. It is very rare for teenagers to live on their own. The highest expectation for children is that they attend school and become successful in their studies. When a child becomes an adult, she or he either continues with education, which is generally supported by the parents, or finds a job to earn financial freedom. These accomplishments can be followed by marriage. Girls are also expected to receive a good education. For them, education is considered the "golden bracelet" that provides not only good job opportunities but also respect as educated women. In addition, this "bracelet" has priceless value in raising their children as educated mothers. Girls who do not attend college are expected to be ready for marriage. Male teens are expected to go to school or to have a job in order to provide for themselves and establish a family.

Teenagers grow up accustomed to their parents being protectors and providers. Even when they become financially independent, teens' familial relations don't change (such as staying close and maintaining respect for their parents). Therefore, parents and teenagers are more involved in each other's lives than those in Western societies.

Since most teenagers are financially and culturally dependent on their parents, only relatively few teenagers—those from predominantly rich families—may own cars or use their parents' cars. Legally, a teenager must be 18 years old to drive in Turkey. However, underage teenagers often break the driving rules. Generally speaking, cars are not affordable for families of lower and middle incomes.

At age 18, Turkish teenagers may vote. They also gain the legal right to drink. Yet they are not likely to drink or smoke in front of their parents, as cultural norms deem this disrespectful. Usually they go to bars or gather in friends' homes to drink or smoke.

In recent years, teenagers' lives have been affected by trends in Western societies, especially in clothing, eating habits, and life choices. Although teenagers are becoming more Westernized, they still maintain some distinctive Turkish traditions and values.

TRADITIONAL AND NONTRADITIONAL FOOD

Eating is a communal ceremony in Turkish culture and tradition. The origins of Turkish cuisine, along with its associated traditional and ritual customs, come from the East and the Mediterranean. Turkish people often have three meals a day. Breakfast includes tea, feta cheese, olives, bread, and jam. Both lunches and dinners have three basic courses. The main course usually has more than one dish, which is preceded by cold and hot appetizers and followed by desserts, served before Turkish coffee or tea. Setting the table is as important as cooking a variety of dishes. Cooking is traditionally assigned to women. Typically, daughters help the mother in cooking and setting the table, whereas sons share the shopping with the father.

Ceremonial cooking and eating is very important, especially during religious holidays called *bayrams* (meaning "festivities"). Weddings, circumcision ceremonies, and big gatherings are still accompanied by feasts. On these occasions, women help each other in cooking and serving, especially in rural areas. Mutual hospitality is very important, and relations between hosts and guests are reciprocal.

Daily homemade meals are prepared with the fresh fruits, vegetables, meats, and dairy products available in Turkish markets. Most popular traditional Turkish foods are variations of meat such as *doner* (broiled lamb), *kebab* (various forms of grilled meat), *tavuk* (grilled chicken), and *iskender* (another variety of minced lamb with tomato, chili sauce, and yogurt) and of vegetable-based foods such as *musakka* (summer dish common with eggplant or cauliflower), *dolma* (rice-stuffed pepper, eggplant or zucchini), and *sarma* (rice-stuffed grape or white cabbage leaves). Every region has unique specialties. Even though Westernization has increased the number of fast-food chains like Pizza Hut, McDonald's, and Wendy's, traditional food is still popular even among the younger generation. One can also find other international restaurants such as Chinese, Indian, Mexican, and Thai in the larger cities. Although eating out frequently as a family is

Turkish teen in traditional costume selling a Turkish dish on the street. Courtesy of Ali Akbar Mahdi.

less common in Turkey for economic reasons, fast-food places, which are more affordable than family restaurants, are quick lunch-break stops for working people. In fact, for many teenagers, traditional places such as old-style restaurants and coffeehouses are no longer in vogue. Traditional dinnertime routines have persisted, and teenagers continue to partake of family dinnertime gatherings and activities.

SCHOOLING

Primary and middle school education is compulsory and free. Primary education is followed by secondary education (3 years minimum), equivalent to general high schools, vocational, and technical high schools. Except for general high schools and some private schools, other special schools, which are based on intensive language, science, or technical education, require entrance exams. There are also special schools for handicapped students as well as for gifted students. The Ministry of National Education is responsible for teachers and the curriculum in all schools, universities, technical and vocational schools, and training centers. Private schools are often free to design their own programs and choose books and materials in consultation with the Ministry.

Students interested in pursuing their education beyond high school have to take a nationally organized exam. The score from this exam, along with the high school grade point average, determines students' admission and disciplinary preferences. Public universities are inexpensive enough that most families can afford them. However, the cost of living in a distant city is a financial burden for most middle-class families. Financial support from the government is available for students in need. Private universities also provide scholarships for students with high scores.

Assessment in schools is based mostly on exams. Private schools are more updated in terms of facilities; students have to pay high tuition and fees. Teachers tend to lecture more than assign hands-on activities or group projects. Memorization is very common, as exams are the main keys to the following academic year or upcoming schools. Students have a great deal of homework, especially in the last year of high school when they prepare for the university entrance exam. Textbooks are standardized for all schools and are approved by the government. Dropping out from primary and secondary schools is rare since students are expected to repeat the year or the courses they fail. On average, there are more boys in schools than girls. However, the gap between female and male education is decreasing.

The number of students who attend public schools is much higher than those in private schools. Typically, parents who can afford private school education send their children there. Most students from middle-class and lower socioeconomic backgrounds attend public schools. There are a limited number of government-supported boarding schools, which accommodate children from low economic backgrounds.

As is common for a secular country, co-education is applied in most public schools except for some vocational schools like nursing. Extracurricular activities in schools are practiced in mixed groups. Public schools require a standard uniform, of which only style and colors change from school to school, sometimes from one region to another. Schools are designed according to the facilities needed, such as computer labs, school libraries, sports facilities, and cafeterias. In poor regions, schools lack many facilities—sometimes even heating systems. Teens walk around or do some activities in the front or back yard of the school in their break in between classes. Senior high school students focus more on their studies than do underclassmen and often attend private institutions designed for university entrance exam studies. Those students who can afford tutoring do so to help prepare for their upcoming exams. As demands for higher education increase by the young population, exams become a greater barrier since the existing schools have a limited capacity. This eventually causes more pressure on the young population, whose future opportunities and welfare depend on having formal educational degrees.

The role of teachers is very important in young people's academic lives since teachers are highly respected in Turkish society. Parents trust teachers' suggestions for their child's school choices and decisions. Parents without an educational background tend to give teachers the primary voice in their child's educational choices. In general, Turkish parents do not get as involved as their American counterparts do in educational activities at school. There has been an increased effort by the government to inform parents about education and to encourage their involvement in school activities.

SOCIAL LIFE

The social life of Turkish teens reflects basic norms and values as well as Western principles. What is considered normal in Turkish culture varies greatly from what is accepted in Western societies. For example, American culture highly values individualism, whereas Turkish culture emphasizes group affiliation in family,[2] school, and work. Thus, social interactions among Turkish teens are more intense and involved. Establishing friendships and socializing among teens are a necessary part of their lives.

Schools and neighborhoods are popular places for teens to socialize with their peers. Rich teens are generally more selective in their interactions with peers than the teens from lower economic classes. Socioeconomic status generally determines not only the social groups but also the different lifestyles among teenagers.

Since Turkish culture promotes socialization among young people, dating usually begins between couples already familiar with each other. It is still not common for someone to ask out a person of the opposite sex directly without having some sort of social connection. Open dating among teens depends on how liberal the parents are and to what extent these parents apply their own cultural values and practices to their children. Although dating is becoming more accepted, such activities, even in urban areas, are often monitored by parents and guarded by various social restrictions far more than one can find in the United States. For teens living in traditional rural areas, where more familial and societal pressure is observed, liberal dating is almost impossible.

When romantic relationships do develop between teens, they are taken very seriously in Turkish culture. Casual relationships, if they occur at all, are more common among teens but usually do not continue until other social obligations are met. Since getting a university degree, completing military service for males, and then finding a job have become important prerequisites for a successful life, no serious relationship is expected to develop beforehand. When relationships develop between young people after they have for the most part met these expectations, it is generally expected that relationships will end in marriage.

Many Turkish marriages still function around traditional and cultural values. One such tradition is that the father of the family decides who his son or daughter marries. The son's family finds an appropriate bride who fulfills the socially assigned roles of proper woman and mother for their sons. They ask the father for the bride's hand. The father decides if the bridegroom and his family are suitable for his daughter. These pre-arranged and family-initiated marriages generally take place in rural areas where dating is culturally and traditionally restricted. In urban areas, it is mostly the couples that decide on marriages. In cities, acquiring education, fulfilling military service, and selecting one's profession often delay marriages. Marriage is not legal for women before the age of 15 and for men before the age of 17 unless the parents' consent is given.

Premarital sex is still taboo in Turkey and is strongly discouraged, especially for women. Traditionally, young women are expected to be virgins at the time of their marriage. This is still a dominant cultural value in rural areas; but in large cities, premarital sex and living together before marriage do occur to a limited extent.

These societal restrictions stemming from cultural, traditional, and religious norms also determine acceptable attitudes and behaviors for teens. Since family ties are very strong and teens are dependent on their families in almost every way, families and community monitor teens' lives closely. However, while family continues to hold on to traditional values, teens are more and more influenced by the rapid social, economic, and cultural changes and tend to show more adaptations to Western lifestyles. This creates a gap between old and young in the family, especially in big cities.

Modern Turkish teens. Courtesy of Ali Akbar Mahdi.

In no other facet of life is this gap more observable than in clothing, through which teens continue resisting the traditional norms. The style of dress among Turkish people varies. People who work tend to wear formal clothing. Women following religious and cultural traditions cover their heads and prefer modest clothing. Young people tend to follow new trends and fashions. They often dress casually, wearing jeans and T-shirts. Although mini-skirts or more sexy outfits are not morally and culturally acceptable, they are becoming popular among upper- and upper-middle-class girls.

RECREATION

Since Turkish youth constitutes a significant percentage of the population, the government provides them with various services through different ministries and private institutions. The government has at least fourteen ministries involved in education, health, employment, cultural activities, leisure time, and youth programs. The General Directorate of

Youth and Sports has branches in every province, plans most activities for youth, and manages youth camps, youth centers, and tours for youth through international organizations. The provincial branches decide the quantity and quality of their activities based on their geographical concerns, local needs, and interests of youth in their region. For example, in the coastal areas, activities are centered on swimming, scuba diving, and snorkeling. In addition, there are various centers and clubs within schools, universities, and dormitories. Teenagers are often encouraged to participate in these clubs. There are also some private organizations within the ministry engaged in similar activities.

Sports are very popular in Turkey, especially with the young population. Among basketball, horseback riding, bicycling, boxing, soccer, billiards, bridge, gymnastics, mountaineering, fencing, wrestling, handball, judo, tennis, volleyball, swimming, and sailing, soccer is the favorite and the most common for teenagers.[3] Galatasaray, Besiktas, and Fenerbahce are the three most famous soccer teams in Turkey. Schools have soccer teams as well. Even every provincial district has its own soccer team. Young people have their own favorite teams and follow their favorite heroes on those teams. They do not miss soccer games on TV and regularly follow sports news. Since not all provinces or districts have recreational facilities, many teens play sports in their neighborhood or even in areas around their apartment complexes.

Schools also provide extracurricular activities such as games, tournaments, and clubs. Games and tournaments are organized among school teams. Sports teams are generally gender-specific. Some teams may consist of both genders. Girls can engage in nearly any sports activities, even soccer, as long as their parents do not object. Generally speaking, girls have more restrictions in their choices due to cultural and religious values. More often, girls spend their time at peers' homes, studying together, walking around the neighborhood, or going shopping. Many girls choose to be in clubs such as chess, folk dance, and theater, as do some boys. Folk dancing is popular, and many schools have folk dance groups representing different regions of the country.

Apart from school-organized sports and other activities, some teenagers prefer exercising for fun and to keep fit. Although exercise centers are not affordable for middle- or lower-class families, it is now becoming more common to see joggers on the street and people in workout clubs. Yet, since schooling is the highest priority for most families, there are some parents who see sports as too time consuming and require their children to focus on their studies instead.

Turkish teens strolling the Bosporus Strait in Istanbul. Courtesy of Ali Akbar Mahdi.

ENTERTAINMENT

There are numerous types of entertainment for teenagers in Turkey. A teen's preference for entertainment varies according to the culture, the family, and the setting in which he or she is raised. In family-based entertainment, teenagers join in outdoor picnics, barbecues at neighbors' homes, and visits to relatives. Girls attend these activities more than boys do. Boys have more liberty in saying "no" to their parents and making their own choices. Yet, nowadays both girls and boys are demanding more freedom to make their own plans.

Going to movies is popular among the young population. Smaller communities usually do not have decent movie theaters. Reading is a less preferred activity since teenagers are so pressured with school assignments that extra reading appeals less to them. Instead, teens prefer going to the movies or staying home and surfing the TV channels.

Watching television is a popular pastime among teens. Boys generally enjoy sporting events, and girls are interested in movies or drama series. There are a number of TV channels. Music channels are a favorite for both boys and girls. There are many types of music in Turkey: traditional folk opera, classical, mystical, arabesque, and pop. Most teenagers enjoy listening to the more trendy pop music and follow the music charts. Foreign music is also popular among teenagers. The older generation generally listens to traditional folk music, whereas teenagers prefer popular music and modern-style folk music. Many teenagers, especially in schools and recreation centers, are interested in playing musical instruments as a hobby and sometimes pursue it as a profession. Many participate in local chorus groups that sing Turkish classical or folk music. Others prefer being part of folk dance ensembles.

Dancing and Western-style dance clubs are common in big cities. In rural areas traditional dancing takes place at weddings—although it is not common to see boys dancing with girls, as it is considered inappropriate. In villages, men and women have different activities at weddings. Women get together at the bride's house and have a "henna party" (a party during which fingertips, palms and toes are tinged with henna), whereas men get together either in the groom's house or at the village coffeehouse. Both teens and adults enjoy these traditional events, even though young people may prefer louder music and more modernized rituals. In urban areas, it is common to see boys dancing and mingling with girls. In large cities, it is easier for boys and girls to escape family monitoring and spend time in discos and clubs. Even though the legal age for attending discos is 18, most are full of teenagers under that age. Drug use is very rare in rural areas, but the popularity of drugs is increasing among teenagers in urban areas, perhaps due to more problems in the family or in school lives or simply emulating what is perceived as a Western lifestyle. Smoking is very popular among young people. They generally start smoking by imitating their elders but mostly in order to be accepted within their circle of friends.

Coffeehouses are very popular as gathering places for adults and are also frequented by teenagers. They are places for men to get together and play cards and games, listen to music, smoke, watch TV, and converse with each other. Some young teenagers end up working in these coffeehouses, especially in rural areas and small towns. Some teenagers enjoy such establishments when there is no alternative setting for them to socialize with their peers.

Recently, Internet cafés have been replacing traditional cafés as places of choice for the young generation in urban areas. Boys especially like surfing the Internet and playing computer games. E-mail communication among teenagers is very popular. A small number of mostly private high schools provide Internet and e-mail access for their students. The other popular communication tool among teenagers is the cellular phone.

Teenagers spend hours talking on the phone and often have arguments with their parents, who carry the financial responsibility.

RELIGIOUS PRACTICES AND CULTURAL CEREMONIES

The official religion in Turkey is Islam. While the Turkish government is secularist, people are allowed to practice the religion of their choice. However, religious activities that threaten the integrity or security of the state are not permitted. The Department of Religious Affairs is responsible for the organization of religious affairs as well as religious education in the country.

Although most Turkish people believe in Islam, not all of them practice Islamic rules and rituals. For some, these rules are considered inconvenient in this modern age. Some practice these rules more liberally, whereas others follow them strictly. Since the secularist system in Turkey inspires a modern way of living, laws do not require veiling and practicing of Islamic rules. Work and school time is not adjusted according to prayers. Covering for women and girls is not allowed at the workplace and at schools. However, Islamic values are still very much intertwined with Turkish culture and influence male-female relationships.

In comparison to other age groups, teens show less interest in religious values and practices, even though some teenagers are very religious and observe Islamic norms devotedly. Many do not follow religious rules in every situation and are prone to interpret Islamic rules very liberally. Their choice of dress, places they frequent, and circle of friends reflect the extent to which their lifestyle adheres to religious-based values.

Teens are exposed to religious principles and teachings in elementary and secondary state schools. The religious courses are based mostly on ethical values and moral teachings as interpreted and taught within the Islamic traditions and belief systems. In order for the state-mandated elementary programs to succeed in serving a wide range of students, the Ministry of Education recently restructured the school system by combining elementary and middle schools and by making attendance compulsory. This restructuring confined religious state schools to being only high schools, which includes grades 10 to 13. In addition to state schools, there are other religion classes in the provinces as well as some private religious schools. In these private schools, students are exposed to strict Islamic rules and practices and are required to learn to read from the Quran, the holy book of Islam, in Arabic.

Some rituals of Islam have been established in the culture not only as a function of religion but also as social norms. Among these, fasting during the month of Ramadan is the most widely observed. Preparing special foods and inviting relatives over for dinner are very popular in this month. A special festivity called Ramadan Feast, Eid al-Fitr, or Sweet Feast, marks the end of Ramadan. This three-day holiday gives people a chance to visit elders, join in gatherings with families, and enjoy socializing with neighbors and friends. The other religious festivity is the Sacrifice Feast, Eid al-Adha, the purpose of which is to sacrifice sheep and give the meat and other food to the poor. This four-day holiday is also widely observed. These are not only religious but also national holidays. Most teenagers follow these traditions by spending holidays with parents, relatives, and friends, much like Americans do at Thanksgiving or Christmas.

Another important ritual in a Turkish boy's life is the circumcision ceremony. This very important passage to adulthood for boys is performed up to the age of 12. The occasion is celebrated with a family feast at which relatives, friends, and neighbors honor the boy for his passage to adulthood by offering him gifts and money. The newer generation of parents seems to prefer circumcision without any rituals, in most cases at the hospital after the baby boy is born. Overall, the new generation prefers limited rituals and simpler practices.

CONCLUSION

Turkish teens form their identities in the frame of the culture, traditions, and values of their country by embracing varying worldviews, lifestyles, and habits. In contrast to other age groups, however, teens are more open to new lifestyles and experiences. The most common challenge Turkish teens experience is trying to establish a balance in their choice of lifestyle. In attempting to bridge tradition and modernity, teens often experience conflict with their elders. To a certain extent, they hold on to old beliefs, traditions, and values while also being bombarded with new technology, Westernization, and changing social norms.

Parents and society view teens as the generation in most need of guidance since they may not fulfill the societal and cultural expectation of responsible and acceptable behaviors. Yet, young people in Turkey need awareness and support on the part of society to keep up with the drastic changes in this modern world. They are increasingly aware of life's struggles while attempting to achieve successful futures. They also learn that in this technology-based modern world there is more competition in education than ever, burdened by exams and followed by intensive job hunting.

As long as the world remains a dynamic place and globalization continues, Turkish teenagers will continue experiencing new perspectives and
values that will enrich their own life as well as their country.

NOTES

1. Mubeccel, Kiray, ed., *Structural Change in Turkish Society* (Bloomington, IN:
Indiana University, Department of Turkish Studies, 1991).

2. Hasan Dindi, Maija Gazur, Wayne M. Gazur, and Aysen Kirikkopru-Dindi.
Turkish Culture for Americans (Boulder, CO: International Concepts, 1989).

3. Office of the Prime Minister, Directorate General of Press and Information.
Turkey, published by the Office of the Prime Minister (Ankara, Turkey: 1993).

RESOURCE GUIDE

Books and Articles

Balim-Harding, Cigdem (Ed.) *Turkey, political, social, and economic challenges in
the 1990s,* Leiden and New York: E. J. Brill, 1995.

Bozdogan, Sibel, and Reset Kasaba, eds. *Rethinking Modernity and National Identity
in Turkey.* Seattle: Washington University of Washington Press, 1997.

Carpenter-Yaman, Carol E., and Thomas Poffenberger. "Family-Size Attitude of
Rural Turkish Youths." *International Family Planning Perspectives* 7, no. 3
(1981): 118–121.

Dindi, Hasan, Maija Gazur, Wayne M. Gazur, and Aysen Kirikkopru-Dindi. *Turkish Culture for Americans.* Boulder, CO: International Concepts, 1989.

Faroqhi, Suraiya. *Subjects of the Sultan: Culture and Daily Life in the Ottoman
Empire.* London: I. B. Tauris, 2000.

Gursoy, Akile. "Child Mortality and the Changing Discourse on Childhood in
Turkey." In *Children in the Moslem Middle East,* edited by Elizabeth W. Fernea, 199–222. Austin: University of Texas Press, 1995.

Jung, Dietrich, and Wolfango Piccoli. *Turkey at the Crossroads.* New York: Palgrave, 2001.

Kagitcibasi, Cigdem. *Sex Roles, Family and Community in Turkey.* Bloomington,
IN: *Indiana University Turkish Studies* (1982).

Lewis, Bernard. *The Emergence of Modern Turkey.* London: Oxford University
Press, 2001.

Orga, Irfan. *Portrait of a Turkish Family.* New York: Hippocrene Books, 1989.

Pope, Nicole, and Hugh Pope. *Turkey Unveiled: A History of Modern Turkey.*
Woodstock, N.Y.: Overlook Press, 2000.

Rasuly-Paleczek, Gabriele. *Turkish Families in Transition.* New York: Peter Lang
Publishing, 1996.

Vergin, Nur. "Social Change and the Family in Turkey," *Current Anthropology* 26,
no. 5 (1985): 571–574.

White, Jenny B. "An Unmarried Girl and a Grinding Stone: A Turkish Girl's Childhood in the City." In *Children in the Moslem Middle East*, edited by Elizabeth W. Fernea, 257–268. Austin: University of Texas Press, 1995.

Fiction

Kemal, Yasar. *Memed My Hawk*. London: Harvill Press, 1997.
———. *The Sea-Crossed Fisherman*. New York: Braziller, 1985.
———. *The Wind from the Plain*. London: Harvill Press, 1996.
Pamuk, Orhan. *My Name Is Red*. New York: Knopf, 2001.
———. *The White Castle: A Novel*. New York: Braziller, 1991.
Walker, Barbara K. *A Treasury of Turkish Folktales for Children*. Hamden, Conn: Linnet Books, 1988.

Web Sites

www.turkiye.org
Arts, resources, media.
www.byegm.gov.tr
Recent Turkish news as well as its press, government, constitutional law.
www.mfa.gov.tr
General information about Turkish foreign policy, recent news, improved relations between United States and Turkey.
www.genckamp.org
Information about international youth camps.
www.gsm-youth.org
Information about GSM-Youth Services Center, its main objectives, main activity areas, international memberships.
www.genctur.com
Information about GENCTUR, one of the leading youth organizations in Turkey with numerous tours and camps.

Pen Pal/Chat

http://www.icep.org.tr/english/penpal.htm

Chapter 11

UNITED ARAB EMIRATES

Judith Caesar and Fatima Badry

INTRODUCTION

The United Arab Emirates (UAE), at the southern tip of the Persian Gulf, is a group of small sheikdoms, each governed by its own ruling family but under the control of the central government. The UAE is at peace with its neighbors, and the Emirati government is stable. Because the Emirati population is small, many Emirati families know or at least know of one another, and many have access to the ruling families. These ruling families are often well liked; some Emiratis even display pictures of their favorite sheikh in the back windows of their cars. In addition, the Emiratis are extremely tolerant of the many ethnic and religious groups living in the UAE. Actually, Emiratis constitute only about 20 percent of the country's population. The rest are guest workers from India and Pakistan (about 50%) and from other Arab countries, Iran, the Far East, Europe, and North America. While Westerners comprise a relatively small proportion of the foreign workforce, the Western influence is disproportionately large. The majority of people living in the Emirates are Muslim, but some foreign workers are Christian or Hindu. All are free to follow their religions; in fact, there are churches in all major Emirati cities, and the newspapers are full of accounts of the celebration of Hindu holidays such as Diwali.

Before 1971, the UAE was called the Trucial States because of the treaties, signed in the early 19th century, that put the country under indirect British rule. Before that time, the Emirates and Oman had been part of a maritime trading network with India and Iran. Under British control, the Emirates were relatively poor, with most of the population making

their living through fishing, pearling, and agriculture. There was no public school system. During this time many Indians emigrated to the Emirates to work with the British administration and to re-establish trade
with India. In the 1960s, when oil was discovered, the Emirates began to
develop, and laborers were imported from India to work in the construction boom.

After independence, the Emirati government began to exploit its oil
deposits and to use the money for the benefit of its citizens, building
schools and hospitals, lending money to Emirati citizens who wished to
start businesses, and providing subsidies for Emirati citizens who did not
have the education or skills to work in the new economy. The Emirati
government encouraged investment and diversification of the economy,
which in turn led to the importation of more guest workers from around
the world to meet the UAE's labor needs. The result of these efforts is that
within the last 30 years the UAE has become a very modern country with
high-rise office buildings, luxurious homes, good roads over which people
travel in high-powered cars and SUVs, and shopping malls featuring
goods from Asia, Europe, and North America. The level of prosperity
allows people to buy computers, cell phones, satellite dishes—all the latest technology. At first glance, the United Arab Emirates looks a great
deal like the United States.

This impression changes as soon as you begin to look at how people are
dressed, which in turn shows the ways in which the UAE blends the modern and the traditional. Most Emirati men wear the traditional long loose
white robe (kandoora, sometimes called a dishdash) and a turban. However,
while teenage boys also usually wear the kandoora, many replace the traditional headgear with baseball caps, worn backwards. The women usually wear a long black cloak (the abayah) in public and cover their hair
with a black scarf. Some of the older, more traditional women also wear a
mask that covers the upper part of the face (the burqa). Underneath their
abayahs, however, Emirati girls may very well be wearing the latest
French, Italian, or American fashions. For other nationalities, some wear
Western clothes, some wear their national dress, particularly the Indian
salwar kamees (Indian loose-flowing shirts), and some combine Western
dress with Islamic standards of modesty. It is not unusual to see a girl in
designer jeans and an Islamic headscarf. People here—especially teens—
seem to pick and choose what they like from Western and Arab cultures.

On the whole, life in the Emirates is not terribly difficult for teenagers,
although, as in any country, there are some problems. The Emiratis are
usually quite well off, and teenagers from other nationalities are certainly
not poor, because their parents must earn a certain minimum income to

bring their families with them. The non-Emirati teenagers growing up in the Emirates are middle class. (The poor in the Emirates are the laborers and servants from Asia and Africa who do not earn enough to bring their families.) The Emirates also has a very low rate of violent street crime, so young people do not have to worry about being mugged or assaulted. There is some petty theft—teens stealing other teens' pocket money and valuables—and burglary, and some UAE teens find access to illegal drugs. The worst problem UAE teens face, however, is the UAE's very high rate of traffic accidents. Young Emirati men are the most frequent victims. The legal driving age in the Emirates is 18, but younger teens often ride with friends or slightly older relatives who have just gotten driver's licenses— and fast new cars. Many Emirati teenagers have had a family member, friend, or classmate killed in a traffic accident.

One more factor has a great influence on life in the Emirates: the weather. From the beginning of May until the end of September, the daytime temperature is between 100 and 130 degrees F. with humidity from the Gulf adding to the misery. At night, it is about 10 or 15 degrees cooler, which means that it is still hot. This makes outdoor activities virtually impossible during the daytime in the summer. Fortunately, homes and public places are air-conditioned. In the winter, the temperature remains in the 70s and 80s during the day, with nighttime temperature sometimes a bit chilly. In short, winters in the Emirates are like summers in Europe and northern North America. It is during the winter months that teens in the Emirates can enjoy outdoor activities. Swimming, boating, picnicking (at the beach, in the desert, or in public parks), and driving SUVs over the sand dunes (wadi-bashing) are all popular with teens.

TYPICAL DAY

The typical day for a teenager in the Emirates varies somewhat according to nationality and area of the country. Almost all teens in the Emirates go to school, either public or private, and these schools generally open at around nine in the morning. There, however, the similarity ends.

In the coastal cities of Dubai, Sharjah, and Abu Dhabi, going to school means a fight with rush-hour traffic, whether teens are driven to school or ride on a bus. In the less populated inland towns, getting to school is a lot easier, and boys in particular might walk to school if it is nearby and the weather is cool enough.

Between one and three o'clock, schools close and the students go home, usually to eat a large afternoon meal with their families. After lunch, many people nap. This is especially true in the summer months, when even the briefest period outside is exhausting. Stores often close around two and open again at four or five. When naptime is over, it is time to start on homework, which schools give in abundance. Homework and relaxing with friends and family take up the remainder of the day. Teenagers watch television and videos, chat with their friends on the phone, or go out. As with American teenagers, shopping malls are favorite hangouts, particularly in cities like Dubai. The evening meal is usually fairly late—sometime between eight and ten. Teenagers, and even small children, often stay up quite late, because the cooler temperature after sundown makes it so much more pleasant to be out-of-doors.

Very few teenagers in the Emirates work outside the home, for various reasons. For one thing, there is no financial need, and many Emiratis and other Arabs would consider the kinds of unskilled work that teenagers in other countries do to be demeaning. The person behind the counter at a fast-food restaurant is likely to be a young Asian adult, not a local teenager. In fact, some Arab teenagers think that the fact that middle-class American teenagers take these kinds of jobs means that their parents don't really care about them or are very stingy. In the Emirates, teens get their spending money from parents or other relatives. Of course, this also makes teens more dependent on their families and gives their parents more control over their activities.

Most Emirati families have servants, because the salaries for foreign housemaids are so low (the equivalent of $300 or $400 a month) that even families who live on government subsidies can afford at least one maid. Wealthier families might employ several housemaids, cooks, drivers, and nannies to look after smaller children as well. These domestic workers have separate quarters within the family home and usually work on two-year contracts, although some stay longer. Many young Emiratis have been cared for by a series of housemaids and nannies while they were growing up. One controversy in Emirati society is whether or not servants have too much of a role in raising children, and some young Emirati women avow that they will raise their own children themselves.

Because Emirati families tend to be large, having servants doesn't necessarily free teens from household responsibilities. In wealthier families, servants might do all the work, but in other households, girls might help their mothers out with cooking and with directing the housework. Boys are not be expected to help out around the house. However, both boys and girls usually spend some time with younger brothers and sisters, even if it is just keeping the children entertained.

Fewer non-nationals have servants, and those who do usually have fewer of them than the Emiratis. Girls might be expected to help their mothers. Again, girls are much more likely than boys to be expected to help with the housework. However, non-nationals are also more likely to live in apartments rather than the large villas Emiratis prefer, so that there would be less work to do. In addition, they would be likely to see it as more important that a girl spend time on her schoolwork than on house-work, although this varies from one family to another.

Non-national boys and girls feel pressure from their parents to do well in school. Unlike the Emiratis, who are guaranteed a job when they grad-uate from high school (usually with the government), non-national boys must find jobs when they finish high school or college if they wish to stay in the Emirates. (Non-national girls can continue to live with their par-ents.) The kinds of jobs a high school graduate can get depend at least partly on how well he or she does in school. Among non-Emirati Arabs, Pakistanis, and Indians, education is considered important for girls as well as boys. Even if a young woman doesn't work after she marries, an edu-cation is considered an asset.

FAMILY LIFE

In family life, there are the biggest differences between nationals and non-nationals. Emiratis sometimes live in extended families. They would have an extremely large house, a mansion by Western standards, or a com-pound containing several houses, often surrounded by a privacy wall. Within these areas, several generations of the same family live—grand-parents, parents, brothers and sisters, aunts, uncles, and cousins. Families not living together visit one another often—at least once a week. Emirati teens almost always know their aunts, uncles, and cousins extremely well and socialize with their cousins as much as with their classmates. For many Emiratis, "distant relative" is a contradiction in terms.

Non-nationals are much more likely to live in nuclear families, since members of the extended family might not live in the Emirates or might work for another employer in another city. However, members of the extended family stay in touch with one another. Family members who live in the same city visit each other often. If a teenager's grandparents, aunts, and uncles live in another country, the family would likely visit them and other relatives at least once a year, often for a visit of several weeks.

Family levels of education also differ between Emiratis and non-nationals. Because mass public schooling did not begin in the Emirates until the 1970s, the Emirati family often reflects different educational lev-els. Unless the family has been wealthy for a long time, the grandparents are likely to have had very little formal schooling. Parents born in the

1950s and 1960s have the basic educational skills for everyday life, but little beyond that, unless they went to a university in another country. Today there are schools in every neighborhood and many public universities, so that the generation of Emiratis currently in high school has far greater educational opportunities than any previous generation. If this creates conflict, it is something Emirati teens do not talk about with outsiders. In fact, many say that although their parents themselves are not well educated, the family values education and wants them to take advantage of the free university education that the Emirati government provides. The teens whose parents come from other countries are in a different position. Many of these parents are college graduates or have had some professional training beyond high school. This makes things a little easier for the non-nationals, because their parents can help them with homework and tell them what to expect when they go to college.

The other generational split among Emiratis is that most teens' grandparents grew up poor and remember when the UAE was a simple and underdeveloped country. Even in the 1960s and 1970s, the Emirates had dirt roads, old houses, and few places of entertainment. Today's teens, however, are growing up rich—often very rich, with every material thing they want and every form of entertainment available, including trips to other countries. Some teens say families were closer in the old days because the whole family worked together, whereas now everyone has his or her own world of work, or school, or taking care of the home. Others say that families are still close and all that has changed is that they have more conveniences.

Certainly, the new wealth and social changes have given girls greater opportunities than their mothers and grandmothers had. Currently, most Emirati women do not work outside the home, although there are educated Emirati women who hold important positions. *Educated* is a key word here, because Emirati girls and women want careers, not just jobs. After all, they usually do not need the money to support themselves, since this is considered to be the responsibility of their families. In addition, since Emirati women often have large families, they are kept busy at home. Women who work outside the home tend to do so for the sense of independence and professional accomplishment that working can give. However, although their mothers do not work outside the home, many young Emirati women are now attending universities and plan to work after they graduate.

There is one important difference between family life in the Emirates and in America. Both Emirati and non-national parents have more control over their children's lives than in the United States. In the Emirates and throughout many traditional societies, an individual is considered a representative of his or her family, and every family member's behavior reflects on the reputation of the family as a whole. This is particularly true of the conduct of young girls. If a girl has a bad reputation, it damages her whole family, not just her own life. For this reason, girls in particular tend to be more closely supervised. This does not mean they never have any fun. However, it usually means that girls spend more of their time with other girls than with boys.

TRADITIONAL AND NONTRADITIONAL FOOD

The traditional foods in the Emirates are rice, fish, lamb, and fresh fruits and vegetables, with Arabic bread on the side and dates as the traditional sweet. The Persian Gulf yields a plentiful supply of seafood, rice has long been imported from India, and the northern Emirates and oasis areas can take advantage of the year-round growing season. However, today, much of the fresh produce is imported from around the world; people buy it in supermarkets or in outdoor fruit and vegetable markets. The latter are somewhat more popular, because the produce is fresher. This is also the traditional way to shop, and many people feel more comfortable with being able to talk to the man who is selling them the produce. Because Emiratis have large families and entertain often, they tend to buy in bulk—cases of fresh fruit, big boxes of vegetables. The fish markets are also popular, open-air markets along the dockside where fishermen display the catch of the day. And many people prefer to buy both bread and pastries from a bakery.

Because there has long been an Indian influence in the Emirates, Emiriti food tends to combine Indian and Arabic cuisines, and the Indians living in the Emirates have no problem finding the ingredients for Indian dishes. Indian-style spices are available in bulk both in the supermarkets and in special open-air spice markets. Emirati food is less spicy than Indian food but is far from bland.

The menu differs according to nationality, with each group usually preparing the traditional foods of its own culture. Except for eating more fish and being somewhat more influenced by Indian tastes, Emiratis eat the same sorts of dishes as other Arabs. Breakfast is often Arabic bread and cheese, tea, and yogurt. For lunch, the main meal, they eat hummus, (puree of chickpeas, *tahina*, lemon, and garlic) parsley and bulgur salad (*tabool*), a kind of dip made from *hummus* and eggplant (*mootabol*, also called *baba ghanoush*), and vegetables like squash or grape leaves stuffed with rice, and grilled meat or fish. People usually end a meal with Arabic coffee, made with unroasted coffee beans, or tea flavored with cardamom.

Dinner, served later in the evening, is lighter; in the winter months when the weather is good, it might be cooked and served outdoors. Most people living in the Emirates are fond of picnics and cookouts, but people generally picnic after dark, not during the day. Public parks, open until ten, provide grills for picnickers from all levels of society.

Traditionally, Emiratis sat on the floor to eat, with the food placed on a low portable table, and ate with their hands. Many families still do this when they do not have guests. This is not as messy as it sounds. People use flat Arabic bread to pick up pieces of food from central platters and wash their hands before and after the meal. However, most non-Gulf Arabs eat at tables, with silverware, and some young Emiratis say they too prefer this to the traditional way of eating. Fast food is plentiful in the Emirates. Every town has stands selling an Arabic sandwich somewhat like a gyro, (*shawarma*), only made with thinner bread. American fast-food chains like McDonald's and Kentucky Fried Chicken are everywhere in the Emirates, especially in the cities, and pizza is as popular with teenagers here as it is in the United States. Also popular is a kind of Arabic pizza called *zaatar*—pizza crust sprinkled with olive oil, sesame seeds, and thyme. Coffee shops selling pastries are a favorite place for teenagers to meet. But fast food is usually a snack, not a replacement for a meal. Usually, families eat their meals at home.

SCHOOLING

Since independence, the UAE has emphasized education and developed an extensive public school system. In the last 30 years, literacy has dramatically increased in the Emirates. In addition, unlike some countries in the Gulf, the UAE has encouraged the education of women. In fact, girls outnumber boys in school, and while the literacy rate for males in the UAE is 83 percent, it is 89 percent among females.[1] Education is free in the Emirates, not only through high school but through university as well. In addition, those who choose to go to private or foreign universities get scholarships to complete their studies.

Most Emiratis go to the government schools, as do non-Emirati Arabs, for whom education is also free. However, non-Muslims and non-native speakers of Arabic seldom attend these schools, although the schools are open to all, both because of the language of instruction, Arabic, and the fact that religious study, which includes memorization of the Quran, the Islamic holy book, is part of the curriculum.

The government schools are strict, and all follow the same rules. At government schools, students wear uniforms. At the end of each term, they have to pass a standardized exam to go to the next level. The Ministry of Education determines the curriculum, which is the same in all government schools throughout the country. In addition to religious instruction, the curriculum includes Arabic, science, math, social studies, and English as a second language. Unfortunately, there are few after-school and extracurricular activities at the government schools; instead, students are expected to spend their after-school time memorizing lessons, since government schools in particular emphasize rote learning. Often, Emirati parents hire tutors to help their children with their schoolwork, so that the work does not stop when the students come home.

Private schools are different from the government schools, and there are several types, although they vary more according to the nationalities they serve than their educational philosophy. The advantage of the private schools is that they provide better instruction in foreign languages such as English. Arab students, both local and non-Emirati, attend bilingual Arabic/English schools, which introduce English in first grade, whereas government schools do not begin English until a year later and teach it as a foreign language rather than using it as one of the languages of instruction. This gives the private school students a great advantage because English is the language of instruction in many of the programs at Emirati universities.

Language is also the reason that many Indians and Pakistanis attend private schools. Students from the subcontinent would find it difficult to attend government schools, since few of them are fluent enough in Arabic in the first place. In addition, the middle-class Indians and Pakistanis who can bring their families with them often speak fluent English and want their children to have the same skill. In the Indian schools, English is the language of instruction. Although some of these schools also teach subcontinental languages such as Urdu and Hindi, many Indian students know English as their first language and speak their parents' language only when they go back to India or Pakistan to visit relatives. In addition, the Indian schools follow a curriculum similar to that of private schools in India and government schools in Great Britain, with students studying for A-level exams like those given in British schools.

Finally, North American and European children attend special English, American, French, and Russian schools, which follow curriculums compatible with those in the students' native countries so that the students can transfer credits when their parents return to their own countries. However, Arab students sometimes attend these schools in order to improve their foreign language skills or because their parents feel that Western teachers and teaching methods are better than those in government or private Ara-

United Arab Emirate teens at school. Courtesy of Judith Caesar.

bic schools. Many Indian families would also like to send their children to British schools, but the British schools use an unofficial quota system "to keep the schools British." British-curriculum Indian schools were instituted in response to this quota system, and thus they have names such as "Our Own English School" and "The Indian English School."

It is more than the curriculum, the memorization, and the many nationalities that make education in the Emirates different from American education. In the first place, most teachers at all levels are non-Emiratis. Thus, the teachers are not part of the same community as their students. In the public schools, the teachers are from other Arab countries, and in private schools, they may also be Indian or Western, particularly in schools where English or another Western language is the language of instruction. In most cases, the teachers in government schools are not well paid by UAE standards but are making much more money than they would in their own countries. Young Emiratis respect education, but they also respect wealth and family background and their teachers are much less wealthy than the Emiratis and do not come from respected local families. By the same token, some of the foreign teachers are in the Emirates primarily for the higher salary and have few ties to the community they are serving. Although many students respect their teachers and many teachers are dedicated to their students, the differences in wealth and nationality are a potential problem. The Emirati government has recognized that this problem stems from the fact that Emirati men generally do not want to become teachers because they can make so much more money in business. In response, the government has encouraged local women, in particular, to take up teaching.

The most important difference between American and Emirati schools, however, is that almost all schools in the Emirates are single-sex. After the fourth grade, boys and girls attend separate schools. This means no school dances, no mixed parties on school property, no clubs or extracurricular activities in which boys and girls can meet and mix. Even universities are single-sex, with separate campuses for men and women students. Only private American-style universities such as the American University of Sharjah are co-educational. Even at these universities, physical contact between the sexes is prohibited. Couples who hold hands may find themselves reprimanded by the dean of students. This does not mean that there is no physical contact; it just means that contact that Western teenagers take for granted is officially forbidden. In fact, co-education at the college level is controversial. Most students say that since men and women work together in business, co-education is helpful in teaching them to become socially comfortable with the opposite sex. Other, more traditional students fear that co-education will lead to premarital sex and ruined reputations (at least this is the view they express publicly). Even at co-educational universities, some conservative students state that men and women should speak only about schoolwork. On the one hand, this sexual segregation means that girls do not have to worry as much about sexual harassment as American girls do, but it also means that boys and girls are less likely to get to know one another as friends.

However, in the long run, while most of the public and private schools seem strict and a bit old-fashioned to most Westerners, these schools (and the society around them) do seem to help prepare students for life in a modern, globalized society. Most young Emiratis, Indians, and Arabs in the Emirates are bilingual and computer literate and have some knowledge of life in other countries and cultures. Most of the under-30 generation in the UAE knows some English—enough to follow an action movie or surf the Internet. In fact, many students learn English by watching television and movies, building on the rudiments they are taught in school. The Ministry of Education strongly encourages the use of modern technology in schools, so that most young Emiratis are computer literate, and their relative affluence enables most Emiratis to have home computers. The omnipresence of American, British, and Indian television, movies, and newspapers also makes it easy to learn something of life in other countries. In fact, it is usually only the children of Western expatriates who remain monolingual, although some of them, too, learn something about Arab and Indian culture while they are in the Emirates.

SOCIAL LIFE

UAE society is a mosaic of nationalities and cultural groups, but most teens socialize with others from their own nationality, or at least within their culture and language. Teens from the subcontinent, from the Levant, from the Gulf, and Western teens tend to mix with one another more than with other groups. Thus, Syrians, Palestinians, and Lebanese are likely to be friends, as are Indians and Pakistanis, despite the political difference between their countries. However, sometimes the boundaries between these culturally defined groups are crossed as teens meet each other in schools, community-based activities, clubs, and shopping centers.

In addition, although young people go to school with others of the same gender, they can meet the opposite sex outside of school, particularly the brothers, sisters, and cousins of their classmates. What happens next depends upon the teenager's family and nationality. Most Arab, Pakistani, Iranian, and Indian girls are not allowed to date because of both religious and social traditions, whereas Western teenagers living in the UAE can date just as they would in their own countries. Non-Western teens do date sometimes, but they generally do so without their parents' knowledge.

There is a very broad spectrum of what teenagers are allowed to do. Western teens, and some non-Westerners from very liberal families, live much as they would in the West. Teenage boys have much more social freedom than girls. Boys can go out with their friends, either by taxi or with a slightly older friend or relative who drives; older boys in particular can stay out late and do not necessarily need to report to their parents where they are going, or with whom. Boys could date if they could find a girl to go out with, but the restrictions on most girls makes this a bit difficult. A girl who is allowed to date would find herself extremely popular.

Although most girls cannot go out with boys, they are usually (but not always) allowed to go out with other girls or with relatives (cousins) their own age. Instead of going by taxi or with a friend who drives, however, a parent or the family driver would take them to the friend's house, to the party, to the shopping mall, or to the movie and bring them back when the event was over. Parents want to know who a girl's friends are, where she is going, and when she will be home. Some parents, both Arab and Indian, object to a girl having a girlfriend with a questionable reputation and do not allow their daughter to be seen in the "bad" girl's company. This is in part because some girls arrange to meet their boyfriends in public places, telling their parents they are going out with their girlfriends. Then, after the date, they return to the mall or café where they were supposedly visiting with their girlfriends all along and wait for their parents or driver to take them home. The girlfriends corroborate the story, and no one is the wiser. However, this arrangement could cause a scandal if it became publicly known; and since families are usually close, most girls try to avoid embarrassing their parents.

The restrictions on girls may sound old-fashioned, but there is a reason for them. Both religion and custom forbid premarital sex, but this restriction applies much more rigidly to girls. It is still a disgrace to the family if a girl is not a virgin when she marries, and if she has a bad reputation (which she can get from dating or even from being friends with girls who do) it may be difficult to find a man to marry her. Most Emirati marriages are arranged by the families, and one of the first inquiries a suitor's family makes is about the girl's reputation. Some conservative families deal with the problem by not allowing a young girl out of the house unless she is chaperoned by an adult relative, especially her mother or an aunt. This used to be the accepted custom a generation ago, but it is less common now.

RECREATION

Teens in the Emirates like sports, but the sport they participate in depends somewhat on gender and nationality. Emirati teenagers, especially older boys, like to go dune-bashing in their SUV's sail, parasail, jet ski, watch horse or camel races, or play golf, as do teens from other nationalities who have the money and interest. Almost everyone follows soccer, although usually only boys play it. However, both boys and girls play tennis and practice team sports such as basketball and volleyball. British, Indian, and Pakistani boys play cricket and rugby, and companies that employ Americans support baseball teams for expatriate boys. Some companies sponsor sports activities that draw many young people such as the "street ball challenge" held every year in Dubai where teens are invited to take part in basketball games throughout a whole weekend in January. Sports tournaments are another opportunity for young people to meet and socialize.

As for swimming, women and girls usually avoid public beaches, where the sight of a girl in a swimsuit invites gawking. However, the UAE has many semi-private beach clubs, or teens can buy a day pass (usually only about $10) to use a hotel beach and swimming pool. The beach clubs and hotels cater to a particular clientele, with the more upscale hotels and beach clubs frequented by Westerners and Emiratis. For conservative families, there are beaches reserved for women only, and many Emirati families have private pools.

On weekends, which correspond to Thursdays and Fridays in the UAE, and on special occasions, families encourage their children to visit family members as a form of recreation that also serves to maintain family bonds. During school holidays, especially in the summer, many families travel abroad, as the extreme heat makes it difficult to go outdoors. Teenagers who stay in the UAE spend most of their leisure time in air-conditioned malls or clubs.

ENTERTAINMENT

Social life starts late in the afternoon and extends late into the night. Teenagers love to hang out in shopping centers, either just walking around or sitting in a café or fast-food restaurant. These provide a good meeting ground. Going to movies in the malls is another favorite pastime. In the evenings, there are several restaurants with open-air seating areas that offer a kind of fruit-flavored tobacco smoked through a water pipe (*sheesha*). *Sheesha* houses, a tradition in the Gulf, are a place for teens to hang out, meet people, and talk as much as a place to smoke.

Many Emirati teens enjoy music, as do teens everywhere else in the world, and in the Emirates they have a wide range of music to choose from—music from the subcontinent, Arabic popular music, and Western popular music. Among Arab teens, both Gulf music and Lebanese singers are popular. Many teens also know and like the folk music and dance of their countries and are proud of being able to do the national dances, such as a Palestinian and Lebanese dance called the *debkah*. They also like Western-style disco. In the big cities such as Dubai and Abu Dhabi, teens go to concerts featuring popular Western and Arabic bands.

Older teens, especially boys, can also go to nightclubs if they live in a city such as Dubai. Starting around 9 P.M. young people start hopping from one nightclub to another. Although clubs are restricted to people over age 21, some 17- to 19-year-olds find ways to get in and dance. Islam forbids alcohol, but alcoholic drinks are available in hotels and in nightclubs located in hotels. In theory, liquor is only for registered hotel guests, but it is served to almost anyone who goes into the club. However, not all of the Emirates allow nightclubs or alcohol. In more conservative districts, such as Sharjah, drinking and mixed social dancing are not allowed in public.

Younger teens and teens in the more conservative Emirates listen to music and dance at private parties on weekends, usually Wednesdays, starting late in the afternoons, either at home or in a hotel. Some of these parties are for girls or boys only, but others are mixed. Adults are usually present during these parties, and parents make a point of knowing the families of their teenagers' friends. Generally the drinks served are sodas. Non-Muslims can purchase alcohol in most of the Emirates, so local teens can pay a non-Muslim servant to buy liquor for them. However, family pressure against drinking is strong.

In other ways, teens in the Emirates enjoy the same kinds of entertainment as teens in the West. Moviegoing is also very popular among young people in the UAE, although they often complain that R-rated movies are severely edited. During the week, young people may watch TV or movies on video. Young teenagers also play video games and listen to music to entertain themselves at home, or they go to game arcades to play billiards. They may choose to spend a day in a water park, go camping, or scuba dive. Access to the Internet is widespread, so surfing the Net and chatting has become a pastime for the young in the Emirates, although some chat rooms may be blocked by the national telecommunications company, Etisalat. Almost everyone possesses a mobile phone in the UAE, and teenagers love to talk on the phone with friends wherever they are.

RELIGIOUS PRACTICES AND CULTURAL CEREMONIES

The majority of people in the Emirates are Muslims and observe all Muslim holidays and festivals. Businesses and schools adjust hours or allow days off for people to celebrate these holidays. Most important for Muslims is Ramadan, the month of fasting when people refrain from drinking liquids, eating, or smoking during daylight hours. One purpose of the fast is to remind Muslims of the suffering of the poor, the importance of charity, and their duty to live ethical and pious lives. By the time young people are in their teens, they are expected to fast just as adults do. Non-Muslims are expected to avoid eating and drinking in front of people who are fasting, but otherwise they go about their lives as usual. Many businesses and restaurants close during the afternoon to give fasting people a chance to rest, and then they open again after dark, staying open until very late. Restaurants offer special Ramadan meals (*iftar*) at sunset, and many families invite friends and relatives to their homes to share the *iftar*.

During other religious holidays, such as Eid al-Adha, government offices and schools close and most employees in the private sector are given time off. Eid al-Adha celebrates God's providing a ram to Ibrahim, allowing him to spare his son Ismail. (A similar story is part of the Judeo-Christian tradition as the story of Abraham and Isaac.) These holidays are times for the extended family to get together to share meals, give gifts to the children, and enjoy each other's company.

Other teens in the Emirates are Hindu or Christian, and both groups celebrate their own holidays, in their homes and in public. Many Indians celebrate the Hindu festival of Diwali, in which houses are decorated with candles and families exchange gifts, particularly of candy. The holiday commemorates the return of Lord Rama and is symbolic of the triumph of good over evil. Indians consider this part of their culture, and even some Indian Christians take part in the secular aspects of the holiday. As for Christian holidays, some Arab Christians belong to Eastern-rite churches and celebrate Christmas and Easter according to the Julian calendar, whereas Indian, Western, and Filipino Catholics and Protestants celebrate these holidays by the Gregorian calendar. In both cases, Christians attend church services and give parties. There never seems to be any resentment or criticism of the public celebration of non-Muslim religious holidays.

Religion is very much a part of teen life in the UAE, but the degree to which people act according to their beliefs varies. For example, most Muslim girls believe that their religion requires them to cover their hair in public, and all Muslims agree that drinking alcohol is contrary to Islam; but some feel that whether or not they cover their hair is a personal matter and that drinking is a forgivable lapse. While they are not following the letter of their religion, they are not rejecting Islam or questioning its tenets, for the most part. Other Muslims follow the letter and the spirit of their religion far more rigorously, and some young people find some of the conservative aspects of their religion attractive as a way of reasserting their cultural and religious identity. Many young Muslim men and boys regularly attend Friday prayers in the mosque, and many boys and girls pray the five required prayers every day. This does not mean that they never enjoy themselves or have fun with their friends, and it certainly does not mean that they attempt to force their views on people who do not agree with them. It does mean that Islam is an important part of who they are and that they respect their religion and culture.

As for the Hindus and Christians living in the Emirates, the degree to which they follow their religious beliefs varies from one family to another. Among Arab and Indian Christians, who have been a religious minority in their countries for hundreds of years, Christianity is very much a part of their cultural identity as well as their personal beliefs, whereas among Western Christians, it is a more individual matter. Among Hindus, degrees of piety also vary. However, most people from the subcontinent, Hindu, Christian, and Muslim alike, are tolerant of one another's beliefs in a country and a culture in which all of them are foreigners.

CONCLUSION

In general, teens in the Emirates enjoy many of the same things that American teens enjoy, but they are a bit frustrated by what they perceive to be Americans' stereotypes about them. After all, they watch American movies and TV shows where the villains are evil Arab terrorists, and they listen to the Western news reports, which they feel misrepresent their religions and the political complexities of the Middle East and the subcontinent. Asked[2] what they would like young Americans to know about them and their countries, they said things such as:

"We are just like you, except that we are closer to our families and don't have sex before marriage."

"We don't live in tents and we don't ride camels (except for fun). We're modern people."

"We like to have a good time just like you do, only we know how to have a good time without drugs and alcohol."

"Women are not oppressed here. No one forces me to cover my hair. I do it because it is part of my religion and I'm proud of it."

"We know about you from watching your movies and television and learning your language and studying your culture. I'm glad you have a chance now to learn something about us."

NOTES

1. I. Al Abed, P. Vine, and P. Vine, eds., *The United Arab Emirates 1996* (London: Trident Press, 1996), 187.

2. Statements in the quotations are from a survey designed and sent out to UAE teens for this chapter.

RESOURCE GUIDE

Books

Abed, Ibrahim and Peter Vine, eds. *The United Arab Emirates 1996*. London: Trident Press, 1996.

Al-Fahim, Mohammad. *From Rags to Riches: A Story of Abu Dhabi*. London: London Center for Arab Studies, 1995.

Callan, Lou, and Gordon Robinson. *Lonely Planet Oman and the United Arab Emirates*. Oakland, CA: Lonely Planet, 2000.

Camerapix, comp. *Spectrum Guide to United Arab Emirates* (Serial). New York: Interlink Publishing Group, 1997.

Crocetti, Gina L. *Culture Shock! United Arab Emirates* Portland, OR: Graphic Arts Center Pub. Co., 1996.

Johnson, Julia. *United Arab Emirates*. Philadelphia: Chelsea House Publishing, 2000.

Kechichian, Joseph A., ed. *A Century in Thirty Years: Shaykh Zayed and the United Arab Emirates*. Washington, DC: Middle East Policy Council, 2000.

Raban, Jonathan. *Arabia, a Journey through the Labyrinth*. New York: Simon & Schuster, 1979.

Thesieger, Wilfred. *Arabian Sands*. New York: Viking Press, 1985.

This Way Gulf States: Kuwait, Bahrain, Qatar, United Arab Emirates, Oman, Yemen. New York and Lausanne: JPM Publications, 2000.

Fiction

Al Murr, Mohammad. *Dubai Tales*. London: Forest, 1991.

———. *The Wink of the Mona Lisa and Other Stories*. Dubai: Motivate Press, 1994.

Web Sites

www.uaeinteract.com

Information about history and archeology, wildlife and environment, culture and heritage, news.

http://www.reach4uae.com

Online business community for UAE with information about market, resources, recruitment, investment, news.

www.hejleh.com/countries/uae.html

Information about the people and country of United Arab Emirates, their business and economy, human rights and politics, education, tourism, governmental organizations.

www.sheikhmohammed.co.ae/Article/article.asp

Information about the Highness Sheikh Mohammed, sports, news, news archive, media, poetry.

www.planetarabia.com

Information about Planetarabia, where millions of Arab people learn recent news of the Arab countries. Also provides opportunities for discussion.

www.arabji.com

Source of links to information, business, economy, government and politics, entertainment and sports, society and culture in the Arab world.

www.lonelyplanet.com/destinations/middle_east/united_arab_emirates/

Historical, cultural, and environmental information, plus some statistics.

Pen Pal

http://www.candlelightstories.com/ClassPenPalListings2.asp?Country-United_Arab_Emirates

Chapter 12

YEMEN

Reuben Ahroni

INTRODUCTION

The Republic of Yemen is located in the most fertile part of Arabia and has a population of over 17 million. Despite the significant progress that Yemen has made in its educational, socioeconomic, cultural, and other fronts since its establishment, it is still considered one of the least developed countries in the world. A significant portion of its inhabitants are still illiterate.

Yemen is situated between Oman and Saudi Arabia, and it includes the Peninsula of Aden in the southwestern corner of the Arabian Peninsula. It is characterized by a diversity of geographical features, varying from low strips of land to highland ranges surmounted by several peaks. A major part of the country's population lives in the mountainous region in the northern part of Yemen. The climate in most of the country is desert-like, hot and humid. Sandstorms and dust afflict parts of the country, mainly in the summer.

Yemen's natural resources are meager. Indeed, because of the poverty of the country, prior to the Gulf War in 1991, millions of Yemenis went to work in Saudi Arabia, Kuwait, and other Middle Eastern countries, sending home a significant amount of money. Many of these emigrants were teenagers. However, Yemen's refusal to join the anti-Iraq coalition, as well as the support it voiced for Saddam Hussein during the Gulf War, brought about devastating consequences for its economy. The United States curtailed its aid to Yemen, Kuwait severed contacts with it and Saudi Arabia and other Gulf states expelled as many as one million Yemeni workers.

This expulsion deprived Yemen of a significant part of its foreign currency income, derived from the workers' remittances, and burdened it with a sudden increase in a population with considerably lower income. This created a harsh economic situation with dire effects on the Yemenis, particularly on children and teenagers, in terms of nutrition, health, and schooling, hampering projects aimed at enhancing the life of Yemeni teenagers in these and other areas.

SPECIAL CONSIDERATION: DIVERSE HISTORY

The life of teenagers in Yemen cannot be understood without a cursory survey of the three widely disparate sectors from which the country evolved. These include North Yemen, which was ruled by a religious leader referred to as *imam*; the British colony of Aden, and the British protectorate of Aden. Of the three, the former imamic (imam-governed) Yemen is the largest and most populated. Until 1962 the autocratic Zaydi imams, who abhorred outside influence, ruled North Yemen. The Zaydi rulers kept the country secluded from the rest of the world, unscathed by foreign infiltration. This isolation accounts for the cultural, economic, and industrial backwardness of Yemen, a fact that has had an adverse effect on Yemeni teenagers' cultural and educational life.

In contrast, the area that constituted the former British Crown Colony of Aden (1839–1967) was the most developed socially, culturally, and economically. Aden town proper, Crater, is built in the crater of an extinct volcano. Despite the stifling climate and the fact that Aden is devoid of agriculture, forests, and mineral wealth, the British recognized the strategic and commercial significance of this town because of its high protective mountains commanding the mouth of the Red Sea and the route to India. With the British occupation, the inhabitants of Aden found themselves thrust into the currents of modern life. The law and order, peace and security that the British rule bestowed upon Aden made it a haven for immigrants fleeing the turbulence of Yemen and the onslaughts of regional hostilities and tensions. Aden also attracted immigrants from diverse parts of the British empire. As a result, Aden rapidly grew from a small village to a thriving city with a population of uniquely cosmopolitan character. In July 1954 an oil refinery was built in Little Aden by the British Petroleum Company, making Aden one of the major oil fueling ports in the world. The British authorities also established a basic cultural and educational infrastructure, benefiting primarily the Adeni teenagers.

Despite its small size, the colony of Aden played a crucial role in the political developments in imamic Yemen. In the mid-1940s the Free Yemenis, revolutionary exiles from Yemen who found refuge in the British colony of Aden, stirred up dissension against the imamic institution. In 1962 a ferocious civil war raged in Yenen, pitting tribesmen on the royalist side against the revolutionaries. The civil war, which lasted seven years, ultimately toppled the theocratic Zaydi imams that had ruled Yemen since 893 C.E. Out of the wreckage of imamic Yemen emerged the Yemen Arab Republic (YAR).

In addition to the tiny colony of Aden, which the British considered an exclusive British possession, Britain had strong control over an extensive area south of imamic Yemen, which they referred to as the Aden Protectorate. This area comprised several Arab autonomous sultanates and sheikdoms. Each of these tiny states was made to sign a peace treaty with the British, according to which the latter extended to their sultans and their heirs, forever, the protection of the British Crown. In return, the sultans committed themselves to utter loyalty to the British and undertook not to cede their territory to, or negotiate with, other foreign powers. The British granted annual stipends to the "well-behaved" potentates and withheld stipends from those who did not display complete loyalty. These tiny states were supervised by British agents, leaving the traditional internal life of their people almost intact. As a result, the cultural, social, and educational life of the protectorate's teenagers was not much different from that of imamic Yemen.

With the British evacuation of Aden and the protectorate in November 1967, these two southern areas were united into a single state, named the People's Democratic Republic of Yemen PDRY (South Yemen). Thus, the current Republic of Yemen (ROY) constitutes, in essence, a territorial merger of the two previously independent, ideologically and demographically disparate Yemeni states, the YAR and the PDRY. Although the two Yemens were formally unified in 1990, the merger was fully implemented only four years later, following a long civil war that erupted in the summer of 1994. Despite its intensity, devastation, and the deep psychological scars it left on both young and old, the civil war helped break down many of the previous barriers and significantly facilitated the unification of the two Yemens into a single state with one flag, one capital, and one constitution. It also helped establish common legislative, executive, and judicial frameworks. Needless to say, the new republic inherited both the accomplishments and the shortcomings of the two Yemeni states that comprise it, including the two educational systems.

Except for a very small number of Hindus and foreigners, Yemen's population is dominantly Muslim with two traditional Islamic sects: the Sunnis, represented by the Shafi'is, and the Shi'a, represented by the Zaydis
and the Isma'ilis. The Shafi'is constitute about half of the general population and are concentrated mainly in the southern regions of Yemen.
The Zaydis occupy the highlands of the center and north of Yemen as well
as the eastern desert regions. Most prominent among the Zaydis are the
Sayyids, who claim descent from the family of the Prophet Mohammad
through his two grandsons Hassan and Husayn. Because of this claim they
are held in very high esteem, their hands and knees are kissed, and their
blessing is sought. Before the 1962 revolution they were an extremely
privileged class in Yemen, serving as government functionaries. Since
then their power and prestige have been declining. The Zaydis, through
their abhorrence of outside influence and their vigilance against foreign
infiltration, managed to keep the traditional social structure of the country intact without any significant alterations.

Both the Zaydis and the Shafi'is are characterized by a pronounced
tribal diversity. The tribes were and still are, to a large extent, guided by
their own conventions and unwritten codes of conduct transmitted from
generation to generation. An important factor in this code of conduct is
the quality called honor (*sharaf*). A tribesman without *sharaf* is deemed
deficient. Any dishonorable conduct on the part of a tribesman—such as
killing a woman or a person of inferior status, or hurting anyone placed
under the protection of the tribe—would be considered an extremely dis-
graceful act. It is for this reason that the Jews of Yemen felt much more
secure under the protection of the tribes than among the townsfolk. The
Yemeni Jewish writings relate numerous instances of bloody intertribal
conflicts prompted by the murder or molestation of a Jew. Although the
Yemeni central government is making tremendous efforts, with significant
success, in expanding its authority to all parts of the country, there remain
some lawless or reluctant tribes in remote areas.

Before 1950 there were some 60,000 Jews in Yemen. According to
Yemeni traditions, the origin of these Jews goes back to certain exiled
tribes of Israel who emigrated to Yemen in 70 c.e and later. Since the dis-
appearance of the formerly very powerful Christian communities in South
Arabia, the Jews were virtually the only non-Muslim community in
Yemen.

The Yemeni Jews were widely dispersed throughout the country. About
80 percent of them lived in villages or small towns. In a predominantly
agricultural society, the Jews provided almost all the services and tools
that were indispensable to the Yemeni farmer. However, following the

establishment of the state of Israel, almost all the Jews of Yemen were air-lifted en masse to Israel.

TYPICAL DAY

The phrase "a typical day" is hardly applicable to Yemeni teenagers. Yemen constitutes a composite and variegated society molded by ancient traditions. Teenagers' lives may therefore vary, at times significantly, from one section of society to the other. Although the Yemeni government aspires to grant education to all Yemeni children and teenagers, education is not compulsory and a high percentage of teenagers, girls in particular, do not go to school. Even if they desired to do so, the educational facilities are too limited to accommodate all of them. The frequent internecine wars that ravaged the country significantly hampered the economy and retarded the country's efforts to build schools for all Yemeni children. Thus, it is safe to say that the current backwardness of Yemen is to a large extent a function of its tyrannical past, a history of willful isolation, a perennial round of intertribal and factional conflicts, and protracted civil wars (the last was that of 1994).

Over 55 percent of the labor force in Yemen is engaged in agriculture and herding. During the agricultural seasons teenagers are called upon by their predominantly large families to help, which causes them to rise very early in the morning and spend some 10 to 12 hours a day in the fields. Moreover, unemployment is pervasive in Yemen, causing a significant number of teenagers, including those from agricultural areas, to emigrate to or seek work in other countries as expatriate laborers. This state of affairs does not leave much time for many of the teenagers for schooling.

Yemeni teenagers who do go to school get up early, eat breakfast, and go to school—the rich go to private schools. Yemenis attach special importance to breakfast, as evidenced by the adage *as-sabuh ruh* ("breakfast is the essence/breath of life"). After school teenagers do their homework, which is generally not very burdensome, read assigned books, and prepare for exams. Male teens may spend their after-school hours roaming the streets, frequenting cafés and fast-food restaurants, meeting in clubs, and engaging in games, sports, and discussions on diverse topics.

While alcohol is strictly prohibited in Yemen, male Yemenis, including teenagers, are known for their fondness for chewing of the leaves of Catha edulis (*qat*), a shrub that grows mainly in the Yemeni hills. The *qat* is mildly narcotic and somewhat addictive. *Qat*-chewing parties constitute a social habit held almost on a daily basis, accompanied by the smoking of hubble-bubble water-pipes (narghiles), which are passed around among the participants. Such parties may last for hours and instill a sense of comfort and relaxation. Within the framework of such parties, literary or political discussions may take place and business may be transacted. Most Arabs view this social habit as a scourge that afflicts Yemeni society. The shrub is expensive, and its consumption may come at the expense of feeding the family. *Qat* parties are also quite popular among male teenagers. They chew the leaves of this shrub either at their homes or at the homes of relatives or close friends. Most teenagers cannot afford this expensive "delicacy" on a daily basis. The frequency of such parties depends on the participants' financial situation.

FAMILY LIFE

Families in Yemen are large and cohesive. Although a Yemeni man can marry up to four wives, as allowed by Islamic law, polygamy is not widespread. The father usually wields authority over all members of his family, who treat him with respect. While he is the one who earns for his family's livelihood, his wife works very hard at household chores. Although electricity is available in most parts of Yemen and bread and other food staples can be bought in stores, most women, particularly in the villages and rural areas, prefer to prepare most food staples at home in the old-fashioned way. This includes the baking of bread (*khubz* or *khubza*).

A heavy yoke of chores, domestic and outdoor, also weighs heavily on female teenagers, particularly in the villages and rural areas. They get up before sunrise, heading to the millstones to grind the requisite amount of flour for the day's needs. They also work in the field, chop wood in the forest, draw water from the spring, bake bread, care for livestock, and perform household duties. Female teen marriages in Yemen are quite common. In many cases girls in their early teens already have children.

While Yemen does not have a caste system of the Hindu type, it nevertheless has class divisions. Two Muslim dark-skinned groups, the *khadim* and the *jabarti*, are considered as belonging to the lowest rungs of the social ladder. They were (until the revolution of 1962), and some are still, treated like pariahs, condemned to the most ignominious manual work, such as roadsweepers, and sewage and refuse cleaners. The *khadim* are of obscure origin. Local tradition views them as descendants of the Abyssinians who ruled Yemen from 525 to 575 C.E. and were later vanquished by the Arabs. The *jabarti*, originally immigrants from the African side of the Red Sea, constitute a Muslim class even lower in caste than the *khadim*. They are concentrated mainly in the area between Zabid and Taᶜizz. In these groups members almost exclusively marry other members of the group. Teenagers from other social classes, like peasants and craftsmen, shun them and do not socialize with them, let alone intermarry with them. While a small percentage of Yemeni teenagers own cars, it would be almost inconceivable for a *khadim* or a *jabarti* to do so. They are poverty stricken. It should be noted that Islam opposes class distinctions and the Yemeni government is trying to improve the social and economic conditions of these groups.

TRADITIONAL AND NONTRADITIONAL FOOD

Even though Yemeni teens are fond of eating Western food, notably pizza and fried chicken, and Indian sweets where they are available, they also adhere to traditional homemade cuisine. Among the favorite national foods are the following. (1) Ground fenugreek seeds soaked in water for a few hours and then whipped by hand into a foam (*hilbah* or *hilbe*). Spices, garlic in particular, are added to it. *Hilbah* may be eaten with bread, dipped in it, or mixed with meat broth or vegetable stew. (2) Homemade butter-fat (*samn*). (3) Flour poured into boiled water (*'asid*). The porridge is continuously and thoroughly stirred until it becomes thick and smooth; salt and spices are added to it. A depression or cavity is made in the middle into which *samn* is poured. *'Asid* is eaten almost daily in Yemen, particularly in the villages. (4) Buttermilk (*laban*). (5) Yogurt (*tharib*). (6) Maize-cake (*kubanah*). (7) Wheat porridge (*haris*). As in the case of *'asid*, a depression or cavity is made in the middle of the *haris* porridge into which *samn* and honey are poured. (8) Salad (*salatah*) consisting of small pieces of tomato, red onion, lettuce, and some vinegar. The Yemenis love to eat their meals with hot chiles. They also eat fish and meat, preferably mutton. Lunch is considered to be the main meal, and families usually have lunch together. Interestingly, food staples such as *hummus* (a pureed garbanzo bean dip) and *tahine*, (a thick paste made of ground sesame seed) which are very popular in other Arab states, are not among the most popular in Yemen.

Although Yemen is known for its high-quality coffee (the best known being the mocha coffee), most Yemenis prefer to drink coffee made from the husk of the coffee berry (*qishr*). The berries are exported. The coffee is usually served with spices such as ginger, cardamom, cinnamon, and cloves.

Despite the innumerable *wadis* (valleys) that crisscross the mountainous region of Yemen, there are no rivers or lakes, causing the country to be almost totally dependent on rainfall. Any scarcity of rain in the agricultural regions causes a general famine. Indeed, famine has scourged

Yemen repeatedly throughout history, occasionally made worse by inva-
sions of swarms of locusts. In fact, owing to the extreme scarcity of food
resulting from drought, anarchy, wars, tribal disputes, and so forth, the
locust has become a source of food in Yemen. Many Yemenis, particularly
in the villages, consider it a delicacy.

SCHOOLING

An educational system was almost nonexistent in imamic Yemen. Education was mostly provided by traditional Quranic "schools" known as *kut-
tabs*, facilities generally associated with the local mosque. These and other
educational frameworks were limited to boys, who would sit huddled
together on the floor, engaged primarily in repeated recitation of the sacred
text (the Quran). At times, the entire class was made to recite a portion of
the text in a choral sing-song, in accordance with traditional diction and
intonation. The loud recitation of the Quranic text, accompanied by
rhythmical physical movements, took place under the vigilance of the
instructor, who usually carried a whip or rod to enhance the child's con-
centration and motivation for learning. Memorization of the Quranic text
was of paramount importance; praise would be showered on those who
managed to memorize large portions. Generally speaking, the instructor
(referred to as *shaykh*) would confine his teaching to the mere recitation of
the text without expounding on it. Only a select few of these children
would pursue a more advanced religious education in the areas of Hadith
(sayings of the Prophet) and Shari'a (Islamic law), with the goal of becoming religious judges (*qadis*) and religious functionaries. Very few sought, if
they could afford it, advanced education in the British colony of Aden or
in other countries, primarily Egypt. However, toward the end of the
imamic rule (prior to 1962) a few primary and intermediate schools were in
existence, but their impact was marginal.

In contrast, the former British colony of Aden developed a basic modern educational infrastructure. As early as 1866, British authorities established the Aden Residency School to provide elementary education. By
the end of the British rule in Aden (1967) there was one high school, the
Government Secondary School, which led to the Senior Cambridge
examination, a technical institute, and two schools for the training of
teachers. In 1950 Aden College, a highly sophisticated school modeled
after the British public school system, was established. Except for religion,
Arabic language, and literature, education was rendered in English.
Although the main goal of education in Aden was the preparation of
clerks to fill the lower ranks of the civil service, it gave Adeni teens lim-

ited access to modern education, which paved the way for many graduates to obtain higher education in Middle Eastern and European colleges and universities. Moreover, the British rule in Aden exposed the rapidly growing population of the colony to European influence.

The new British subjects of Aden soon became aware of the significant advantages that could be derived from general secular education, mastery of the English language, and a basic knowledge of mathematics and science. Furthermore, cultural clubs, such as the Arab Reform Club and the Islamic Arab Reformation Club, were established. Also, Arabic newspapers, including *Fatat al-jazira*, were published. In addition to the British schools, Christian missions, such as the Danish Mission and the Roman Catholic Mission, contributed to the Adeni educational and cultural spheres. These and other intellectual frameworks helped create an intellectual elite that took over the leadership and administration of Aden and the protectorate following their evacuation by the British.

Thus, whereas the People's Democratic Republic of Yemen (PDRY), a merger of the former colony of Aden and the British protectorate, had the advantage of the basic Adeni educational infrastructure to build upon, the Yemen Arab Republic (YAR), formerly imamic Yemen, had to establish an educational system almost from scratch.

Following a bitter and destructive civil war between Royalists and Republicans, which lasted for eight years (1962–1970), the YAR made immense efforts to establish a modern educational system. Egypt's school system served as a model: 6 years of primary, 3 years of intermediate (in Yemen called preparatory), and 3 years of secondary schooling. Of the foreign teachers, the large majority were, and are still, Egyptians. Some of the schools had to operate on a shift system to accommodate the growing student enrollment demands. A significant milestone in the YAR's educational efforts was the founding (in 1970) of the University of Sanaa, which comprises diverse colleges, including the Faculty of Education, which provides training for teachers. Vocational, commercial, and technical schools have also been established. However, despite significant progress on the educational front of both Yemeni states, a major section of the population remains illiterate.

Yemen is facing enormous challenges in the educational field, chief of which is the scarcity of teachers, notably native teachers. Foreign teachers constitute over 50 percent of the teaching staff. Yemen still relies heavily on support from other countries. Indeed, many expatriate Arab teachers are financed from oil-rich states as a form of aid. These and other factors lead Yemeni youngsters to prefer the more competitive employment opportunities in the private sectors or seek better-paying government administrative posts. Moreover, many of those who graduate from teacher-training programs abandon their positions as teachers and join other professions. Thus, the continuous loss of teachers to other professional sectors is detrimental to significant improvements on the educational front. Teachers are also discouraged by overcrowded classrooms resulting from the acute shortage of educational facilities. Given that the Yemeni population growth rate is estimated at 3.7 percent per year, and that there is an extremely low rate of native graduates produced by universities and other teacher-training schools, the educational system will continue to rely heavily on foreign teachers. Moreover, many of the books assigned for students are authored by non-Yemeni Arabs. Needless to say, a heavy load of foreign educators along with teaching materials that do not reflect the students' background and milieu can be quite alienating.

Due to the strict separation of the sexes, there are schools for boys and schools for girls. Although in some private schools and public schools in rural areas boys and girls may study together in the same room, boys sit on one side of the class and girls on the other side. This is also true of most Yemeni universities. Girls are generally confined to their homes, particularly in the evenings. Although Yemen has seen a major improvement in the education of girls, it still has a very low female enrollment ratio. In 1999 the number of students registered in secondary schools was 323,124, of whom 242,580 were males and only 80,544 were females. Thus, males constituted 75.1 percent of the high school students. According to a 1996 report to the United Nations Development Program, Yemen "has also the lowest basic education completion rate, the highest primary education dropout rates by grade 4 and the largest dropout differential between girls and boys."[1] Conservative and traditional views still lead many parents to have their daughters leave school and get married; females are not expected to pursue public careers. In 1994–1995 there were more than 2.5 million students enrolled in basic education. Of these, 1.8 million were males and only 0.7 million were females. The report also notes that there is a significant difference in enrollment ratios between rural and urban areas. Communities that maintain traditional or conservative lifestyles tend to have low female enrollment ratios.

The 1996 report also lists the social and cultural factors that are detrimental to girls' schooling in Yemen. Among them are the following: schools are often located in isolated or faraway areas, making it inconvenient for girls to walk unaccompanied; schooling interferes with early marriage; fathers of large families generally tend to accord priority to their sons, who are expected to be the breadwinners. These and other factors and attitudes account for the large disparity between the educational rates

for males and females. However, a gradual increase in girls' school attendance is discernible, particularly due to changing attitudes.

SOCIAL LIFE

A high percentage of teens do not attend school; they prefer to work to
support themselves and their families. This is particularly true of teenage
girls, who either get married at a young age or stay home helping their
mothers. Male teens usually socialize with other teens from their
extended families or teens whom they get acquainted with in school,
clubs, and other gathering places. The genders are strictly separated from
an early age; no dating is allowed. To preserve the chastity of girls, no
social interaction is permitted between boys and girls. Indeed, every
aspect of a girl's life is strictly controlled by her parents or husband. Marriages are negotiated and contracted by family agreements, and parents
tend to marry off their daughters at a young age. It is not uncommon to
see a 15- or 16-year-old girl, particularly in the villages, already a mother.
Women do not drive and cannot obtain driver's licenses. Complete veiling of girls is mandated in public.

Like teenagers in other Arab countries, Yemeni male teenagers prefer
the style of American clothing—jeans and shirts—particularly when they
go to school. They also like to wear Yemeni traditional clothes, which in
Sanaa (the political capital; Aden is the commercial capital) include a
long dress (zanah), a rectangular piece of designed fabric put on the head
in a special way (somateh), a coat, and the ubiquitous dagger that Yemeni
insert in their belts (jambiyyah). Clothing varies from one region to
another.

Like all Muslims, Yemeni males are circumcised; the age for circumcision varies widely between and within regions. The completion of the
reading of the Quran is a memorable event to be celebrated and rewarded.
Beyond that, no religious or cultural ceremonies accompany the Yemeni
children's passage to adulthood.

RECREATION

Sports in Yemen are in the process of development. Most Yemeni
schools are not equipped with adequate sports facilities. The favorite
sports among Yemeni male teenagers are soccer, basketball, volleyball,
handball, and track. Swimming is confined to areas close to the sea.
Yemen has no lakes, and swimming pools are rare. Among girls, volleyball
is the most popular. Boys and girls do not play together.

Yemeni students go to school only five days a week. The rest of the week, together with after-school hours, provides ample time for recreational activities. So do the national and religious holidays.

ENTERTAINMENT

Yemen is an integral part of the Islamic world. Its people, Zaydis and Shafi'is alike, are dominated by a devoutly Islamic culture and cherished traditions that have framed their life since the inception of Islam. Teenagers generally follow the footsteps of their forebears, and no meaningful cultural conflict is discernible between the generations. Wine and other alcoholic drinks are prohibited in Yemen; teen drinking of alcohol is very rare. Moreover, there are indications that fundamentalist and extremist attitudes are on the rise in Yemen, particularly among teenagers. Given this highly conservative background, one cannot expect to find many modern activities characteristic of teenagers in most other societies, including those of several Arab states. Western music is not popular in Yemen. Teenagers prefer Arabic music, mostly Yemeni. This is also true of films: Yemenis prefer Arabic films, predominantly Egyptian ones. Dance clubs are almost nonexistent. Male teenagers usually meet in private houses, engage in discussions on diverse topics, and chew *qat*. Yemenis are known for their reverence of poets and poetry. This is also true of teenagers. Thus, teens' cultural activities include recitation of Arabic poems composed by celebrated poets and by the teenagers themselves.

In view of the limited number of movie theaters and the scarcity of other cultural and entertainment facilities, Yemeni teens frequent cafés and restaurants that serve dishes such as pizza and fried chicken. Girls like to associate with other girls, particularly from the extended family. They listen to Arabic music, watch television, and visit girlfriends. Although radios, particularly transistor radios, are ubiquitous, television sets are not. There were only 470,000 television sets in Yemen in 1997.[2] Newspapers are not readily available. There are no railways, and the road system is very poor, which impedes the timely distribution of newspapers throughout the country.

During school vacations, teens work to earn money. Those who can afford it, travel within Yemen and to other Middle Eastern and European countries.

RELIGIOUS PRACTICES AND CULTURAL CEREMONIES

Yemeni society is strongly religious and generally adheres to established Islamic tenets, particularly the five pillars of Islam. Teenagers strictly observe the fast of Ramadan, the ninth month of the Muslim calendar. The two major Muslim festivals, Eid al-Adha (sacrificial festival) and Eid al-Fitr (festival of ending the fast of Ramadan), are celebrated with much festivity and jubilation. Teenagers put on colorful attire, and social parties with festive dishes are held within the extended family. The mosque plays a major role among Yemeni male teens in terms of after-school religious education and social gathering. Most Yemeni male teens observe the five daily prayers (*salat*), considered to be the most important duty of a Muslim. Although the *salat* need not be held in a mosque, Yemeni teenagers love to frequent the mosques, particularly on Fridays because it provides them with another opportunity to socialize. Many teenagers who do not study in government public schools attend the Quranic schools, which are held either in mosques or in frameworks associated with mosques.

Even though the Yemeni national holidays commemorate recent historical events associated with liberation and unification, they have a religious component in terms of offering thanksgivings to Allah. The most important national holidays are May 22, proclamation of the republic on May 22, 1990; September 26, commemoration of the 1962 revolution that put an end to the imamic regime; October 14, the anniversary of the 1963 revolt against the British occupation of Aden and the protectorate; November 30, the British evacuation of Aden and the protectorate (in 1967). October 14 also commemorates the 1989 signing of the unification agreement between the two Yemens (the YAR and the PDRY). National holidays are celebrated with intensity and almost religious devotion. They also constitute an occasion for socialization and family reunions.

CONCLUSION

Yemen faces a formidable demographic problem. Its population, which already exceeds 17 million, has an annual growth rate of 3.7 percent, one of the highest in the world. This imposes severe budgetary strains on the government. Although Yemeni citizens are entitled to education at all levels free of charge, the limited resources and the shortage of schools and teachers severely limit access to education. In 1997 there were only 1,924 secondary schools. About 30 percent of teenagers (age 16–18) are enrolled in secondary schools; of these, girls constitute only 25 percent. Civil wars greatly hampered the government's efforts to build modern schools, modernize the curricula, and improve the educational services provided for students There is a need to expand teacher training, extend education to urban and remote areas, diversify higher education, and combat illiteracy. Yemen is facing enormous challenges of poverty, ignorance, disease, lack of health centers, and lack of clean water supplies. Moreover, the country's road system is one of the least developed in the world. There is much more to be done in (1) paving roads to accommodate the rapidly growing vehicular traffic, (2) developing drainage systems, and (3) supplying piped water and electricity to villages and remote areas. The government is making commendable efforts in promoting national unity, reinforcing law and order, and coping with unemployment, which causes teenagers to leave the country in search of work.

The wind of change is coming to Yemen. There are efforts to transform the character of Yemeni society and culture by building a modern infrastructure that blends the modern and the traditional. Revenues from the increased production of petroleum and gas will help facilitate the accomplishment of social, economic, technological, and cultural goals. Moreover, the Yemeni people are endowed with vitality and determination. This, together with the willingness of the government to address the country's problems, reinforces the hope for a better future for Yemeni teenagers.

NOTES

1. Sharon Beatty, "Basic Education for Girls in Yemen: Country Case Study and Analysis," submitted to UNDP, February 1996.

2. CIA, *The World Factbook*. "Yemen" at www.odci.gov/cia/publications/factbook

RESOURCE GUIDE

Books and Articles

Dorsky, Susan, and Thomas B. Stevenson. "Childhood and Education in Highland North Yemen." In *Children in the Moslem Middle East*, edited by Elizabeth W. Fernea, 309–324. Austin: University of Texas Press, 1995.

Friedlander, Jonathan, ed. *Sojourners and Settlers: The Yemeni Immigrant Experience*. Salt Lake City: University of Utah Press, 1988.

Stevenson, Thomas B. *Social Change in a Yemeni Highlands Town*. Salt Lake City: University of Utah Press, 1985.

Fiction

Abdul-Wali, Mohammad. *They Die Strangers; A Novella and Stories from Yemen*, trans. Abubaker Bagader and Deborah Akers. Austin: University of Texas Press, 2001.

Franck, Derek. *A Yemeni Passage*. New York: Azimuth Press, 1998.

Web Sites

http://www.yemenembassy.org/
Information about the country, its people, culture, government, economy,
    Yemeni-U.S. relationships.
http://www.yementimes.com/
Official site of the *Yemen Times* newspaper, the only English-language Yemeni
    paper, published since 1991.
http://www.aiys.org/webdate/fiction.html
Yemen Fiction. Fiction written by Yemeni or non-Yemeni authors about aspects
    of Yemeni society.
http://www.lonelyplanet.com/destinations/middle_east/yemen/
General information as well as links to other sources. A great source for tourists.

Pen Pal/Chat

http://www.yemennetwork.com/english.shtml
http://www.geocities.com/yemenonline/
Free e-mail services, search engines, discussion forums, chat rooms, links to Ara-
    bic newspapers and media.
http://www.yemennetwork.com/english.shtml
Yemen Electronic Media Network is a full-menu directory offering information
        and links on poetry, media, culture, art, health, government, and many
        more aspects of Yemeni society. Also provides discussion and chat rooms.
http://www.YemenWeb.com
A very informative and resourceful site containing information on a variety of
        issues from politics to culture, tourism to art, and so on. A great photo
        source as well.

INDEX

ABOUT THE EDITOR
AND CONTRIBUTORS

REUBEN AHRONI is a Professor in the Department of Near Eastern Languages and Cultures at Ohio State University, Columbus, Ohio.

NADJE AL-ALI is a Lecturer in Social Anthropology in the Institute of Arab and Islamic Studies, University of Exeter, England. She is a founding member of "Act Together: Women against Sanctions on Iraq" and a member of "Women in Black." She is the author of *Secularism, Gender and the State in the Middle East: The Egyptian Women's Movement*; "Gender Writing/Writing Gender: The Representation of Women" in *A Selection of Modern Egyptian Literature*; and coauthor of *New Approaches to Migration: Transnational Communities and the Transformation of Home*.

TAGHREED ALQUDSI-GHABRA is Associate Professor and Director of Library and Information Sciences in the College of Social Sciences at Kuwait University. She is the author of two books: *Alraha Alghareeba* (*The Strange Comfort*) and *Mundhu Nu'mat Adhfarihim: Adab Alatfal Al'arabi Alhadeeth Fi Alqarn Al'ishreen* (*A Content Analysis of Arabic Children's Books Published in the Twentieth Century*).

FATIMA BADRY is Chair of the Department of English and Professor of English and Linguistics at the American University of Sharjah, United Arab Emirates.

JUDITH CAESAR is Associate Professor of English at the American University of Sharjah and has written two books: *Crossing Borders: An American Woman in the Middle East*; and *Writing Off the Beaten Track: Essays on the Meaning of Travel and Culture*.

RAWAN DAMEN and DIMA DAMEN are students at Birzeit University, Ramallah. They have contributed a number of working papers to Arab and international conferences on oral history and children's issues.

NAHED EMAISH teaches French language and culture in the Department of French Language at the University of Jordan.

LAILA HOURANI is a Palestinian journalist residing in Syria.

YASMIN HUSSEIN is a Ph.D. candidate at the Institute of Arab and Islamic Studies at the University of Exeter, England.

MERAL KAYA is a native of Turkey and a Ph.D. candidate in the College of Education at Ohio State University.

MALIHE MAGHAZEI is a native of Iran who has written several articles and translated several books.

ALI AKBAR MAHDI is Professor of Sociology at Ohio Wesleyan University. He has authored numerous articles and reviews in various sociological and Middle Eastern scholarly journals. His books include *Sociology in Iran* (co-authored); *Sociology of the Iranian Family; Resources for Teaching Sociology of Development; Women in International Development;* and *Iranian Culture, Civil Society, and Concern for Democracy.*

M. A. NEZAMI is Professor of Sociology at King Saud University, Riyadh, Saudi Arabia.

MUSA SHTEIWI teaches in the Sociology Department and the Women's Studies Program at the University of Jordan. He has published many books and articles on various aspects of Jordanian and Arab society.

REBECCA TORSTRICK is Assistant Professor in the Department of Sociology and Anthroplogy at Indiana University, South Bend.